What Is a Book?

"Through his readings of two centuries̶ ̶̶.̶̶.̶̶.̶̶u̶̶e̶̶r̶̶i̶̶c̶̶a̶̶n̶ fiction, poetry, and criticism, Kirby answers his own question, 'What is a book?,' with a nuanced, comic, and profound account of what it means to be human."—Edward Mendelson, author of *The Things That Matter: What Seven Classic Novels Have to Say About the Stages of Life*

"Kirby has a flair for combining scholarship, earthy wisdom and humor in his work. His impulse is to seek connections between literature, academia, popular culture, and the moral dimension."—Floyd Skloot, *Harvard Review*

"Kirby's book is full of interesting principles, hard-earned on the front lines of academia."—*Los Angeles Times Book Review*

"Essays so clear, relevant, and far-reaching as to address all the major working parts of literature . . . An important and useful book that is also surprisingly pleasurable and entertaining to read."—*Library Journal*

"This altogether enjoyable, enlightening, and reassuringly human collection radiantly celebrates our unceasing love and need for books."—*Booklist*

"Kirby's well-oxygenated prose ultimately clears our heads for good reading, brightening our understanding of why literature matters."—*The Tennessean*

The House of Blue Light

"The loquacious style of David Kirby's poetry can sometimes resemble the riffs of a brainy stand-up comedian. . . . Yet in relating seemingly autobiographical, spryly digressive sagas about work, marriage, travel and even the joys of mediocre movies, Kirby makes the narrative poem—a form often proclaimed to be outdated—amusing, lively and relevant enough for contemporary tastes." —*New York Times*

"Talky, jokey, and carefully lineated, Kirby's vignettes unabashedly celebrate middle-class writing life, middle-aged male life and middle-to-highbrow cultural life, while simultaneously deflating all three."—*Publishers Weekly*

"Kirby is a spieling genius of the compound sentence and laugh-aloud funny." —*Booklist* (starred review)

The Ha-Ha

"Kirby is a brilliant narrative poet who gives enormous and, in the end, deeply serious pleasure: his poems deliver surprise, thoughtfulness, and delight. . . . These poems are tender, funny, talky, full of bad jokes brilliantly told; they are at times unabashedly sentimental yet somehow earn their sentiments."
—*Chicago Tribune*

"The stream-of-consciousness and jazz-based rhythms of Kerouac and Ginsberg meet the surreal, philosophical musings of Wallace Stevens, with an occasional dose of cathartic confessionalism a la Robert Lowell."
—*New York Times Book Review*

"Kirby's poetry is a comic slaughterhouse where nothing goes to waste."
—*Boston Phoenix*

"Kirby has evolved a poetic vision that seems able to include anything, and when he lets it sweep him across the face of Europe and America, the results are astonishing."—Philip Levine, *Ploughshares*

Ultra-Talk

Johnny Cash,
The Mafia,
Shakespeare,
Drum Music,
St. Teresa Of Avila,
And 17 Other Colossal Topics
Of Conversation

Ultra-Talk

by David Kirby

The University of Georgia Press
Athens and London

Acknowledgments for previously published material
appear on pp. vii–viii and 237–41.

Published by The University of Georgia Press
Athens, Georgia 30602
© 2007 by David Kirby
Set in Adobe Garamond by Newgen
Printed and bound by Thomson-Shore
The paper in this book meets the guidelines for permanence
and durability of the Committee on Production Guidelines
for Book Longevity of the Council on Library Resources.
Printed in the United States of America
11 10 09 08 07 c 5 4 3 2 1
11 10 09 08 07 p 5 4 3 2 1

Library of Congress Cataloging-in-Publication Data
Kirby, David, 1944–
Ultra-talk : Johnny Cash, the Mafia, Shakespeare,
drum music, St. Teresa of Avila, and 17 other colossal topics
of conversation / by David Kirby.
    p. cm.
Includes bibliographical references and index.
ISBN-13: 978-0-8203-2908-6 (hardcover : alk. paper)
ISBN-10: 0-8203-2908-8 (hardcover : alk. paper)
ISBN-13: 978-0-8203-2909-3 (pbk : alk. paper)
ISBN-10: 0-8203-2909-6 (pbk : alk. paper)
1. Civilization, Modern—Miscellanea.
2. Popular culture—Miscellanea.
3. Quality (Aesthetics)—Miscellanea.
4. Quality (Philosophy)—Miscellanea.
5. Conversation—Miscellanea.
6. Kirby, David, 1944– . I. Title.
CB358.K47 2007
909.08—dc22   2006023755
British Library Cataloging-in-Publication Data available

Contents

Acknowledgments *vii*

First Words *xi*

On Titles *xxi*

I Shot A Man In Corleone: How Sicily Explained
  Johnny Cash To Me *1*

The Meaning Of Everything *27*

Chekhov's Influence On Shakespeare *31*

Give Me Life Coarse And Rank *55*

An Army Of Chitterlings *74*

"Why Does It Always Have To Be A Boy Baby?" *92*

The Goat Paths Of Italy: Dante's Search For Beatrice *110*

Looking For Leonardo *125*

The Naturalist And The Narrative *142*

I Brake For Richard Petty: Black Water And Boredom
  In The Talladega Infield *147*

Bang The Drum All Day *159*

Shrouded In A Fiery Mist *174*

Like A Twin Engine Bomber *189*

Poetry, Television, And The World Wide Web:
  Art In A Time Of Terror *199*

I Never Said What They Say I Said, Or Everything You
   Always Wanted To Know About Pull Quotes But
   Were Afraid To Ask *211*

Mornings With Travis, Evenings With Dick, Or Lucky Buck
   At The Questura *216*

Notes *237*

Index *243*

Acknowledgments

This book poses a simple question—what's good?—and plows through a ceiling-high stack of examples to support a single answer: it's good if both the elite and the general public embrace it and do so repeatedly over time.

Goethe and Leopardi both said that a book is valid only if it has been accepted by an intellectual elite and a vast public, and that if it fails on one or the other count, there's something wrong with it; to their formula, I add a third requirement, which is that the book (or singer or saint or sport or dish or musical instrument) have a track record. Consistent with my desire to keep both the elite and the public in mind, roughly half of these pieces appeared in literary magazines and half in newspapers. I saw my name in print the first time as a freshman writing for my college newspaper, and although I quit the paper after a term, I never forgot the lessons all journalists master: don't go over the word count, get your piece in on time, learn to live with the fact that you're going to be edited. Even during the years when I wrote little but poetry, I tried to write economically (which doesn't always mean briefly), to set deadlines for myself, and to appreciate that a good editor makes a good writer into a better one. Later, when the idea for *Ultra-Talk* came to me, I returned to newspaper writing and began to mix journalism with literature with the confidence given me by my worthy antecedents: Whitman wrote for the papers, as did Twain and Melville, though all three wrote for posterity as well.

Permission from the following to reprint some of these pieces, often in very different form, is gratefully acknowledged; a couple of titles are attributed to more than one publication because they appeared first as short newspaper pieces and then were expanded into full-length essays. The journals and newspapers that originally published portions of *Ultra-Talk* include the *Chicago Tri-*

bune ("I Never Said What They Say I Said, Or Everything You Always Wanted To Know About Pull Quotes But Were Afraid To Ask," "The Meaning Of Everything," "The Naturalist And The Narrative"), the *Christian Science Monitor* ("I Brake For Richard Petty: Black Water And Boredom In The Talladega Infield"), the *Cincinnati Review* ("Bang The Drum All Day"), *Denver Quarterly* ("I Never Said What They Say I Said, Or Everything You Always Wanted To Know About Pull Quotes But Were Afraid To Ask"), *Mid-American Review* ("Like A Twin-Engine Bomber"), *Northwest Review* ("The Goat Paths Of Italy: Dante's Search For Beatrice"), *Pleiades* ("The Goat Paths of Italy: Dante's Search For Beatrice"), *Shenandoah* ("I Shot A Man in Corleone: How Sicily Explained Johnny Cash To Me"), *South Florida Sun-Sentinel* ("I Brake For Richard Petty: Black Water And Boredom In The Talladega Infield," "Like A Twin-Engine Bomber"), *Southwest Review* ("Poetry, Television, And The World Wide Web: Art In A Time Of Terror," "'Why Does It Always Have To Be A Boy Baby?'"), *TriQuarterly* ("Shrouded In A Fiery Mist"), and *Virginia Quarterly Review* ("An Army Of Chitterlings," "Chekhov's Influence On Shakespeare," "Give Me Life Coarse And Rank").

None of these pieces would have appeared anywhere were it not for the editors who sometimes sought me out and often were approached by me and then not only said yes but saw my prose into print, gently questioning a loose fact or a questionable word choice, offering kind words where appropriate or necessary, and putting up with my queries about payment: James Cummins, Mike Czyzniejewski, Ted Genoways, Susan Hahn, Judy Lowe, Chauncey Mabe, Nicola Mason, Kevin Prufer, Bin Ramke, Ron Silverman, Rod Smith, Willard Spiegelman, Tom Swick, Elizabeth Taylor, Teresa Weaver, Eric Miles Williamson, and John Witte, you've all made me a better writer. To my childhood friend Bill Bertrand and my colleagues Jimmy Kimbrell and Mark Winegardner, thanks for your good will, good humor, and good sense of direction; keep a bag packed, because there are more trips to come.

And to my truest friend, Barbara Hamby, who loves movies and parties and books and rambles, who writes poems so electric that when you read them you feel you've stuck your finger in a wall socket, and who occasionally arches an eyebrow as I hunch over a notebook instead of appreciating the thing of beauty before me: when the waiter fills our glasses and touches a match to the candle that lights your lovely face, you always have my full attention.

First Words

One afternoon Barbara and I arrive in Florence, fall exhausted into bed, and stroll out later in search of a trattoria. But there is crowd noise from the Piazza della Signoria, so we wander over to see what's going on. It's the orchestra of the Maggio Musicale, the city's music festival, playing Beethoven's *Ninth Symphony* to a crowd of several thousand listeners of every type: backpackers from all over Europe, young parents pushing prams, schoolchildren chasing each other around the legs of the big people, carabinieri, Africans peddling Gucci knock-offs, Asians selling bamboo birds, teenagers who can't keep their hands off each other, drunks, older couples strolling arm in arm, gypsies, the homeless, business people pausing on the way home to whistle a bar or two.

The crowd is so big and varied that of course it commits the music lover's cardinal sin of clapping and cheering lustily when the orchestra pauses between movements. But so what? It's summer, it's outdoors, and it's Florence, where the great modern experiment begins, where architects and scientists and political thinkers and artists and poets like Brunelleschi and Leonardo and Machiavelli and Michelangelo and Dante lived and worked within a few streets of one another and almost at the same time, banked by wealthy merchant families like the Medicis who, far from finding art and learning mysterious or daunting, competed with one another to buy the most books, commission the loveliest paintings, and erect statues most likely to strike the viewer dumb, like those still standing in the piazza today. Art, ideas, beauty: they're for everybody, the crowd seems to be saying as it sends skyward its own odes to joy.

The idea for a book on king-sized cultural monuments had been buzzing in my head for several years when I came across these words in an interview with Primo Levi, Auschwitz survivor and one of the greatest (and, considering his achievement, one of the most neglected) writers of the twentieth century: "Both Goethe and Leopardi said that a book is valid only once it has been accepted by an intellectual élite, followed by a vast public. If it fails on one or the other count, there's something wrong with it." Isn't the same true for songs, plays, movies, food, pleasures of every kind? What is most valuable is not that which is "great" (because experts say so) or "popular" (because people buy a lot of it) but both. My subjects are things which are valuable because everybody values them: poets and waiters, journalists and mechanics, scientists and short-order cooks. And I would add a third element to Goethe and Leopardi's formula: for a cultural phenomenon to be truly colossal, it has to be valued by everyone not just briefly but repeatedly and over time.

How do we know when someone knows that a work is "good"? It's not necessarily good if that person says, "I like it," but it's definitely good when he or she says, "I want to read (or watch or look at or do) it again." So a phenomenon must not only appeal to both the elite and the public, as Goethe and Leopardi required; it must also have a track record. "I've seen it twenty times" or "I read it again every year" are statements I see and hear variations on in papers and class discussions and talks with audiences of every type all over the world, from preschoolers to disadvantaged kids to teens, college students, peers, retirees. Fandom is everything, and every topic touched on in this book, whether it's music or theatre or sculpture or religion or the human body itself, is good not because the elite and the public say so but because they say it again and again.

My original idea had been to write personally about great writers, ones I went out after because I couldn't do otherwise: Shakespeare and Whitman were giants looking in my window, so I walked out to meet them. Then a piece on television (included here) was more or less forced on me when, improbably, one of my sons won half a million dollars on a reality show. Novelist Robert Stone says, "The world will come for you if you don't go out and get it," and since I was already straying from the academic cloister, I decided to write about any subject that presented itself to me as long as it passed the test of Goethe and Leopardi: it had to be appeal to both intellectuals and the public. Advertising, auto racing, Dante, the English language, folk music, food, France, Leonardo, movies, poetry, recreational vehicles, religion, storytelling, striptease, television, travel, the world wide web: they're all in this book.

The idea isn't to include something for everybody but the opposite: these are topics that people in the developed world, regardless of income or class or level of education, have studied, read about, been to, sought avidly, resisted vigorously, and discussed passionately in coffee houses and saloons and chat rooms. Billionaires walk through the Paris that I write about, but so do beggars. In Rome, heads of state kneel before Bernini's statue of Saint Teresa in ecstasy, and so do people who can't read. Everyone watches TV. We live in the post-theory age, as pretty much everybody seems to be saying these days, which is to say that we benefit from what theory has taught us but don't rely on jargon and rigid argument any more. What I offer in these pages is a way to read, see, and savor, a post-theoretical world view that everybody can share.

Across the lintel of the Teatro Massimo, the opera house in Palermo, are carved these words: L'ARTE RINNOVA I POPOLI E NE RIVELA LA VITA, or "Art renews people and reveals life to them." Those very people—music lovers, candy sellers, passersby—fill the sidewalk in front of this beautiful building, and if everyone can't afford the price of a ticket to that evening's performance, at least they can look up at the theater's dome as the sun sinks behind it and the swallows soar and dip and a string quartet plays an air from Bellini or Verdi. In *A Few Good Voices In My Head*, Ted Solotaroff says that a piece of writing is often a writer's "only way to organize and to some extent comprehend life's fullness and perplexity." Surely that's equally true for readers. And not just readers, either: surely anyone who takes the time to look at a painting or listen to music or watch a TV show is organizing their experience and, to use Solotaroff's modest phrase, "to some extent" comprehending it.

And it's not as though culture is going to become *less* democratic. When do modern times begin? One might start with the European Renaissance, when books became cheap and widespread. ("With twenty-six soldiers I have conquered the world," said Johannes Gutenberg.) During the Technological Renaissance that began in the nineteenth century, books became even cheaper and more widespread, and, thanks to telegraphy, the radio, and the telephone, a revolution in communication began to change the world. Now there is a Global Renaissance centered around computers rather than books, which means that the spread of information will be cheaper, faster, easier still.

◆

Most of these pieces involve research but also my physical presence, my walking around and talking to people who often know more than they're given credit for. Each piece begins in the library, but I always go out into the streets and boulevards—or the other way around. "This is the city and I am one of the citizens," as Whitman says in "Song of Myself," and "Whatever interests the rest interests me, politics, wars, markets, newspapers, schools. . . ." If that's good enough for Whitman, it's good enough for me. At the end of a good day, both my head and feet are tired.

Like Melville's Ishmael, sometimes I just want to stretch out in my hammock with a good book, and some of these pieces reflect that quiet, measured exchange that can only take place between two people, the one who is reading and the one who is read, and than which there is little more satisfying in this life, especially if there's a fire burning and it's cold and rainy outside. More often, though, I hear chatter and singing coming from the deck of the *Pequod,* so I go up to see what's going on. Even when the weather's bad, and even though my shipmates are speaking in a dozen tongues, it's worth it to be amidst "life coarse and rank," as Melville's contemporary Whitman said. The pleasures of reading and writing about a single topic in a book-lined study are not to be underestimated, but here I've sought to walk and talk and read and listen like my old masters.

The phrase "ultra-talk" is not only not original with me but comes from an essay by Mark Halliday called "Gabfest," the subject of which is my poetry. Halliday says a typical poem of mine "includes several detailed anecdotes from his own past, bits of pop culture culled from past and present . . . , and explicit references to books he has read." My prose isn't as much of a gabfest as my poems are, but the same principles apply, the same desire to hear many voices and make them my own.

In a profile in *The New Yorker*, writer Michael Frayn is quoted as saying, "'The German playwright Friedrich Hebbel said that in a good play everyone is right.'" Frayn goes on: "I don't suppose he meant that you had to morally approve of everyone, but I take it he meant that drama is people presenting themselves with the same force as they do in life, and feeling as justified as they do in life. If the playwright is taking sides, it's not very interesting, because in life it's not like that—there's no directorial figure, no writer, no God figure saying this guy's right and this guy's wrong." *Ultra-Talk*'s title may come from poetry, but the better metaphor might be drama: people talking to each other, and "everyone is right."

I'm aware that what I'm doing could be called reader-response criticism by some of my learned colleagues, and Bakhtinian heteroglossia by others; there is much here of the "carnivalesque" and "polyvocal," to use terms borrowed from European criticism (or the "riotous" and "many-voiced," as I'd prefer to say). But I read Melville and Whitman long before I and everyone else discovered the European sages who came to dominate critical thinking in Western universities. The writings of Foucault and Derrida struck many as startlingly new; to me, what they wrote seemed brilliant and provocative and also rather familiar, since

I'd already encountered many of their ideas in American writings. Roland Barthes proclaimed the death of the author in 1968, but a hundred and twenty years earlier, Emerson wrote in his essay "History" that "a Gothic cathedral affirms that it was done by us and not done by us. Surely it was by man, but we find it not in our man." Mikhail Bakhtin wrote in midcentury that "during carnival time life is subject only to its laws . . . the laws of its own freedom," but Hawthorne had already shown that in 1851 "My Kinsman, Major Molineux," his portrait of feverish, torchlit unrest in colonial times.

◆

It's impossible to separate critical stance from self; critics who say they are objective and disinterested are ascribing to themselves qualities no human can claim. My starting point as a consumer of culture is my accident of birth. For the time being, at least, I belong to the majority in this country, which is to say I am of European stock but was born in America. Like those early settlers, I tend to want to see things pragmatically (let's get that stockade up before we write our sonnets) and outward-looking (now that the stockade's up and we've finished the first drafts of those sonnets, let's see what's on the other side of the river).

Centuries after the settling of this country, that paradigm still prevails. As a teacher, I've noticed over the years that students like best those works which contain both the familiar and the unfamiliar, the known and the un-. I've taught every age group, from kindergartners to people older than myself, and I've learned that everyone likes it when the work starts in the known world and proceeds to the unknown, when the poet or painter or filmmaker first establishes intimacy and then moves toward the new.

One technical term for this movement is defamiliarization. The war memoirs of the Russian Formalist writer Viktor Shklovsky, for example, are an almost childlike recounting of horrors in which the events are described in the offhand tone

one uses to recount a bad dream, as when Shklovsky writes of walking out of his door one morning and finding a dead baby on his doorstep: every morning, we all walk out of our doors (the known world) but never expect to find anything as unsettling as the body of a baby (the unknown). Then again, watching something as predictable as a football game, which takes place on a carefully lined field and is governed by a thick rule book, can take a turn toward the unpleasant (a player's injury) or the breathtaking (a Hail Mary pass into the end zone).

When I work with others, I like to proceed inductively, that is, to get everyone to read lots of examples and then discuss what the favorites have in common. Again and again, I find audiences like work that isn't small or snide, that tries to be big, to have heft, to go somewhere. Readers keep coming back to works that aren't impressionistic, abstract, or fragmented but have narrative elements, rely on images, and use traditional syntax.

This doesn't mean that readers feel comfortable only with the familiar. Far from it: they want the work to take them into the unknown. Octavio Paz described his own poetry as "the apple of fire on the tree of syntax": the tree is what we know, the apple the flame that contains all mystery. In a recent paper, a student wrote about watching a beautiful woman in a long skirt; she's leaning back with her legs crossed, and she's sipping a glass of wine, and the observer writes that "it was as though I knew absolutely everything about her and nothing about her at the same time."

This interplay between the known and the unknown in the cultural phenomena I write about in these pieces puts the intellectual elite and the general public on an equal footing. Irrespective of education, class, and economic status, everyone likes the familiar, just as everyone likes to be surprised. That carnivalesque and riotous Florentine piazza in which modern times began was old then, even as it is young now, and we are all in it, our jaws agape.

What I've learned is that audiences like to use the familiar elements in a work as a base camp: you set up your tent, get a fire going, and then walk out over the ice and hope you don't (or do) run into the Abominable Snowman. I see art as the deliberate transformed by the accidental: story, image, and sentence are the deliberate aspects, and what happens after that is unpredictable. The known is always the same—same tent, same fire—but the unknown changes, because you never know what you'll find when you climb the peak. That peak experience has been given many names over the years. Edmund Burke called it the sublime, which, as opposed to the merely beautiful, inspires awe, even fear. Freud called it the unconscious; he also called it *fort* or "there!" when describing the game his grandson delighted in, crowing *Fort!* when he threw his plaything away and *Da!* ("Here!") when he brought it near him again. Lorca called it *duende,* loosely translated as "the shadow of death." The Italians call it *terribilità,* which needs no translation. In plain English, they're all talking about the unknown.

◆

Part of seeing the world from an American standpoint is recognizing that our culture is as many-sourced as the English language itself. Europe is vital to me, and as I've indicated several times, Florence in particular is important to this book. There I found time to write most of it, just as there I found myself pining for my own culture in a way that sharpened and focused its contours and made it seem all the richer to me; as Barbara says, there's nothing that makes you feel more American than trying to get your dry cleaning back in a language you can't speak all that well. You can walk across the face of the entire modern experiment in Florence, from the anonymous symmetry of Brunelleschi's Brancacci Chapel through a Piazza della Signoria full of statues of gigantic naked people waving their weapons (and their egos) in the air—talk about king-sized cultural monuments!—to the little church of Santa Felicità on the other side of the Arno, where the helpless figures holding Christ's body in Pontormo's *Deposition* look down as though saying, "Nothing works any more—what do we do now?" The chapel and the church bookend the piazza, one of the greatest gathering places in the world and an old place yet one so very much of our time that I half expect to see a statue of Johnny Cash there, his guitar strap on his shoulder like David's sling, or Janis Joplin instead of Donatello's Judith sawing the head off Holofernes.

Florence is also the city of Dante, the greatest of those who walked and looked and listened before they took up their pens. Down to hell he goes, not alone but accompanied by *his* master, the Virgil who guided him as Dante guides us, and there he sees every manner of creature: bad popes, virtuous pagans, heroes from legend like Odysseus, three-headed dogs, harpies, centaurs, imps and demons and Satan himself, his beloved Beatrice, angel-headed hipsters, saintly motorcyclists. Okay, I'm quoting from Ginsberg's *Howl* at the end of the list, but those two poets would have much to say to each other: they would disagree violently on much, and Dante would not have hesitated to put Ginsberg in Circle Seven of his Inferno with the other sodomites, but they would have conversed brilliantly, because each had a large mind and loved learning.

As I abandoned my original idea of writing only about giants like Shakespeare and Whitman and expanded my approach to include colossal cultural phenomena of all kinds, I also changed the way I wrote. In some cases, I sought commissions for big subjects, as with the final piece I wrote for this collection, the one on NASCAR. In other cases, I sought or was given books to review, such as the one on the *Oxford English Dictionary,* and in these instances, I wrote two pieces: one the shorter version that would appear in the newspaper that had commissioned it, the other a longer one intended for inclusion here. Alternatively, sometimes a review turned into a full-fledged article, as when I added my reminiscences of my youthful awareness of sex to a short piece I'd written about a book on striptease. Other pieces I wrote cold and sought publication for them later; these include the first and last items in this book.

As different as they are, each piece has behind it a similar methodology. Take the piece on NASCAR as an example. I'd read articles by intellectuals about NASCAR culture, but none by anybody who'd actually been to a race. So I got commissions from a Boston and a Florida newspaper; I wrote a straight news story for the one and a longer life-in-the-infield treatment for the other; and I combined the two and added additional material to make the essay included here. As I set out for Talladega, I had no idea what I was going to say, but I applied the same principles I used when I wrote on all the other topics in *Ultra-Talk*. First, read—read everything. (At the time, I didn't know a thing about car racing.) When you get to the infield, start walking, and don't worry about getting lost, because it will almost certainly be better if you do. Talk to everyone you meet. Above all, listen. Then retrace your steps and begin to write.

For only after reading and walking and talking and listening to people on every avenue are you ready to begin answering the only question worth asking—what's good?

On Titles

As I sent earlier drafts of these pieces to the editors of the journals and newspapers where some of them first appeared, I capitalized the first letter of every word in their titles. When the work appeared in print, though, usually the capitals of the so-called minor words had been made lowercase, even though I had resisted the change during the proof stage; house style is an enemy not easily defeated.

Here, though, the caps are restored. Is not every word as worthy as every other? If, say, "professor" and "blacksmith" are equal, are not "a" and "the"?

Ultra-Talk

I Shot A Man In Corleone

HOW SICILY EXPLAINED JOHNNY CASH TO ME

I'm sitting on a rock in the archeological park at Selinunte, on the southern coast of Sicily, when I hear three shots:
"Pop-pop . . . pop!" I was raised on a farm and know the sound
of a small-bore weapon, a .22 rifle, say, or a .410 shotgun. But
from books and movies, I also know the pattern of a lethal take-
down: two shots to stop your man as he runs, one for the coup
de grâce.

A few minutes earlier, Barbara had said she wanted to sketch
the ruins of one of the Greek temples that dated to the sixth
century BC; looking around for something to occupy myself,
I see a sign for the "Malophoros" and announce, "I'm going to
go take a look at the Malaphoros," and set off in that direction.
It'd been a long day—we'd taken the train from Palermo to the
airport, picked up a car, and driven to Segesta to see the temple
and theater there before ending up at Selinunte, whose park is
immense. It was almost dark, and after fifteen minutes or so, I
hadn't seen anything looking even vaguely like what I imagined
a malophoros to be; the word itself means apple or pomegranate
bearer, I learn later, and the site I can't find is a sanctuary where
rites were practiced away from the sight of the profane, including, apparently, me.

The gunfire woke me from my drowsy musings on the classic
order of the temples. Books brim with these kinds of juxtaposi-
tions between serenity and chaos, restraint and mayhem: back
in Florence, where we're living for four months, I'm teaching
The English Patient at my university's study center, and the war-
ravaged characters of that book reflect on the difference between
Lorenzo de Medici's Renaissance villa, where Politian and Pico
della Mirandola and the young Michelangelo argued about Plato
all night, and the ruined lives they live there.

Later, I ask a hotel desk clerk if it's hunting season, and she says yes, for rabbits and birds, animals calling for the kind of light fire I heard in Selinunte. Yet the town where the Greeks once prayed to Apollo and Hera lies between the great mafia centers of Palermo, Trapani, and Agrigento. Where I was sitting, the olive groves and vineyards had given away to thickets of wild maquis, evergreen shrubs like sage, juniper, and myrtle that provide dense coverage for bandits. Under the Sicilian sun, it was a dark as night beneath all that brush, and there was no way to see what had been killed there. It could have been a rabbit that was shot so a family could have dinner that night. It could have been a dog with distemper or maybe one that just happened to cross the path of somebody in a foul mood. It could have been a man.

◆

The heart has many chambers, and it can be dismaying to realize how quickly, even gleefully, we are able to move from the beautiful to the bloody. The most famous recorded live-concert line ever occurs in "Folsom Prison Blues," when Johnny Cash sings he shot a man in Reno just to watch him die, and his inmate audience responds with a rowdy "Yeahhhh!" that has brought a guilty smile to more than one listener's face. On the one hand, it's not nice to shoot people. On the other, most of us have wanted to shoot somebody at some point, so it's easy to agree with the convicts, who are just saying what the rest of us don't have the nerve to.

I've always wondered about that audience reaction, though. I attended a live performance in a Florida prison once, and the inmates at it were a lot better behaved, at least up to a point. A theater troupe was putting on a performance of *Waiting for Godot,* and I was supposed to lead a discussion afterward. Before the curtain rose, the warden stated in no uncertain terms that the slightest misbehavior would result in an immediate cancellation of the show; the guards seemed angry already, and the audience was intimidated into a respectful silence for the first part of the play.

But the roles of Pozzo and Lucky were played by women, and when the two actresses appeared, first one and then half a dozen inmates responded with slurpy kissing noises and the kind of how's-it-going catcalls you might expect to hear from a passing car on a small-town Saturday night. It wasn't that bad—I've heard worse from traditional playgoers—but the guards came down on the audience like storm troopers, throwing inmates against the wall and kicking chairs across the room. I got on the floor and covered my head; when I looked up a couple of minutes later, the hall was empty. So I've always had trouble understanding how the Folsom audience could get away with that anarchic "Yeahhhh!"

It turns out that they didn't. In *Johnny Cash at Folsom Prison*, his note-by-note reconstruction of Cash's historic January 13, 1968, Folsom prison concert, Michael Streissguth reports that the inmates listened silently, enthralled by the look and music of the "black circuit rider" who had appeared before them, yelling clamorously only as the song ended. The version the rest of us hear was pumped up by Columbia Records sound engineers who moved audience noise around to create a moment of musical fiction as thrilling as it is specious.

Yet this bit of legerdemain is one of those artistic lies that tells more truth than any fact ever could. For no matter when and where you live, if you've been starved and beaten all your life, if you've been worked past the point of collapse and not paid for your labor, if you've watched your wife and kids shiver and sicken and die for lack of firewood and food and medicine while the guy who lives in the big house on the hill strolls by every day in his new suit, then you, too, might let out an animal yelp of joy on hearing that someone else has committed a random murder, regretting only that you hadn't picked up that gun yourself.

◆

My first impression of southern Italy mirrored the image most people get from the movies: this was in Bari, a couple of years before, where we'd driven from Rome and stopped for dinner. As we got out of our car, an older man shouted for me to lock it and then added *"La mano nera!"* ("The black hand!") as he gestured in a menacing fashion. I'd already figured that southern Italy wasn't Kansas; earlier that day, we'd taken a side road and, when we tried to get back on the autostrada, found ourselves at the end of a highway that went nowhere. Literally: the pavement just stopped, with no warning, and, like David Balfour climbing his murderous uncle's stairs in *Kidnapped,* we "found nothing but emptiness beyond it." If, like him, I hadn't stopped in time, the last hundred feet of our southern Italian idyll would have been straight down.

The more I traveled in the south, the more I went down roads that led nowhere or, at best, to buildings nobody lived in. At another archeological park in Sicily, the stunning Valley of the Temples in Agrigento, I walked to the Temple of Juno at the eastern end and looked south toward an unfinished sports complex, then north toward a gigantic cluster of one ugly building after another, some of a dozen stories or more. In *Excellent Cadavers: The Mafia and the Death of the First Italian Republic,* Alexander Stille puts at six hundred the number of *case abusive* ("abusive houses") that had been built illegally there, almost certainly as a way of laundering Mafia drug money. The view I had could have been worse; in October 1999, officials began to demolish at least some of Agrigento's *case abusive,* though plenty of the eyesores remained.

From the Temple of Juno, Agrigento looked ratty, but then Sicily has always been poor. Ancient Rome used Sicily as a breadbasket, deforesting much of the island to plant grain. Like Islamic Spain, Sicily enjoyed a period of prosperity under Saracen rule, but as the Renaissance swept across the rest of Europe, the French and Spanish who succeeded the Moors kept the island in a state of feudalism so deeply entrenched that it lasted, in different forms, well into the twentieth century. The Sicilian novelist Leonardo Sciascia recalls how his grandfather labored in the sulfur mines, where boys as young as five were sold to "pickaxe men" to carry extracted material to the surface; the boys worked naked because of the tremendous heat and were sexually abused by their masters. Some of these children were able eventually to buy their freedom, while others remained slaves all their lives. The Franchetti-Sonnino report of 1876 was followed by a law forbidding the use of children under ten in the mines, though the law was often ignored. In his groundbreaking *Poverty in Sicily*, Danilo Dolci quotes a 1953 government report which says that 47.1 percent of Sicilians are "completely destitute or semi-destitute persons." Today, the rate of unemployment in all of Italy is around 9 percent; in the south, including Sicily, it is nearly 25 percent.

Where there is poverty, there is brigandry, and where brigandry is rampant, deals with the devil become an everyday way of life. It would be four hundred years before crime became organized, but as early as the sixteenth and seventeenth centuries, there were robber bands referred to as the "mafia." By the nineteenth century, mafiosi were necessary middle men who settled the disputes between absentee landlords who preferred Palermo, Naples, Rome, and Paris to the hot and dusty farm country and their hapless tenants.

The best road map through the complicated web whose main strands are the mafia, the government, and the Catholic Church is Peter Robb's *Midnight in Sicily*. Among other things, Robb explains why almost all developed countries are divided into a prosperous industrial north and an impoverished agricultural south. In Renaissance Italy, city-states like Florence, Venice, Bologna, Genoa, and Milan were democratic, entrepreneurial, and outward-looking; customers had to be sought and contracts signed, so commerce organized life horizontally. But in the Mezzogiorno (the country south of Rome, including Sardinia and Sicily), the wealth came from the land, and agriculture tends to organize life vertically, in a hierarchic and autocratic way with a hundred peasants at the bottom for every rich person at the top. Between these extremes, armed guards controlled estates run by tenant farmers who leased land to sharecroppers who hired day laborers who worked mainly for bread, pasta, and beans and led lives little better than those of slaves.

Robb quotes the protagonist of Giuseppe de Lampedusa's magnificent *The Leopard* as saying, "For at least twenty-five centuries, we've been carrying magnificent . . . civilizations on our backs, all of them coming fully perfected from outside, none sprouted from ourselves, none that we've made our own . . . for two thousand five hundred years we've been a colony." A character in another novel, Elio Vittorini's *Conversations in Sicily*, says Sicilians are "always hoping for something else, for something better, and always despairing of being able to attain it." Everything I read about the Sicilian language says that, while you might say "I have to do this or that," there is no separate tense to express the future, as though there's no point in breaking your heart by pretending your life is your own.

•

Johnny Cash, too, had seen the face of hopelessness when he was young, and he never forgot its features. He was raised amidst terrible poverty in Dyess, Arkansas, and as country boys and girls still do, he took the surest route out, choosing the meager pay, prosy if plentiful chow, and free dental care of the U.S. armed forces over a life that offered none of that. Within months, he'd formed his first band: the Landsberg Barbarians, a group of airmen at the base in Germany that gave the group its name. Country boys who all knew the same standards by Ernest Tubb, Jimmy Rodgers, and Roy Acuff as well as the gospel songs of their youth, the Barbarians played and sang in their free time. Melville's Ishmael says that the *Pequod* became his Yale College and his Harvard; according to Michael Streissguth, the Landsberg base was Cash's Juilliard School. Before long, the young airman got up enough nerve to write a few songs himself.

One of these was "Folsom Prison Blues." In 1953, two years into his air force hitch, the twenty-year-old Cash saw Crane Wilbur's film *Inside the Walls of Folsom Prison,* one of Hollywood's "uninspired melodramas," according to the *New York Times,* though the plot involving conflict between a crusading prisoner and a sadistic warden struck a spark. Lifting the tune and many of the words from Gordon Jenkins's "Crescent City Blues," Cash also based the song's most famous line on one from Jimmie Rodgers's "Blue Yodel No. 1 (T for Texas)," in which the singer boasts "I'm going to shoot poor Thelma / Just to see her jump and fall." In doing so, he tapped into a mean streak in blues, folk, and country music that is seldom heard in the more genteel airs of the pop charts. From the hellhounds on Robert Johnson's trail to the adultery and murder of "Long Black Veil" (another Cash arrangement of a traditional favorite), there is a river of blood in American music that usually stays in its channel, though from time to time it even flows into the lyrics of rock songs like "Hey, Joe," the tale of a guy with a gun in his hand who's going down to shoot his old lady 'cause he caught her messin' 'round.

♦

Our first night in Palermo, we stay at a hotel in the Quattro Canti area, which is the heart of the city. Here, sidewalks are so narrow that we have to walk single file, and shady characters abound. Peter Robb reports that ten thousand deaths were attributed to organized crime in southern Italy between 1983 and 1993. In 1981–82, there were two hundred murders in Palermo and three hundred disappearances; given the choice, I'd rather be killed outright, since the disappeared often were held in underground bunkers for years, tortured, their severed body parts sent to hysterical family members, then strangled and covered in lime or set in concrete and tossed into the bay. When we go out for dinner, we lock our passports and extra money in the safe in our hotel room, just taking a single credit card and a bit of cash. Of course, nothing happens; we are bumped and jostled, but by passersby hurrying to their own dinners, not cutthroats and thieves. And just north of us, near the Teatro Massimo opera house, the city opens up into wide piazzas where young parents push baby carriages and old timers stroll arm in arm, just as they do in Milan or Verona.

Where is the mafia? The bad guys may not be gunning down each other on the sidewalks, but it's hard to pick up a newspaper without seeing an item on an old or new story about a mafia figure. One of the oldest stories still current is that of Giulio Andreotti, whose picture appears in the *International Herald Tribune* one morning. Andreotti was never a robust figure in the first place, so the image of the seven-time prime minister's shrunken face sparks an I-didn't-know-he-was-still-alive reaction. But the news is all good, at least from Andreotti's perspective: in its final ruling on the matter, Italy's highest court clears Andreotti of charges that he conspired with the mafia during his several terms of office; even better, the court permits a statute of limitation to exclude any further delvings into his activities prior to 1980.

The charges against Andreotti were leveled in a five-year trial that began in 1994 after a *pentito* or repentant mafioso testified he had seen Andreotti exchange a kiss with godfather Totò Riina, the semiliterate head of the world's largest drug syndicate who kept his accounts in pencil in a child's notebook; surely, said the journalists, a peasant like Riina couldn't possibly run a multibillion dollar business without protection from those in power. Long assumed on the street to be in the mafia's pocket, Andreotti walked away a free man in 1999. Later, a friend tells me that Italians refer to Andreotti as a *sughero* or cork, though others speculate that the first court simply didn't have the nerve to convict an obviously guilty man who nonetheless had been at the heart of the government for years. Now, perhaps, the highest court has agreed that is better to let the old man live out his last days in peace rather than deliver yet another blow to a country whose corruption scandals have, in recent decades, been endless.

A newer mafia story involves a much younger man, a killer

named Giovanni Brusca who boasted once of committing at least a hundred murders. Incredibly, Brusca had been given days out with his family because he, too, had become a *pentito* and had behaved well during his eight years of prison. But during our Sicilian sojourn, Brusca was seen using a cell phone during the course of an outing, a violation of the terms of his temporary release. One of his murders was a revenge killing of another *pentito*'s eleven-year-old son, whom Brusca kept in a bunker for two years before strangling him and dissolving his body in acid. But the crime for which he was imprisoned was the bombing death in 1992 of prosecutor Giovanni Falcone; this, as well as the killing less than two months later of Falcone's colleague Paolo Borsellino, put an abrupt end to the public's indifference to the mafia, and the outrage that erupted in every Italian city at the murders ushered in a new era of accountability.

Well, sort of: Andreotti is still free, and Brusca, a pudgy man with a scruffy beard, merely looks annoyed in the photo in *La Repubblica* which shows him being taken back to prison by policemen wearing stocking masks over their faces to conceal their identities. Outside Palermo, planes now land at what is now known as the Falcone-Borsellino Airport. Reader, can you think of any other airport in the world that has been named for two slain judges? Most visitors to Sicily pass through Falcone-Borsellino, and should any of them think the mafia is, as even many government figures maintain, mythical or insignificant or no longer active, they have only to brush up on recent history to realize that *La Mano Nera* still has a deadly grip on Sicilian life.

Not my life, though. Exhausted from travel and a bad if almost certainly unnecessary case of the jitters, I check the contents of the wall safe after we get back to the hotel and slide into bed to read another chapter of Peter Robb's *Midnight in Sicily* before sleeping. An hour later, the phone rings. Somehow Barbara's sister has got hold of our number, and the two women chat excitedly as I groan and burrow into the pillows: midnight in Sicily, indeed. Silence and darkness return, and then—I must be making this up, I think—from the heart of the hotel I hear a note-for-note rendition of Gene Vincent's "Be-Bop-a-Lula."

Vincent died years ago, but his band reunited in the 1990s for a successful tour—in Europe, musical trends having long since bypassed them in the States. Could they still be on the road? Somewhere under my rumpled sheets, could the real gangsters of Palermo be bopping and twisting to the music of the faux gangsters of my youth, the black-leather-jacketed and duck-tailed rockers who stood for the harmless threats our parents dreaded: hotrods, switchblades, bottle blondes in tight sweaters? Robb writes that the Ucciardone prison, which looms above the bay of Palermo, is ruled by mafiosi who order in meals from the city's finest restaurants. Having ratted out their comrades like Giovanni Brusca, could these killers have been granted an evening in town? Can they have made their way to the ballroom of the Centrale Palace Hotel, and were they even now plotting their next outrages as they shimmied to "Blue Jean Bop" and "Woman Love"?

◆

Whether it's rockabilly or *Rigoletto,* art makes us shiver with delight and horror when it describes what really happens to people—other people, that is. Lancelot falls in love with the king's wife, and a kingdom crumbles, but we didn't do it. Macbeth slays his rivals and is himself cut down bloodily, but not us. And a thick substratum of American music tells the true stories of the millions of men and women in prison, people most of us don't even think about unless we get off the highway and take the side road that goes past the big gray buildings surrounded by wire and guard towers. But Johnny Cash was aware of the convict's lot and backed up his concern by playing some thirty prison concerts during his career. He was convinced that, far from re-forming its unwilling guests, the prison system only made them more criminal. In the 1960s and '70s, a time when the legitimacy of every institution was being called into question, Johnny Cash spoke through his music for the hardened, bitter men inside rather then their jailers.

In Michael Streissguth's account, the entrance into the prison of Cash, June Carter, Carl Perkins, and the Statler Brothers early on that January morning resembles a visit of epic heroes to the underworld. Cash himself comes across as wily Odysseus, slow to fear and more than a little willing to take a chance if the result might be glory or at least a good tale. It would have thrilled him if he had been taken hostage, said Don Reid, another performer that day. ("If they held him for about five days. He wouldn't have had anything to eat. He would have loved that.") In the winter-lit photos outside the prison gates, the entertainers look grim in their severe black clothes, Cash's face gaunt from drug use.

On the way in, producer Bob Johnston recalls an encounter with a character who might easily have been one of the shape-shifters in *The Odyssey:* "I think his name was Chester," recalled Johnston, "little bitty guy, bad teeth, hundred and forty, eye glasses, and I said, 'What are you in here for?' And there were three guards standing there, and he said, 'I beat three men to death with a baseball bat. By God, I'd do it again if I had the chance. Fucking people.' And the guard said, 'Calm down, calm down.' And I said, 'Wow.' And he didn't even look like he could win a fight, much less beat three people to death with a baseball bat."

Once musicians and crew were inside, though, the dark mood lifted as the band loosened up and rehearsed. By the time the first of the two shows kicked off at 9:40 a.m. and tape rolled, Cash was singing and playing like "an out-of-control train that never seemed to wreck." The so-called "insurance policy" show at 12:40 couldn't measure up to the excitement of the first; Cash himself was sagging at that point. Only one track from the second show, a song called "Give My Love to Rose," made it onto the *Johnny Cash at Folsom Prison* album, though Columbia technicians did move announcements and crowd sounds to the other recording to sex up an already high-energy show.

At one point on the album, Cash can be heard referring to the guards as he chortles, "Them mean bastards, ain't they?"

◆

Almost everyone in prison is poor, but that's all right, because we don't really like to look at or think about poor people anyway. It's the rich we admire; they're prettier to look at, in general, and certainly they are who we aspire to be. Like rich people at every point in history, the well-to-do have always done all right by themselves in Sicily. Of the ancient Sicilians, the most enviable was Roger II (ca. 1105–1154). His father was one of the original Norman rulers, but young Roger was born in Sicily and spoke several Mediterranean languages, including Greek and Arabic; moreover, he wore Arabic and Byzantine robes and even kept a harem. His court was known for its splendors, though it wasn't all fancy costumes and multiple bed partners for Roger. Described by one commentator as a man who accomplished more while asleep than most men did while awake, Roger patronized the arts generously, introduced the first written legal code to Sicily, and enlarged his kingdom to include Malta and parts of southern Italy and North Africa.

Even before Roger's day, high-living invaders worked hard and played hard, always on the backs of the nameless drudges who never quite make it into the history books. At the Villa Romana di Casale near the present-day town of Piazza Armerina, I rent an audio guide that leads me not only around the remains of the complex of buildings with its stunning floor mosaics (including those of the bikini-clad beauties in the Room of the Ten Girls) but also through the daily lives of the *dominus* and *domina* and their children and their many guests, all of whom reveled in the "magnificent lifestyles enjoyed by wealthy Romans." But you have to go to the Lonely Planet guide to Sicily to read of the "extensive slave quarters" where the wretches dwelled who made those magnificent lifestyles possible.

The hard-luck cases who poured wine for the villa's high rollers and gave them rubdowns in the *thermae* (complete with gym and massage room as well as baths of cold, tepid, and hot water) may not have left much of a legacy, but their colleagues in the wood-cutting trade left a visible mark on today's Sicily; the deforestation may have taken place centuries ago, but the empty fields we passed are still a testament to Roman efficiency and ruthlessness. The road from Caltanisetta to Piazza Armerina crosses a huge dust bowl where cactus becomes the dominant plant, and signs everywhere warn about the *fango* or mud. Before, hillside fields rich with greenery swooped down to the road from such vertiginous heights that you wondered how they could possibly be tilled; now, the decline from peak to roadside is just as steep, yet the low stone walls in which every field ends seem like dams holding back acres and acres of dust—not clay but metric tons of fine powder that sift in the occasional breeze like desert sand. If ever there were a source for *fango,* this is it; just add water.

Yet it's *fango* that saved the Roman villa at Casale; the Lonely Planet guide says that the buildings were covered by a mudslide in the twelfth century and weren't excavated until 1950, thus saving them from the fate of so many other ancient monuments that were looted by Sicilian rednecks: the mean, the venal (sold to a rich Palermitano, those Ten Girls would have turned a nice profit), or the merely thrifty who might make a sturdy pig pen, say, from the old house's *frigidarium.*

Because everything is used and reused in Sicily; once I saw a gap in a fence that was filled with a set of rusty bedsprings. All parts of every animal seem to find their way into the food chain, and while that's true everywhere in Italy, this omnivorousness attains the level of art form on the island. In Palermo, I stop for a sandwich of *panelle* or fried strips of chickpea flour, a cheap, savory, poor man's breakfast. An hour later, I get a *pane co' la meusa,* which is a sandwich of sliced beef spleen.

A mound of purplish flesh, the spleen itself sits on a block behind the counter, looking much as one might expect a cow spleen to look though certainly larger than I would have guessed. The sandwich maker is chipping slices of it into a cauldron that bubbles gently. When I place my order, he slices a roll in half, pitchforks through his slices as though custom-selecting the right ones in exactly the right order, adds a sprinkle of rock salt and a squeeze from a huge green lemon to the towering stack of meat, and then, with a grin at me, holds the whole affair at arm's length over his cauldron and squeezes it like a sponge, though it's still chin-dripping juicy when he hands it to me.

In Piazza Armerina, I have a meat dish that is unarguably delicious on every count, a *castrato* or castrated kid—goat, I should say. (No matter how poor, every culture draws the line at children.) It tastes like the best lamb I've ever had: a little gamey yet in a complex way, moist but crisp around the edges, a delight to the eye, nose, and taste buds. Since it was a *castrato,* I didn't get all the parts of this particular animal, though I assume the thrifty cook put the unused portions into a stew or gave them to a deserving dog.

Most of the dogs we saw in the countryside deserved a big meal. Whereas the piazzas in every town appeared to be run by cats, dogs were everywhere in the country, and I've seldom seen a scruffier bunch of curs. There are two main types, a blondish dingo-like creature and its dark twin. The two breeds band together and compete for food as well as opportunities to make mischief; looking down at that unused sports complex in Agrigento, I see three dingos in pursuit of three black dogs in pursuit of . . . a rabbit? Whether the dingos intend to wrest the prize from their foes or simply settle their hash in brutal noisy doggy fashion is unclear. In fact, when the rivals come together around a bend where I can't see them, there is a startling silence, as though the two warring families have made peace the way their human counterparts do, agreeing that life will be better for everyone if enemies live together like the fingers of a single hand, each separate yet all acting together so as to seize more.

At Segesta, an especially mangy dingo makes sorrowful dog eyes at Barbara as we eat our salads at a picnic table, so she nips back into the snack bar and returns with a ham sandwich for him. The dog takes that sandwich apart with impressive economy of gesture: flipping it once so that it falls into its constituent parts, he scarfs the ham in a single gulp, bites both chunks of bread in half and swallows them, eyes the lettuce suspiciously, and looks up at Barbara as if to say, "Got another?"

The dog was emaciated, as all dogs on the island are and as the people used to be; now the people are fat, as the poor are everywhere. A few miles down the road, we stop so Barbara can take pictures of a wrought-iron gate outside a decaying villa that looks as though it might belong to either a mildewed aristocrat or a middle-rank mafioso, and within seconds four black dogs roar up and create a fuss that would wake the dead, leaping against the gate and thrusting their snarling muzzles through the bars. But when Barbara hits her zoom-lens button, the mutts begin to howl like demons sprinkled with holy water and all but do back flips as they clamber over each other in their haste to get away. Obviously they've taken the zoom lens for a gun barrel; these are dogs that have witnessed shooting and either been shot at themselves or seen a comrade dispatched by an ill-tempered marksman. In the first photo Barbara takes, the dogs are rushing the gate, seething with valor and righteous fury, and in the next you see their rears as they hightail it for the safety of the villa's crumbling portico. In the photos, the dogs are indistinguishable; inbreeding has made them imbeciles as well as cowards.

One night we stay at an *agriturismo,* or working farm that takes in tourists, and there we meet two dogs, Leon and Tina, who, the owner assures me with a chuckle, are *due grandi rufiani.* But since they're not chasing our chickens or tracking mud all over our carpets, they don't seem like ruffians to us, and Barbara and I find them pleasant companions indeed. Neither belongs to one of the two prominent breeds: Leo, as befits his name, is a sort of oversized fluffy collie-lab mix, whereas Tina, with her brindled coat, seems a little bit of everything; clearly there is no inbreeding here but a healthy influx of new blood from old races. Both are affectionate and good-natured, greeting us enthusiastically every time we return from an outing in the car and willing to walk with us as far as we like in any direction.

By contrast, the dog across the road, who is behind a fence, loses his mind every time we go past. Like the fenced dogs at the villa, he's a coward as long as there are bars between him and us but runs when I pretend to throw a stick at him. At intervals, he barks throughout the night, leading me to ponder one of the central paradoxes of Canine Ownership, Bad Dog Division: if the barking dog is waking me, who is one hundred yards away, how can he not disturb the *dominus* and *domina* under whose window he makes his hullabaloo? Somehow, the warden is deaf to the cries of the inmate. At one point I gaze out into our courtyard, and there, under a full moon, Leo and Tina sleep dreamlessly.

◆

In the turbulent 1960s and '70s, Cash stood up for the caged men in Folsom and their denim-clad brothers in other prisons, yet he disappointed the left when he failed to check all the necessary boxes on the job application to become a political icon like Woody Guthrie and Bob Dylan. He may have fit the rebel mold, but Cash was a Christian and, for a time, a Nixon supporter. Jack Newfield of the *Village Voice* wrote that "A lot of us—Ralph Gleason, Nat Hentoff and myself among others—have been guilty, I think, of glibly trying to force too close an alliance between radical politics and rock music, to view the music as a surrogate for a political movement. We have tried to leech support and significance from groups, musicians, and lyrics when none exists." Part of the confusion stems from the fact that, along with protest singers and counterculture rock bands, Cash was played widely on the so-called underground stations that rebelled against Top 40 AM radio.

The difference between more political singer-songwriters and himself can be seen in the bewilderment Cash expressed when Columbia executives sought his permission to edit "Folsom Prison Blues" following the June 5, 1968, assassination of Robert F. Kennedy. Deejays were refusing to play the song with its shot-a-man-in-Reno line and its gleeful if dubbed-in audience response, yet Cash couldn't understand why Columbia wanted to "mess with" his song. No political correctness for the Man in Black: he knew that the doctored version of the song was more true to life than the raw tape. But eventually he relented, and thousands of fresh copies of the record were shipped to radio stations across the country.

◆

One decision we made early in the trip was not to go to Corleone. It just seemed like bad manners: thousands of American tourists have surely passed through it, and one thing I've learned over here is that my countrymen and -women will, in the certain knowledge that they'll never return, say the most outrageous things to people they probably regard as just "a bunch of Italians." As Barbara and I are a head taller and several shades pinker than most Sicilians, it'd be obvious that we've come to Corleone to check out the godfather vibes rather than sample *il vino della zona* or buy local handicrafts. Even though my Italian seems to be stuck permanently in what I'd call High Basic mode, I don't mind talking to people and trying to find out what's going on. But just about every book you read says that Sicilians don't like questions; in a town like Corleone, my guess is that you can multiply that reluctance several times.

Besides, Sicily isn't one big mafia theme park filled with brooding dons and murderous foot soldiers. It's a beautiful island with stunning vistas, yet its cities are pocked with unsightly slums; it's a cornucopia of rich food and complex wines which many of its own people can't afford. It's a land of contrasts, as are all lands, though Sicily is so small and the topography so varied that you can see all those contrasts in the course of a morning's drive.

You can see Africa, it says in our guidebook, and we are certain we do in the archeological park at Selinunte; though there is fog on the water, clearly there is a land mass on the horizon that stretches east and west as far as we can see. At our hotel there, the *signora* who registers us (or me, since Barbara stays with the car) is young and pretty and has an unwashed ripeness that wouldn't work for the aged and charmless yet somehow comes across as an asset in the young and pretty. Her hair is pulled back in a way that says, If you think I look good now, wait till I pull the pins out. She has the classic Snow White color scheme: creamy skin, black eyes, red mouth. She has a Mona Lisa smile and a Mona Lisa way of speaking, which is to say she listens but does not speak at all, and when she does, it's only to say something like "You speak Italian beautifully" or "I'm sorry I'm not getting to meet your wife." Since the first statement is patently untrue, I have my doubts about the second. Still, there is an intensity to her gaze that I'd mistake for something else if I were younger.

The next morning, there is no fog on the water. There is no Africa, either; the evening before, we had talked ourselves into a fictitious view of the Dark Continent. Then again, as Lampedusa says in *The Leopard*, "Nowhere has truth so short a life as in Sicily."

On our first day of driving, I wave at a guy on a tractor who just scowls at me, probably practicing his own version of *omertà*, which, contrary to popular usage, doesn't mean "silence" so much as something like Yiddish *Menschkeit*. You don't have to have a Ph.D. in Italian linguistics to guess that there's a connection between *omertà* and *uomo* or man; *omertà* is what a man does, which means taking care of business in an efficient and decisive manner, and that means no whining or complaint or unnecessary chatter.

The farther we get from Palermo, though, the friendlier the people are. Not initially: whereas northern Italian towns often seem empty during the day, people are out and about in the Sicilian heartland, and they'll stop, put both hands in their pockets, and look at you as though you're a new TV channel that's just been added to their basic cable package. But when you talk to them, the spell is broken and they come to life, often in surprisingly warm ways. In the north, the people you try to get directions from give answers on the fly, like New Yorkers, but in Ragusa, when I asked an older fellow how to get to a restaurant, he not only told me the way but walked there with me, keeping up a one-sided conversation in Sicilian, which is similar to Italian but is softer and more sing-songy (*il gatto* or "the cat" becomes *lu 'attu,* for example).

In the same city, I park in a tiny courtyard, and a woman with a broom watches me suspiciously as I back and fill, and when I ask her if it's okay to leave the car there, she scolds me for not leaving enough room for the others. When I move the car, I get out and apologize and ask again if it's okay, softening my request even more by telling her that I wouldn't want to take her son's place. Leaning on her broom, she eyes me for a minute more before breaking into a grin that suggests I'm either crazy or a genius, and then she, too, begins to walk with me and says, Yes, sure, it's fine, where are you from, where are you staying, and did you know there's a shortcut to the hotel just down here on the left?

It doesn't take long to figure out that relations between men and women are more rigid and conservative in Sicily than elsewhere in Italy, though this is probably attributable less to Roger II's pro-Islamic legacy than to the usual reasons, poverty and religion. One morning in Piazza Umberto I in Caltagirone, I count forty men and two women. The latter are there strictly temporarily: one has her purchases at her feet and is clearly waiting to be picked up, even though she isn't standing at a bus stop, and the other is stopping briefly to chat with a man on a bench, someone more likely to be a father than a husband, as he, like most of the others, is gray-headed and thick in the middle. Where are all the women? Being dutiful, I suppose: making dinner or caring for little ones or just staying out of sight.

There's a certain ceramic store Barbara wants to find that's supposed to be just off the piazza, so she goes in one direction and I in another. When I get back, the two women who were there before are gone, and Barbara, the only female there, is obviously a subject of speculation. From where I stand, she looks like a shore bird who has mistakenly lit in a forest full of quizzical, aging bears.

At the farmhouse where we stay, we are given two steaks at dinner, and Barbara puts the bigger one on my plate. But when the *signora* brings dessert and slides the larger slice of *cassata alla siciliana* in front of Barbara, she keeps her slice, even though it's twice the size of mine. As I glare, she grabs her fork and wades in, so I start to pick at mine. Five minutes later, I'm done with my slice, and she's only halfway through hers; the time it takes her to finish seems endless. Pouting, I agree to go on a moonlit walk. As Tina bounds ahead and the older Leo ambles after her, Barbara says, "I know you wanted me to give you that big piece of cake, but I'd already given you the bigger steak, so I figured, do I have to give him the bigger everything?"

◆

When June Carter came on stage in Folsom, the prisoners were restrained. There was no hooting and cat-calling the way there had been at the production of *Waiting for Godot* I had seen. Cash had won the inmates over by that point; it was obvious that day that Johnny Cash was the man and she his woman. He proposed to her in February of this same year, and they married within a month.

June Carter Cash would have been a remarkable woman even if she had never met Johnny. Born into the legendary Carter family, she performed as a child on their radio broadcasts; later she studied acting in New York with Sandy Meisner, who trained Gregory Peck and Robert Duvall, and she was an accomplished writer as well. When she married Johnny Cash, though, she abandoned her career for decades to devote herself to him and their family. The choice was voluntary, according to her: "I chose to be Mrs. Johnny Cash in my life. I decided I'd allow him to be Moses, and I'd be Moses' brother Aaron, picking his arms up and padding along behind him. . . . I stayed in submission to my husband, and he allowed me to do anything I wanted to. I felt like I was lucky to have that kind of romance." Lucky or not, it would be more than thirty years before she came out with an album on her own, the Grammy-winning *Press On,* though she and Cash recorded duets together, including "If I Were a Carpenter," a catchy tune I have always found creepy; in one verse, the male voice asks the female to imagine if he were a tinker and then wants to know if she would mind him, carrying the pots he made and following behind him.

Okay, so Johnny Cash was no feminist, either. But if he wasn't a cafeteria-style leftist, what was he? He must have known that most of the prisoners he appeared to romanticize were really like the baseball bat killer recalled by producer Bob Johnston. The answer may lie in his hardscrabble childhood. In briefly reconstructing the years Cash spent in Dyess, Arkansas, before joining the air force, Streissguth relies on the singer's comments to biographer Christopher Wren, and his memories of his boyhood put an American face on Peter Robb's critique of the vertical organization of agricultural life in every country. As a boy in Dyess, Cash knew best the lowest stratum: "Across the road on the Stuckey plantation," he recalls, "was a three-room shotgun shack. Every year, a different family would move in and ask us if they could farm part of the crops. They were in dire poverty. They'd come with rags on their backs and maybe a skillet tied on their wagon. Mostly they just walked in"

Cash also told Wren stories that seem to come out of the dark forests of European folk tales: of the father who buried his child in a ditch bank, the six-year-old who poisoned his father. As an adult, says Streissguth, Cash "carried these scenes with him as if they were sacred beads, invoking Christ's golden rule as he walked with Indians, common people, and prisoners."

Here Cash sounds less like Bob Dylan than an earlier American original, Walt Whitman, who, in "Song of Myself," walks with priests and politicians but also bastards, amputees, opium eaters, runaway slaves.

♦

In the end, we decide to go to Corleone anyway. Our Palermo jitters have dissolved in the countryside, and besides, we've seen all but one or two of the Greek temples and Roman amphitheaters which were our real reason for visiting Sicily. On our last day, then, we decide to finish up with a Mob Tour, beginning with Lercara Friddi, the town where Lucky Luciano was born. His family, too, was one of the countless that emigrated to New York, where Luciano lived out his own version of the American Dream: he became a crime boss, went to jail, was freed during the war to help Allied forces take Sicily, and died peacefully in Naples in 1962.

Today Lercara Friddi is much like any of the other little towns we've seen: a piazza or two, a duomo, lots of people in the streets, mostly men. Maybe I'm imagining it, but as the men on the sidewalk fall silent and even stoop slightly to peer into our car, it seems to me that The New People From Elsewhere are getting a more intense once-over than they got earlier. The interior of the duomo is lit not by floodlights hidden in high wall sconces but by a dozen chandeliers in need of a vigorous dusting. There is a Figli Sinatra garage; a sign promises that the Sinatra Sons will tackle any problem on any type of car. For a moment, I think about asking a barman for the *guida telefonica* so I can see if there are still any Lucianos in town, but anyone looking over my shoulder is liable to figure out why I've got my nose in the Ls. We'll only be in Sicily one more day; why step on somebody's toes now?

The closer we get to Corleone, the more surprised I am at how nervous I feel. Barbara always says there are two ways she can tell when there's another car behind us in Italy—I sit up straight and I stick my shoulders in my ears—and I'm driving high and tight now, even though the road behind us is empty. When we reach the town, though, suddenly we're through it and on the other side: most towns have signs saying "To the center" or "To the Duomo," but if there are such signs outside Corleone, we've missed them. So we go back and try again, and still we can't find Corleone. The third time, we use the never-fail method: instead of looking for signs that aren't there or that we can't see, we just do the opposite of what we did earlier, turning left where we went right and vice versa.

Out of nowhere, suddenly we found ourselves in the middle of Corleone. I'm relieved: far from being a Sicilian version of Dodge City, the town is disappointingly tame. Food and drink venues have the same bland English names they have everywhere in Italy: Sweet Temptations, Big Burger, Black and White Pub, Excelsior Bar. There is a sandwich shop called Strange Days, and I think, okay, the owner is a Doors fan, but who'd buy a *panino* at a place called Strange Days? A man walks in front of me with a shotgun under his arm, and I think, "Pop-pop . . . pop!" But he's a hunter, not a button man, and the heft of his game bag suggests that the rabbit and bird population around Corleone is significantly smaller today.

Then I see it, just as we are driving out of town: a ragged plastic ad banner that says "BEVETE AMARO DON COR-LEONE." In the town he made famous, I'm urged to try the after-dinner drink named after the fictitious don; other than that, I could be anywhere.

Besides, the other little towns just south of Palermo—Partinico, San Cipirello, San Giuseppe Jato—are just as likely to breed killers and *pentiti* as Corleone. A half-literate graffito in San Giuseppe Jato says "*GIOVANNI BRUSCA SI PENTE / 18 CARATI*," which might be rendered along the lines of "GIO-VANNI BRUSCA, 18-CARAT RAT." Since the penitent ma-fiosi have to go through a long process of proving themselves, the writing might be saying that Brusca hasn't completely sold out—yet. Or simply that he's not a very good rat. Or, more sinisterly, and as his re-imprisoning the week before suggests, that he is one of the many *pentiti* who may be playing a double game and cooperating with legitimate authorities only in order to retain as much as possible of their dark power.

◆

Though the two shows at Folsom Prison never bordered on the mayhem that the edited recordings suggest, there were spontaneous exchanges between entertainers and audience, notably when Cash reached down to shake the hand of a convict named Glen Sherley, whose song "Greystone Chapel" he had just performed. Sherley had done time in the juvenile system before embarking on a career of small-time stickups; following jailbreak and recapture, he had been sent to the maximum security facility at Folsom. The prison was actually "an artistic beehive," writes Streissguth, where inmates painted, sculpted, wrote poetry, sang, and played every instrument. Like the young Johnny Cash at Landsberg Air Force Base, Glen Sherley used music as a way to fly over the walls.

With Cash's support, Sherley was eventually paroled. As an American *pentito,* he profited nicely: having testified at senate hearings on prison reform, Sherley married, bought a car (or more than one, since his inexperience at driving led to several wrecks), and even recorded an album that reached number 32 on the country charts.

But old habits die hard for thugs in every country. Sherley's unease with his new life surfaced as he began to disappear unexpectedly or lose his temper on stage. Bassist Marshall Grant recalls talking with Sherley in his room one day when the ex-con looked up and said, "'Marshal, let me tell you something. I love you like a brother. I really love you like a brother. You've been so helpful with me. . . . I appreciate that.' But he said, 'You know what I would really like to do?' I said, 'No, man. What would you like to do?' He said, 'I'd like to get a knife and cut you all to hell. Let you lay there on the floor and bleed to death.' He said, 'Now that's what I'd like to do to you. But I can't. Unfortunately, I can't do that, so let's try to be friends.'" Sherley eventually left Nashville, rattled around the country for a few years, took up his druggy ways again, and, in 1978, shot himself to death on his brother's porch.

A few days after Cash died in 2003, it was Hallowe'en, so I dyed my hair black, made an eight-foot long cardboard guitar, and wrote on it in spangles the names of his hits: "Ring of Fire," "I Walk the Line," "Folsom Prison Blues," and the song that I now realize is Cash's most Sicilian work, the woeful, resigned "I Don't Like It But I Guess Things Happen That Way." Halfway through my round of parties, though, I realized I wasn't having as much fun as I thought I would.

In the end, there was nothing fun about being Johnny Cash. I've never been to Dyess, and even if I had, it wouldn't be the same Dyess that Cash grew up in. But the more I learned about Sicily, the more I saw what poverty and hunger and abuse can do to the human spirit. Cash was an entertainer, but he was a witness as well; he had seen what millions of others have seen in every country and every time, and he gave voice to their despairing vision. Johnny Cash didn't have to be who anyone else wanted him to be. He simply had to remember where violent, unhappy men came from and sing about it.

◆

The night before we leave Sicily, we stay in a coastal town called Cefalù, a name with unsettling associations for one who grew up where I did. There were lots of Cefalus (the accent had been dropped long before) in South Louisiana, and they were just part of the sizeable number of Sicilians who had emigrated in the late nineteenth and early twentieth centuries to escape hard times. Not, at least in the beginning, that the times were any easier in America. The new arrivals were poor and dark and wore strange clothes and ate food no one had ever heard of; they spoke a language that no one could understand and practiced a religion that, with all its saints and bloody icons, seemed idolatrous, almost pagan to the Pentecostals of Hammond and Amite. The Sicilians and other southern Italians were feared and mistrusted, and my mother, who was born on a farm in Tangipahoa Parish in 1902, used to recall with tight-lipped shame the brutal treatment that these new arrivals received in the Land of Promise. People still talked, she told me, of the eleven Italians who were accused of murdering police chief David Hennessey in nearby New Orleans in 1891; after they were acquitted, a mob dragged them from jail and hanged them.

Our last morning in Sicily, we had breakfast at our hotel in Cefalù before driving through Lercara Friddi and Corleone and leaving the car at Falcone-Borsellino Airport outside Palermo and flying north. From where we sat in the dining room, we could see the Mediterranean. The sun on the water was blindingly bright; it would be a good day for driving. I took a bite out of my *cannolo* and looked up again and almost fell out of my chair in surprise. In the time it took to nibble a pastry, the water had been covered with a thick, yellowish fog. What had happened to the light? It had been there just a moment before. And then, as quickly as a song ends, as a man falls to the earth when a bullet enters his heart, it was gone.

The Meaning Of Everything

For months after Barbara bought the second edition of the *Oxford English Dictionary,* the boxes the twenty volumes came in littered our stairs. I can see why she kept them, since they're both beautiful and sturdy; from volume I ("A–Bazouki") to volume XX ("Wave–Zyxt"), the boxes are of durable sky-blue cardboard stamped with cobalt lettering, and each has a no-nonsense lid that snaps open and shut like the door of a tiny but well-made car.

No doubt numberless word lovers bought the OED the year Barbara did, thanks to a holiday promotion; normally priced at $3,000, the sale price was about a third of that, if memory serves. It's actually a little cheaper right now; as of this writing, all twenty volumes are available at a special seventy-fifth anniversary price of $895. This may be the last chance to get the OED so cheaply, since the world's biggest dictionary is going to get a lot bigger. As Simon Winchester points out in *The Meaning of Everything: The Story of the Oxford English Dictionary,* the revised edition now being compiled could run to as many as forty volumes and thus be so ungainly that it can only take on-line form.

The Meaning of Everything is an entrancing read because, while it takes the quantitative approach that a multiyear, multivolume project employing thousands of workers requires, it also resonates with all the chauvinism and misgiving, the self-congratulation and self-doubt that emerge when we think about our language. A word is just a cluster of black marks on a white page, and almost every word we read is familiar to us, or reading would be impossible. Yet there's a story behind each word—or more than one story, if one takes the historical approach, as did the OED editors when they decided to follow each definition with as many quotations as are necessary to show how usage changes over time. Multiply this by the 625,100 words in the second edition and the 2,436,600 quotations used to illustrate them, and the result is not just a dictionary but also an anthology containing every nuance of every tragedy and comedy to befall us Anglophones.

At the heart of any dictionary is a question about language itself: does it define us or we it? Certainly such studies as Wm. C. Hannas's *Asia's Orthographic Dilemma* and Richard E. Nisbett's *The Geography of Thought: How Asians and Westerners Think Differently . . . and Why* suggest that how we read and write determines how we think, and both books have been misread so as to seem to say that Western languages are somehow "superior" to others.

Yet one point experts agree on is that English, like the boxes the OED comes in, gets high marks for being both beautiful and practical, thanks first to its unique double-sourcedness and then to its friendliness toward words from elsewhere. English has two primary faucets, one gushing Old English and the other Norman French; the first language is notably blunt and candid, the other flowery and ornate. As with much else in contemporary culture, a huge debt is owed to Shakespeare for using so many now-familiar words for the first time, as when, for example, he added the Norman French *-able* to Old English *laugh* to allow Salanio in *The Merchant of Venice* to declare a jest *laughable*. And the rich stew of English has been further thickened by words from dozens of other languages, including Malay (*bamboo, ketchup*), Turkish (*kiosk, sofa*), Algonquian (*raccoon, wampum*), and Dutch (*cruise, knapsack*).

Now not every *ayatollah* (Persian) or *mullah* (Urdu) is likely to endorse Winchester's chest-thumping description of English as "so vast, so sprawling, so wonderfully unwieldy, so subtle, and now in its never-ending fullness so undeniably magnificent." Yet no one can deny the language's "foxy and relentlessly slippery flexibility."

The task of corralling this tricksy, ingenious tongue fell to one James Augustus Henry Murray, an unlikely prospect for such work yet no more unsuitable than any of the other gifted eccentrics who devoted themselves to the dictionary over the years. A linen draper's son from Scotland, he had been brought up in rural isolation, though he developed a precocious interest in, well, pretty much everything: geology, botany, astronomy, history, archaeology, manuscript illumination, and, not surprisingly, languages. Unable to afford college, he left school at fourteen, though eventually he became a teacher, and by age thirty-eight found himself, during what he later called "the happiest period of my life," teaching at Mill Hill School in London, happily married and a father. All this changed on March 1, 1879, when he was appointed senior editor of a new dictionary projected to be some seven thousand pages, to cost nine thousand pounds, and to take no more than ten years to complete.

One wonders what he and his colleagues would have thought had they known that this first edition of the OED would ultimately require sixteen thousand pages, three hundred thousand pounds, and fifty-four years of steady toil. That it was completed at all is testimony to Murray's calm, cheerful persistence, especially given the quirky nature of so many of the others involved in the enterprise. There was Nottingham farmer's son Henry Bradley, for example; Bradley was said to have learned Russian in fourteen days, though he could identify only one tune, "God Save the Queen," and only because everyone stood when it was played. Another key figure is Frederick James Furnivall, an indifferent mathematics student at Cambridge yet, as an adult, an impassioned devotee of rowing whose hobby was to teach busty waitresses how to scull; Winchester refers to the sepia photographs of Furnivall "speeding along the river, a pretty girl behind him, with his long white beard flowing in the wind, the two of them a picture of goatish contentment."

Murray and the other editors wrote the definitions, but the bulk of the OED consists of the illustrative quotations that follow every word, and these were provided by hundreds upon hundreds of unpaid volunteers. Winchester has written more fully of one of these, William Chester Minor, in his 1998 book *The Pro-*

fessor and the Madman, the story of the surgeon who murdered a stranger during a schizophrenic episode, yet for twenty-one years supplied the OED with quotations from his cell in the Broadmoor asylum for criminal lunatics.

If Minor was the least likely of volunteers, the most engaging may well be the American Fitzedward Hall, who was about to start his studies at Harvard when his father sent him to India to find a brother who had run off. Hall's ship foundered in the Bay of Bengal, and with neither ship to return home on nor brother (whom he never found), the would-be scholar slaked his thirst for learning by becoming fluent in Hindustani, Bengali, Sanskrit, and Persian. Eventually Hall made his way to England and became professor of Sanskrit at King's College, London, though, following a mysterious row with another academic, he fled to a remote cottage in East Anglia. When he learned of Murray's project, he volunteered his services in 1881, and "from that moment onward he wrote every single day" for decades, working so assiduously that Murray became frantic on the few occasions that Hall fell ill.

With few exceptions, these volunteers, who seem to have come from every country, profession, and walk of life, labored selflessly and with the expectation of no other reward than a footnote mention in eight-point Clarendon type. Winchester prefers not to guess at the reason behind this tireless altruism, though my guess is that it has something to do with what sociologists call familiarly "the urge to merge," a desire to join an enterprise larger than oneself, and, in this case, a cause that, like English itself, is rooted in a love of precision as well as a dreamy artiness.

The boxes Barbara's OED came in are now stacked neatly in a corner of her office, and she says she's thinking of using them to package gifts. With one exception: the box for volume XVI, "Soot–Styx," is surely destined for someone's ashes. James Murray was known to crack a half-smile whenever some piece of meaningful silliness came to his attention, and Winchester's wonderful book reminds us why English will always have the capacity to make its hearers shiver and laugh.

Chekhov's Influence On Shakespeare

Something Recognizably His

It's a chilly autumn evening in London, and I've just returned from a production of *Twelfth Night* at the Donmar Warehouse, the charming pocket-sized venue where Sam Mendes directed so many memorable plays (of which this is the last) before he decided to give up London theatre and instead make mediocre Hollywood movies like *American Beauty* and *Road to Perdition*. All in all, a stunning performance of the best comedy written by the world's greatest comic writer.

And yet how different this performance was from the other London *Twelfth Night* that had closed just a few weeks before, the enormously successful all-male production that had run all summer across the river in Shakespeare's Globe. In fact, if you were Sam Mendes, you might well ask yourself what you had in mind when you decided to go up against this riotously funny people-pleaser.

But that's what made Mendes such a gifted theatre director: that he chose not to compete with the Globe production but to mount a version that was so opposite as to seem a completely different play. Well, not *completely* different, but different as a twin is from its sibling, the same thing yet its opposite.

For one thing, whereas the Globe players had audiences capsizing with laughter, the Donmar Warehouse play was wistful to the point of melancholy. When these older actors (most of whom were in their forties and fifties rather than their thirties and forties, like the ones at the Globe) agree in act 2, scene 3, that "Youth's a stuff will not endure," that became a main theme in this version, whereas I don't remember even noticing it in the Globe production. One particularly effective aspect of Mendes's minimalist set was the use of an outsized picture frame at center rear; when one character spoke longingly or fondly of another, often that other would walk on slowly and then turn and stand in the frame, gazing fondly at the lover as one might from a distance or perhaps even from heaven—the beloved sometimes seem so totally unobtainable in Shakespeare that they might indeed be dead.

In addition to the actors and the set, even the music supported this bittersweet staging. I'll say more about the Globe's music later, but suffice it here to say it was raucous and boisterous; you couldn't hear the rustic trumpets and pipes and drums without thinking of the nonsensical yet expressive word "razzmatazz" as well as its Bronx-cheer cousin "raspberry." By contrast, the Donmar Warehouse music was honeyed and sorrowful. There were only three instruments there: a piano, a guitar, and, most important, a cello, whose low moans and banshee sobs were an aural match for the grays and blacks of the players' costumes.

Twelfth Night wasn't Mendes's only success at the Donmar Warehouse this season. A month earlier, I'd seen a superb *Uncle Vanya* there. Now *Uncle Vanya* is universally acclaimed as one of the best plays ever; it's on most actors', directors', and producers' top-ten lists of plays they want to be part of. But it's a play that has never really got under my skin. Certainly there are juicy lines, but the characters all seem to come from the same street in the same neighborhood, and the plot goes in one direction until it runs into a (not very imaginative) challenge and then lands quietly, like a plane coming to rest following a bit of midflight turbulence.

In fact, having seen a merely wonderful *Uncle Vanya* first and an extraordinary *Twelfth Night* shortly thereafter, I couldn't help thinking what Shakespeare might have done with Chekhov's play. With rare exception, he derived all his plays from earlier sources, which he then complicated, sometimes almost beyond recognition. At the very least, he would have added several plot lines to *Uncle Vanya* as well as the necessary new characters to flesh them out, and he would also have sped up the pace.

Now no doubt I was taking my thought a bit farther than other viewers would, but I wasn't alone in making connections between the two plays. A couple of days after I saw the Shakespeare play, Sheridan Morley noted in the *International Herald Tribune* how the play staged first affected the one performed second, that this *Twelfth Night* was "in Russian mood" and therefore was no "mindless frolic of mistaken identity but a strange, soulful tragi-comedy about bisexuality, depression, and misplaced power, closer to the later Shakespeare of *Winter's Tale* or *Cymbeline* in its many moods and internal conflicts." Of course, the connection was made easier by the fact that the cast was the same in both *Uncle Vanya* and *Twelfth Night:* Simon Russell Beale was Vanya and Malvolio, Emily Watson was Sonya and Viola, and so on.

No wonder, then, that one viewer might think that, had Shakespeare come across the text of *Uncle Vanya* in some old book, he might have seen in it the raw potential he saw in so many of his other sources and, with characteristic speed and dexterity, turned it into, not *Twelfth Night* or even a play as marvelous as that one, but something recognizably his.

A Quilt Is One And Many Things

And what would something "recognizably his" be, exactly? What does Shakespeare do that is not only different from what other playwrights do but also better? I can begin answering that question by quoting something I heard a guide say at Shakespeare's Globe just before the performance there of the other, rowdier *Twelfth Night,* namely, that, with each play, Shakespeare issued to his audiences "an invitation to an elaborate game that's both absolutely realistic and total make-believe at the same time."

Every playwright, filmmaker, and novelist—every mimetic artist, in other words—does this, of course. In *Mimesis as Make-Believe,* Kendall Walton suggests that literary works are best seen from the point of view of children's acts of make-believe. Thus a child pretending to build a fort will say "I built this big fort today" rather than "I pulled some branches and boards together and pretended it was a fort." To be effective, though, the totally believable fort must continue to partake of its unbelievable aspects. A child might be delighted momentarily if a millionaire parent had a ready-made fort installed in the backyard, but he or she would probably become bored quickly; hence the truism familiar to every father and mother of the child discarding the expensive toy and devoting hours to play with the box it came in.

Okay, so we all do that, all of us writers: we all offer readers a paradox requiring a perception of total artificiality combined with an utterly unself-conscious sense of engagement. But what makes Shakespeare's paradoxes better than my paradoxes or your paradoxes or anyone else's paradoxes? It's not as though we haven't been trying to figure him out for centuries, often throwing in the towel after rounds of futile struggle. Thus Emerson, who, in *Representative Men,* pronounced Shakespeare "inconceivably wise; the others, conceivably. A good reader can, in a sort, nestle into Plato's brain and think from thence; but not into Shakespeare's. We are still out of doors. For executive faculty, for creation, Shakespeare is unique. No man can imagine it better." I don't know about nestling into Shakespeare's (or anybody else's) brain, but I think I can offer some insight into why he appeals to all sorts of audiences and continues to inspire other artists as no writer has.

Or at least I'd like to try, beginning, since we're dealing with paradox here, with a fundamental contradiction: this most original playwright's lack of originality. First, with such exceptions as *The Merry Wives of Windsor,* Shakespeare borrowed his plots from sources contemporary and historical: *As You Like It* from Thomas Lodge's 1590 prose romance *Rosalynde, Coriolanus* from Plutarch, and so on. Indeed, the more dependent he was on sources, the better the play; *Merry Wives* is a whole lot of fun, but nobody ever called it one of Shakespeare's greatest. Second, he collaborated; his work with George Wilkins on *Pericles* and with John Fletcher on *Two Gentlemen of Verona, Henry VIII,* and *Cardenio,* the so-called "lost play," are well documented, but it's hard to believe that a playwright who was as gregarious as Shakespeare and who had so many playwright friends (Ben Jonson, Christopher Marlowe, Beaumont and Fletcher) didn't "talk shop" and reap the benefits thereof. Third, he recycled characters (kings, queens, fools, young lovers, heartless murderers, trailer-trash minor nobility), language ("The Wind and the Rain" song in both *King Lear* and *Twelfth Night,* almost identical lines in that play and *The Winter's Tale*), and plot devices (shipwrecks in a dozen plays, the miraculous off-stage preservation and reappearance of Emilia in *A Comedy of Errors* and Thaisa in *Pericles*). I mean, he wrote nearly forty plays, most of them masterpieces, in a little over twenty years; how could someone write so much and so consistently *without* borrowing, collaborating, and recycling? The plot of the movie *Shakespeare in Love* is ludicrous, but the more you find out about Shakespeare's compositional habits, the more the scenes depicting his writing processes—the starts and stops, the happy accidents, the verbal sparring with peers, the magpie plucking of a line heard here or a character spied there, and above all, the intensely collaborative nature of it all—seem almost documentary.

So there you have the supreme paradox of this most paradoxical of playwrights, that the most original of writers is the least original. No wonder he has not only delighted but baffled (and, in some cases, enraged) his would-be explainers over the years. The quote from Emerson about not being able to nestle into Shakespeare's brain expresses most of what those who have tried and failed to explain Shakespeare have felt; three stories, the first by Henry James and the other two by Jorge Luis Borges, cover the rest.

In James's "The Birthplace," a man named Gedge and his wife become the caretakers of the house in which Shakespeare was born. A capital-B Bardolater, Gedge can't believe his good fortune: "The shrine at which he was to preside—though he had always lacked occasion to approach it—figured to him as the most sacred known to the steps of men, the early home of the supreme poet, the Mecca of the English-speaking race." At first, he tells visitors that we know nothing about Shakespeare, and at least one fellow worshiper, a young American, offers a sympathetic ear: "'He escapes us like a thief at night, carrying off—well, carrying off everything. And people pretend to catch Him like a flown canary, over whom you can close your hand and put Him back. He won't *go* back; he won't *come* back. He's not'—the young man laughed—'such a fool! It makes Him the happiest of all great men.'" Gedge, however, is the unhappiest of men, since the tourists who visit the birthplace know nothing about the plays yet want to know everything about the man:

"That's just what They won't do—not let *me* do. It's all I want—to let the author alone. Practically"—he felt himself getting the last of his chance—"there *is* no author; that is for us to deal with. There are all the immortal people—*in* the work; but there's nobody else."

"Yes," said the young man—"that's what it comes to. There should really, to clear the matter up, be no such Person."
"As you say," Gedge returned, "it's what it comes to. There *is* no such Person."

The evening air listened, in the warm, thick midland stillness, while the wife's little cry rang out. "But *wasn't* there—?"

"There was somebody," said Gedge, against the doorpost. "But They've killed Him. And, dead as He is, They keep it up, They do it over again, They kill Him every day."

In the end, though, Gedge gives in. He begins to make up stories about Shakespeare, including details of the playwright's private life. Of course, he becomes a huge success with the visitors and receives a raise in salary.

There is a similar theme in Borges's much-discussed story

"Everything and Nothing." The Shakespeare here has acted many parts but has never had a self. He speaks of this to God—if you're going to have Shakespeare as a character, why not go all the way?—but Borges's God is a postmodernist. "'Neither am I anyone,'" says the Deity. "'I have dreamt the world as you dreamt your work, my Shakespeare, and among the forms in my dream are you, who like myself are many and no-one.'" Borges is typically playful and indirect in his identification of Shakespeare with God and avoids the bluntness of Heine, whose statement in praise of Aristophanes might be paraphrased to say that "There is a God, and his name is Shakespeare."

"Everything and Nothing" is mentioned often in writings about Shakespeare. Yet the more complex and engaging by Borges is "Shakespeare's Memory," whose narrator, Hermann Sörgel, is a Shakespearean scholar. Sörgel attends a conference and meets a man named Daniel Thorpe, a former military physician. In that role, Thorpe once attended a dying enlisted man named Adam Clay in some far-flung outpost of the Empire. Just as Clay dies, he offers Thorpe Shakespeare's memory, on these conditions: "'The one who possesses it must offer it aloud, and the one who is to receive it must accept it the same way. The man who gives it loses it forever.'"

Thorpe gives the memory to Sörgel but explains that "'The memory has entered your mind, but it must be "discovered." It will emerge in dreams or when you are awake, when you turn the pages of a book or turn a corner. Don't be impatient; don't *invent* recollections. Chance in its mysterious workings may help it along or it may hold it back. As I gradually forget, you will remember. I can't tell you how long the process will take.'" Among the many things Sörgel learns is that "Shakespeare's apparent instances of inadvertence . . . were deliberate. Shakespeare tolerated them—or actually interpolated them—so that his discourse, destined for the stage, might appear to be spontaneous, and not overly polished and artificial. . . . That same goal inspired him to mix his metaphors: 'my way of life / Is fall'n into the sear, the yellow leaf.'" (Or, as Simon Russell Beale said when he came to our Study Centre to talk with the students, "Shakespeare was famously oblivious to his inconsistencies.")

In the end, Sörgel decides to give the gift away: Spinoza, he remembers, says "the wish of all things . . . is to continue to be what they are. The stone wishes to be stone, the tiger, tiger—and I wanted to be Hermann Sörgel again." So he dials telephone numbers at random until he finds someone to give the gift to. First, though, given that he now knows everything about Shakespeare, including what happened during the so-called "lost years" after the playwright-to-be left school and before he appeared on the London scene, Sörgel contemplates writing a biography but ultimately decides not to (significantly, he points out that Daniel Thorpe had and abandoned the same idea). Why? Because "I do not know how to tell a story," says Sörgel. "I do not know how to tell *my own* story, which is a great deal more extraordinary than Shakespeare's. Besides, such a book would be pointless. Chance, or fate, dealt Shakespeare those trivial terrible things that all men know; it was his gift to be able to transmute them into fables, into characters that were much more alive than the gray man who dreamed them, into verses which will never be abandoned, into verbal music. What purpose would it serve to unravel that wondrous fabric, besiege and mine the tower, reduce to the modest proportions of a documentary biography or a realistic novel the sound and fury of *Macbeth*?"

As different as is the Emerson essay, the story by James, and the two by Borges, all four of these—not "attempts to explain Shakespeare" but something like "engagements with the idea of explaining Shakespeare and ultimate rejections of that idea"— not only lead away from the playwright's life but also point to the text that is, like Poe's purloined letter, so obviously right in front of our eyes that we keep overlooking it, namely, the plays themselves. The first paradox we have examined here is that Shakespeare achieved originality by being unoriginal; the second is that every single work of his is no single work but a pastiche of sources, plots, subplots, songs and poems, special effects, vaudevillian high jinks, tableaux, set pieces, choruses, and borrowings from himself and others. In other words, Shakespeare is literature's supreme quilt-maker, and just as a quilt is one thing and many things, so is each of his plays.

"Do Not Saw The Air Too Much With Your Hand"

A third sort of paradox in Shakespeare is the one I'll call the paradox of thematic assymetry, which means that the comedies tend to be marred by unhappiness at the end just as the tragedies usually conclude with some sort of optimistic uptick. To give just two examples from each genre, *The Comedy of Errors* ends with the reconciliation of the two Dromios but a baffling chill between the two characters named Antipholus; *Twelfth Night* concludes with marriages all around but also the spiteful handling of Malvolio and his angry vow of revenge. And among the tragedies, *Macbeth* concludes with bloody deaths as well as Malcolm's speedy restoration of order and convincing promise of a better day to come; similarly, the final word in *Richard III* goes to Richmond, who delivers a virtual state-of-the-union address in which all of Richard's bloody crimes are erased in the promise of a harmonious future.

But the paradox that is most essential to an understanding of Shakespeare is the one I'll call twinning. As I've said already, a pair of twins is a paradox, one thing yet two. Within the general population, twins exist among us as synecdochic signposts pointing toward the myriad other paradoxes that zigzag through the human comedy as surely as the drips and splashes in a Jackson Pollock painting exist as themselves as well as parts of an aesthetic whole. As the father of the twins Judith and Hamnet, Shakespeare must have had plenty of occasions on which to consider that each pair of twins is a paradox, two creatures yet one. Or, as the astonished Orsino says in act 5, scene 1, of *Twelfth*

Night when Sebastian and Viola are revealed to be brother and sister, "One face, one voice, one habit, and two persons!" At the Globe production, Orsino was played by Liam Brennan with a broad Scottish accent which with he underscored the baffled joy this paradox produces in him (and us), pausing before the last two words, turning to the audience in wide-eyed astonishment, and all but roaring "TWO PAIR-SONS!"

And that's just zygotic twinship. Other forms of twinning in Shakespeare include literal disguises (Bottom is an ass in *A Midsummer Night's Dream,* Viola a boy in *Twelfth Night*) as well as the kinds of disguising that take place from the inside out. Thus there are two Hamlets, the sane one and the one who feigns madness (at least act 3, scene 4, by which time the two Hamlets have become one). And Macbeth disguises himself not only to others but also, in order to accomplish his terrible deeds, to himself, as he indicates when he says, "False face must hide what the false heart doth know" (act 1, scene 7) and "Make our faces vizards [visors] to our hearts, / Disguising what they are" (act 3, scene 2). Directors can further Shakespeare's penchant for twinning by giving actors two parts, as in the Albery Theatre production of *Macbeth* I saw in which Julian Glover plays Duncan and then, just seconds after Duncan is slain, makes an uncanny if appropriate appearance as the drunken Porter who thinks he's at the gates of Hell. (Afterwards, Glover become a triplet in my eyes as I walked toward the Leicester Square tube station and saw this sixtyish actor duck out of the stage door, don a motorcycle helmet, and roar off on two wheels to skirt the portals of the underworld on London's crowded, rainy streets.)

And as if the twinning of characters were not enough, Shakespeare makes twins of his plays as well: In *A Midsummer Night's Dream,* the *Pyramus and Thisbe* playlet, with its comical lovers' confusion over death and suicide, mimics tragic versions of this same scenario in *Romeo and Juliet* and *Antony and Cleopatra.* And this same playlet at least refers to what might have been a similar scenario in *The Mousetrap,* the play-within-a-play in

Hamlet whose outcome will never be known because the performance is halted by a guilty Claudius. *Henry V* begins with a Chorus announcing that what follows will be a simulacrum of reality rather than the thing itself, and the entirety of *The Taming of the Shrew* is preceded by an often-ignored Induction which says that everything which follows is "false." In *Twelfth Night,* when Fabian says in act 3, scene 4, that "If this were played upon a stage now, I could condemn it as an improbable fiction," he winks at us and lets us in on the game at the same time that he is telling us he and the other players can do what they want.

In fact, in the hands of a skilled director, each play is made to become multiples of itself. In the *Midsummer Night's Dream* program, notes by Master of Play Mike Alfreds describe his approach to directing, how he not only breaks the play into units ("Theseus expresses his impatience for his and Hermia's wedding night," for example) but also rehearses each unit from what he calls a different "point of concentration" each time. Thus, if the actors are rehearsing the scene in which the Rude Mechanicals are practicing their play, the Master might ask the players to concentrate on the fact that they are in a dark wood filled with wild animals but also wondrous fairies. At the next rehearsal, the Master would ask the players to concentrate on a different point: that they are practicing a play which will be presented before the Duke of Athens, whom they are fearful of offending, but whose preferment will assure their success. "The process is a sort of layering," says Alfreds, in which all the paradoxes of the play are brought to bear even if they are not discussed explicitly in the text.

In live production, even the music can contribute to the perception of doubleness in Shakespeare's plays. I've already pointed out how the wistful string music of the Donmar Warehouse version of *Twelfth Night* supported the bittersweet quality of the entire production. In contrast, the loud, blaring, period instrument music for the Globe *Twelfth Night* couldn't have been more different. The program notes to this production included a discussion of the use of a so-called "broken" consort to accompany the text, one that provided not strict polyphony or "whole noise" but a division of musical labor in which the viol, violin, and flute were responsible for the principal melody while the lute, cittern, and bandora contributed a jazzy ornamentation. Thus, for example, a dance involving both sober and comic characters could be both stately and erratic at the same time.

One of the most interesting types of twinning we see in Shakespeare involves what Harold Bloom calls "self-overhearing" in *Shakespeare: The Invention of the Human*. For when we talk to ourselves, we become two people, speaker and listener. All of Shakespeare's great soliloquies are examples of self-overhearing, but there are opportunities in live production for introducing less obvious examples. Thus, in the Globe production of *Twelfth Night* I saw, Orsino could be seen to hesitate and search for the right word in his private moments, as did Olivia; both were talking and listening to themselves as they sought clarity in a world of confused identities and muddled love matches. In contrast to these two uncertain, fumbling, self-overhearing characters, the supremely self-satisfied Malvolio did not merely utter his words confidently; no, he all but caressed them, as though each were something separate from himself, a child or darling pet.

It's important for a director to give actors and audiences this opportunity for self-overhearing. In her 1996 *New York Times* article "Helping Shakespeare Make an Easy Crossing," Margo Jefferson observes once that American actors are incapable of saying Shakespeare's words as English actors do. Her particular focus is on one of those Shakespeare in the Park productions involving a short run and celebrity actors, and it's easy to see how nervous, overprepared players might speak their lines quickly and unmusically, especially if they're going to do a only limited number of performances.

Jefferson has a point, but I don't think she's quite right. In an essay entitled "All's Well" (collected in *Berryman's Shakespeare*), John Berryman notes that, as Shakespeare developed as a playwright, he came to rely more and more upon timing for his humor. "This is in accordance with life," notes Berryman, for "the things at which we have laughed hardest are hardly every worth repeating—it was *when* they were said, *after* what, by whom." (He illustrates his remark with a recollection of *Twelfth Night* in which Laurence Olivier as Sir Toby Belch and Alec Guinness as Sir Andrew Aguecheek played the drinking scenes so slowly "they might almost have been dead.") Shakespeare's plays *read* quickly; on stage, they *play* slowly. Or should, as Theseus says in act 5, scene 1, of *A Midsummer Night's Dream.* And surely Hamlet is asking the Players, in act 3, scene 2, to pay attention to their timing when he asks them to "speak the speech . . . trippingly in the tongue; but if you mouth it, as many of our players do, I had as lief the town-crier spoke my lines. Nor do not saw the air too much with your hand, thus, but use all gently; for in the very torrent, tempest, and, as I may say, whirlwind of your passion, you must acquire and beget a temperance that may give it smoothness."

A final (and crucial) form of twinning in Shakespeare comes in the language of each play itself, and here each of us lucky enough to have English as our native tongue must thank Harold for taking that arrow through the eye at the Battle of Hastings in 1066. When William the Conqueror's Norman troops occupied England, they combined with the native population rather than supplanting it, and the result is a language that has all the advantages of an Anglo-Saxon vocabulary as well as a Latinate one. (I'm not just being patriotic here; when Gabriel Garcia Marquez said he preferred the English translations of his novels to the originals, he made a comment about the supple expressiveness of English that no Anglophone could.) What Shakespeare does is use both types of vocabulary in a studied yet graceful way. In his 1990 *Virginia Quarterly Review* article "Shakespeare and the Norman Conquest: English in the Elizabethan Theatre," George Watson argues that the playwright tosses a bone to educated courtiers and groundlings alike when he uses a polysyllabic

Latinate word and then a crisp Anglo-Saxon synonym; thus in act 2, scene 2, of *Twelfth Night,* Sir Andrew Aguecheek listens to a song sung by Feste and pronounces his voice "mellifluous" and then, in his next line, "sweet."

Like Hamlet's "What a piece of work is a man" speech in act 2, scene 2, twins are a reminder of everything that is remarkable about humanity. A twin is part of a whole that is always threatening to break into its parts, and from that tension spring all the surprises that define the human comedy.

The King's English

As one pauses in this consideration of Shakespeare's myriad tricks to catch one's breath and dry one's eyes of the tears that come from laughing or weeping or both, it becomes easy to see how the playwright may come to stand for too much of a muchness in the minds of those who don't like to chuckle or cry or wheeze—who, for whatever reason, simply don't like Shakespeare. The antis can be divided into two large groups. The first, the anti-Stratfordians, be they Oxfordians, Baconians, or of some other ilk, can be disposed of briefly. The questioning of Shakespeare's authorship didn't begin until the mid–nineteenth century; if this skepticism is valid, why doesn't it occur earlier? Delia Bacon is a representative if poignant example of one of the early anti-Stratfordians; convinced that the true author of Shakespeare's plays was Francis Bacon (to whom, incidentally, she was not related), she traveled to England, and, with the bemused support of Nathaniel Hawthorne, who recounts his time with Delia in *Our Old Home,* undertook several late-night vigils to Shakespeare's tomb, where apparently she awaited an announcement from the spirit world that she was right and the collected works hadn't been penned by someone she described as a "stupid, ignorant, third-rate play-actor." Delia died believing she was the Holy Ghost surrounded by devils, which pretty much says everything we need to know about her.

Unfortunately, she has been replaced by numberless latter-day skeptics acting under the guise of sanity. One of these, a professor in another discipline, cornered me at a party recently and asked, "But how do we know that Shakespeare wrote any of these plays at all?" I include the question mark here as a point of standard punctuation, but there was no rise at all in the professor's voice at the end of his statement; the question was a rhetorical one, and it was accompanied by a raised-eyebrow gaze which suggested that the mere asking of it was enough to torpedo centuries on the subject. I began by pointing out that Ben Jonson and plenty of Shakespeare's other contemporaries refer to him and his work plentifully, but the owner of the eyebrows merely lowered and raised them in a dismissive flourish before going in search of another drink.

What makes the anti-Stratfordian view particularly repellent is its built-in snobbery, its assumption that, because somebody didn't get his Ph.D. from an Ivy League university, he couldn't have written the plays—as though, in order to be able to write the plays, the playwright would have to have an education equal to that of those who have been trained to interpret him. (This view means that Keats, Dickens, Twain, and Whitman couldn't have written their work, either.) Probably the first to turn up his nose at Shakespeare's résumé was his contemporary Robert Greene, who sneered that he was "Maister of Artes in Neither University," though apparently this enmity didn't bother Shakespeare, who cheerfully filched the plot of *The Winter's Tale* from Greene's *Pandosto: The Triumph of Time.*

But despite the gaps in his biography, the historical record is quite clear on just how well Shakespeare, like other middle-class boys of his day, would have been schooled. A. L. Rowse's *Shakespeare the Man* tells how, in elementary school, Shakespeare would have learned his ABCs and numbers; more important, he would have been required to memorize the catechism with its big questions of creation, resurrection, and so on, as well as Psalms—all this before turning seven and going on to grammar school, where he would have studied classic plays (the comedies of Terence and Plautus, the tragedies of Seneca) and mastered the rules and practices of rhetoric.

Too, he would have learned to converse in Latin; in *Shakespeare for All Time,* the most recent Shakespeare biography, Stanley Wells gives evidence for the currency of Latin in this period by noting the existence of a 1599 letter in Latin to Shakespeare's Stratford friend Richard Quiney from his eleven-year-old son asking that Quiney bring some books of blank paper from London for the boy and his brother. After Shakespeare dropped out to help his beleaguered father with his glove-making business, the schooling ceased, but not the education: Wells suggests that Shakespeare joined an acting troupe during the so-called "lost years" and learned everything he could from his fellow thespians before finding out he was better as a writer.

Okay, so Shakespeare didn't go to Cambridge—Marlowe did, but then Marlowe but wasn't as a good a dramatist. As for those who claimed Christopher Marlowe faked his death in 1593 but continued to ghostwrite Shakespeare's plays thereafter, they'd have to believe that someone as volatile as Marlowe would have provided Shakespeare with, by my count, thirty-three plays without winking at least once or twice and saying, "I' faith, I wrote *Hamlet* and—promise not to tell?—*Lear, Macbeth,* and *Othello,* among others."

In addition to the anti-Stratfordians, the second big group of Shakespeare denigrators is made up, and here's another paradox for you, of those who teach him. Not that these people are picking on Shakespeare, of course; to them, all writers (except themselves) are frauds. Thus Christy Desmet, in *Shakespeare and Appropriation,* which she edited with Robert Sawyer: "The author, *no longer regarded as the origin of writing,* becomes simply a proper name by which we describe a piece of discourse" (italics mine). This sounds a bit like what Michel Foucault says in his essay "What Is an Author?" though even Foucault points out that it will not do to "repeat the empty affirmation that the author has disappeared."

Besides, his reputation being what it is, Shakespeare is a little harder than other writers to reduce to "simply a proper name." Thus, in *William Shakespeare*, Terry Eagleton sandwiches his dismissal between the bread of praise when he says "though exclusive evidence is hard to come by, it is difficult to read Shakespeare without feeling that he was almost certainly familiar with the writings of Hegel, Marx, Nietzsche, Freud, Wittgenstein and Derrida. Perhaps it is simply to say that though there are many ways in which *we have thankfully left this conservative patriarch behind,* there are other ways in which we have yet to catch up with him" (my italics).

People who can fix their mouths to call Shakespeare "this conservative patriarch" remind me of the art critics—and this includes most of them, as far as I can tell—who complain about Picasso's misogyny. Sure, Picasso expresses an anger toward women that borders on violence, but mixed with that is playfulness, humor, eroticism, and deep love. Or they're like the diner who choked and coughed and spat out the wine he'd ordered and who, when asked if it was sour, said no, he simply couldn't stand the stuff.

Hey, if you don't like wine, don't order it. But then if you got tenure and regular merit raises for guzzling something you couldn't stand, you'd probably do it, too. In "Alas, Poor Shakespeare! I Knew Him Well" (also in *Shakespeare and Appropriation*), Ivo Kamps points out that Shakespeare is big box office not just for his admirers but his detractors as well. You'd think a radical scholar would base a career on a revolutionary author like Brecht. But there's no money in Brecht. Instead, it makes sense to attach oneself to Shakespeare and chip away at him; the stratagem increases one's visibility and, since the host is indestructible, he'll never disappear, no matter how many parasites attach themselves. This is why, says Kamps, "feminists, Marxists, and cultural materialists seem very much at home these days in the reading rooms of the Folger Shakespeare Library—and I do not see any of them trying to tear the place down, the way

Protestant reformers smashed Catholic icons, nor close it down as Stalin did the churches."

Of course, Shakespeare helped his critics by his indifference, like that of every other playwright of the era, to the publication of his plays. In *Shakespeare Alive!* Joseph Papp and Elizabeth Kirkland note how Elizabethan acting companies violently opposed the printing of texts; in an era without copyright laws, publication amounted to giving a popular play to a rival acting company for nothing. Thus Shakespeare's body of plays didn't appear until seven years after his death. John Fletcher, who succeeded Shakespeare as ordinary poet for the King's Men, was equally indifferent. And their contemporary, playwright and actor Thomas Heywood, noted in the preface to his 1624 play *The English Traveller* that his plays weren't published because his acting company "think it against their peculiar profit to have them come in print"; in addition, says Heywood, "it was never any great ambition in me, to be in this kind voluminously read."

In the end, the truest thing one can say about Shakespeare's detractors has already been said by Kingsley Amis in *The King's English,* namely, "To say or imply that the man of this name is not our greatest writer marks a second-rate person at best."

All Roads Lead To Shakespeare

And yet, and yet . . . the snobs and the School of Resentment types are right, in a sense, when they say there's no such person as Shakespeare, just as Harold Bloom, the greatest of all living bardolaters, is wrong when he says that, in Shakespeare, "here at last we encounter an intelligence without limits." Because it's the plays that have limitless intelligence, not the playwright. He wrote them, sure, but when the curtain comes down and we professors begin chatting, Shakespeare remains the dreaming gray man in Borges's story "Shakespeare's Memory," and it is his dreams that contain more things in heaven and earth than are dreamt of in our philosophy.

Another way to answer the question of Shakespearean biography is to say that, if he's nobody, then he's everybody. And here I invite readers to take their pick, to associate Shakespeare with anyone and everyone he bears some kind of relation to. Conventionally, he's put in the same pigeonhole as the other great poets (Virgil and Dante), the other great English authors (Chaucer and Milton), the other great humorists (Molière and Mark Twain). But why stop there? The final Shakespearean paradox is that our greatest writer communicates directly with the least of us, so that this exercise in associating him with others is one that cannot fail.

Just in the few months I've been in London, I've thought of Shakespeare in the same breath as, for example, Pontormo, the eccentric Renaissance painter artist of whom Vasari wrote "had strange notions," but "when he had made up his mind he was not deterred by anything from carrying out what he had proposed, like a clever and skilful man." I think of Pontormo when I think of, not the majestic or tragic or even the comic Shakespeare but when I think of the one who's odd and goofy (and mixes his metaphors, for example, or refers in *The Winter's Tale* to "the seacoast of Bohemia") yet who, for all that, makes big statements about his time as well as ours. The greatest of Pontormo's paintings is the *Deposition* in the little church of Santa Felicità in Florence. A deposition is a depiction of the removal of Christ's body from the cross, typically a solemn, formal, somewhat abstract event akin, say, to the state burial of a revered leader. But the *Deposition* of Pontormo is another matter altogether. Whereas many church paintings are dark, heavily varnished, or otherwise obscured by the exigencies of age, this one is light, bright, and colorful; it is as though Pontormo used not paint but melted Life Savers to daub his figures with lime, pomegranate, peppermint. And the figures themselves are the precise opposite of the bold, resolute ones we see in other Renaissance paintings. The two who hold Christ's body and are closest to the spectator have a decided caught-in-the-act air to them; they look over their shoulders at the viewer as though to say, "What do we do now?"

And I've thought of Shakespeare as akin to Giovanni Battista Piranesi, mainly because, during my stay in London, there was an exhibit of Piranesi's engravings of imaginary prisons in the British Museum that I used to go down and look at during my lunch hour. Speaking of twinning, there were actually two sets of engravings; the first were done in 1749–50 and the second, in which Piranesi added line and detail to the originals, in 1761. In their creation of fantastic architectural interiors, the first engravings are remarkable on their own. But in the second set, the artist added not only prisoners being guarded and punished and even tortured but also depth and shadow that give these drawings a solidity that the originals lack. As I looked at the individual engravings, each of which is displayed side by side with its twin, I thought of the interior worlds of Richard III and Iago and Edmund and Macbeth. I also thought of the process of revision and how Piranesi had changed his original conceptions eleven years later. Shakespeare, too, began with a few strokes on the page and then more and more, though Shakespeare's revisions came all at once, the terrible shadows appearing as suddenly as a thunderstorm on a sunny London day.

In fact, Shakespeare's breathtaking speed (*Julius Caesar*, *As You Like It*, and *Twelfth Night* in one year, *Othello*, *King Lear*, and *Macbeth* in another) reminds me of Jackson Pollock, whom I've mentioned earlier. And since, thus far, I've mentioned only the visual artists Shakespeare reminds me of whose names begin with P, let me avoid a bookish consistency by saying also that he makes me think of Algonquin J. Calhoun, the verbose lawyer of *The Amos and Andy Show* who dazzled his opponents with new coinages and is the only person I know of, fictional or real, to have used the verb "absquatulate," a dog-Latin formation meaning "to depart in a hurry," "to die," and, in the sense that Calhoun uses it in the episode I recall, "to argue."

The American Heritage Dictionary from which these definitions come note that there is a precedent for jocular pseudo-Latin words "in the language of Shakespeare, whose plays contain scores of made-up . . . words." Thus, in *The Winter's Tale,* Antigonus declares that, could he identify the villain guilty of slandering the virtuous Hermione, he would "land-damn" him. According to the note in the little pocket edition of the play I took with me when I went to see it performed in Stratford, the origin of this phrase is likely "landan," identified by the editor as a Gloucestershire word still in use which describes "the punishment meted out to slanderers and adulterers by rustics traversing from house to house along the country side [*sic*], blowing trumpets and beating drums or pans and kettles; when an audience was assembled the delinquents' names were proclaimed, and they were said to be landanned." Okay, but obviously the original word wasn't up to snuff, so Shakespeare altered it so that its meaning would be clearer and that we'd know Antigonus is so angry he wants to find out who the slanderer is and then "damn him throughout the land."

One afternoon during my fall in London, I took the tube downtown to see a Brazilian movie that sounded promising, though when I arrived at the theatre, I found the listing in *Time Out* had been wrong and something else altogether was playing. As I walked around Soho, wondering how to amuse myself, I found myself in front of the Prince Charles Theatre, where *Mamma Mia* was playing. Like most people who listened to their car radios during the 1970s I can sing the chorus and a verse or two to half a dozen Abba songs, but I wasn't really interested in going in until, at exactly 2:56 p.m., a well-turned-out woman from Ketchum, Idaho, asked if I'd give her thirty pounds for her ailing husband's forty-pound ticket. Shortly after the three o'clock curtain, then, I too found myself clapping to and singing along with the cheesy but irresistible score in the company of approximately 1,500 of my fellow theatre lovers.

Since I have kept this information secret until now from family and friends, I reveal it here only to advance my argument, which is that, once you know what Shakespeare's up to, it's impossible not to see virtually everything else as a forerunner to his plays. *Mamma Mia* is a play about marriage, as are, one way or another, most of Shakespeare's plays; its plot is built around identity confusion, as are virtually all of his comedies; and it's set in Greece, one of Shakespeare's favorite settings. Shakespeare could have easily improved the simple story line of *Mamma Mia* with several more characters and a couple of additional plot threads—indeed, it's inconceivable that he wouldn't have. It also goes without saying he would have complicated the script verbally, leaving in many of the original broad jests but layering the language elsewhere and thus creating subtler wordplay. If, as is said, that Shakespeare used 21,000 words and Racine around 4,000, the *Mamma Mia* writers used—well, no more than Racine, let's say.

In good conscience, I can't really recommend *Mamma Mia*, at least not at full price. There are too many wonderful West End productions of great plays, classic and modern, as well as all the cheap, energetic fringe productions that cost practically nothing and take place in truly bohemian venues, more often than not a black-walled room with a few benches situated over a noisy pub. Still, hundreds of thousands of Americans flock to London every year to see such perennials as *Cats, The Phantom of the Opera, Les Miserables* (which the English, with their talent for deflation, call "The Glums"), and other shows they can more easily see at home. I mean, why not see *Chicago* in Chicago?

But here I'm making an objection that Shakespeare wouldn't. For just as he loved the court, he loved all things outdoors, and as he knew how to keep the nobility happy, so too did he show, again and again, his abiding affection for ordinary people. This universal applicability explains why Shakespeare not only inspires others as no other artist has but also brings out the best in them.

Thus Verdi's greatest operas are based on the stories of Macbeth, Othello, and Falstaff, and there are hundreds of ballets, symphonies, and other musical pieces which derive from the plays, not to mention sculptures, paintings, films, and musicals like *West Side Story* and *Kiss Me Kate.* The two greatest U.S. novels would not be the same without Shakespeare's influence. *Huckleberry Finn* would have been a mere sequel to *Tom Sawyer* had not the two Shakespearean actors the King and the Duke appeared to put a smiling face on evil. And Melville was all set to write yet another travel book when he discovered Shakespeare and created Ahab. If Faulkner had not encountered *Macbeth,* at least *The Sound and the Fury* would have had a less memorable title. In the realm of oratory, it's difficult to say which is quoted more, Shakespeare's work or the Bible, though it's easy to remember that the latter is the work of many hands instead of one. When Saddam Hussein learned that Yemen had sided against him in the recent weapons inspection dispute, he said, *"Et tu, Brute?"* When the BBC aired the Shakespeare segment of its *Great Britons* series in 2002, it was reported that Nelson Mandela and the other political detainees in their South African island prison maintained their civility in the face of state barbarism by reading to each other from a copy of the collected plays.

In the course I taught in London this fall, I ended with a play by Shakespeare's collaborator John Fletcher called *The Woman's Prize, or The Tamer Tamed.* My intention was to show that Shakespeare couldn't be improved upon, and my students agreed, though by this point in the term, Fletcher struck me as a better playwright than I'd thought earlier. The women characters are magnificent, and if the writing is not up there with that of the great tragedies, it's certainly as good as any in the midrank comedies. Of course, I argued that, Fletcher's achievement notwithstanding, the fact that he started with *The Taming of the Shrew* must have had more than a little to do with the success of his sequel.

The text of the Fletcher play we used is in an anthology edited by Daniel Fischlin and Mark Fortier entitled *Adaptations of Shakespeare: A Critical Anthology of Plays from the Seventeenth Century to the Present.* If that title sets up an echo, if it seems a twin of one that came earlier in this essay, that original would be Desmet and Sawyer's *Shakespeare and Appropriation,* the essay collection whose contributors, like many critics these days, appear baffled by, irritated at, envious of, and, in their more extreme expressions, contemptuous toward their subject. Like the good-bad twins of the Superman comics, the books exist as though in parallel universes. The one is populated by those who love the plays but probably give little thought to "the gray man who dreamed them," whereas the other is the world of those who use the plays as indictments against a "conservative patriarch" they should ignore but can't.

Fletcher's *The Woman's Prize* is the first play in the anthology; from this simple one-to-one twinning, the Shakespeare corpus splinters into a funhouse mirror of replicas, from Nahum Tate's "improved" version of the Lear story, *The History of King Lear,* to *Lear's Daughters,* which is by the Women's Theatre Group and Elaine Feinstein. The other plays in it include a Zulu version of *Macbeth,* Welcome Msomi's *uMabatha;* Heiner Müller's *Hamletmachine;* Paula Vogel's *Desdemona;* and other reinventions of Shakespeare by Keats, Lorca, and Brecht, among others. This is to say that somehow the narrow-minded bigot that hard-core theorists denigrate yet cling to is still able to speak to women and men of every color, in every country, in every period of time from his own until now. One last paradox, then, one final twinning: if it's true that all roads lead to Shakespeare, it's equally true that Shakespeare leads to all roads.

Give Me Life Coarse And Rank

Give Me Now Libidinous Joys Only

To get from Haleiwa on Oahu's north shore to Hono-
lulu, you have to drive over a little bridge near Waimea. To get
from the San Polo section of Venice to San Marco, you'll need to
walk over the Rialto bridge. And the way to get from the world's
oldest poetry to the newest is by means of a bridge whose name
is Walt Whitman. In all three cases, there are other routes you
can take, but these are the most direct.

As *the* American poet, Whitman is scrutinized, taken apart,
reassembled, and categorized more than any other. Yet I find
that often he ends up in the wrong pigeonhole. Some readers
type him as an American original who sprang fully formed from
the brow of Ralph Waldo Emerson; others take him for a Civil
War hippie, a no-holds bard playing tennis without a net or even
a racket. In this essay, I'll connect Whitman to two traditions
that tell a lot more about him and his poetry, the ancient tradition of dithyrambic verse and that of "the old, weird America."

Because Emerson posted a job description for a uniquely
American poet in his 1837 "American Scholar" address ("We have
listened too long to the courtly muses of Europe") and Whitman
answered the call, far too many readers think that he sprouted
from his native soil shortly after Emerson concluded his remarks.
This assumption endures in part because cultural historians tend
to think the world begins at the point that their own interests do;
a lot of American scholars haven't read anything written before
"The American Scholar." But the poetry of Whitman goes back
to the dithyrambs of ancient Greece and, while we can't plausibly
link recorded work to unwritten literature, surely even further, to
the earliest unrecorded chants. When the first edition of *Leaves
of Grass* appeared in July 1855, Emerson wrote Whitman to praise
the book as "the most extraordinary piece of wit and wisdom

that America has yet contributed," saying also "I greet you at the beginning of a great career, which yet must have had a long foreground somewhere."

"Long foreground" doesn't even begin to express Whitman's literary pedigree. Originally, a dithyramb was "a frenzied, impassioned choric hymn and dance of ancient Greece in honor of Dionysus," according to the dictionary definition, though it has come to mean "a wildly enthusiastic speech or piece of writing" or "poem written in a wild irregular strain." Neither lyric nor narrative, the dithyramb embraces both the emotional heat of the former and the sprawl of the latter.

Euripides' *Bacchae* is a good representation of Dionysian ecstasies and the dithyrambs that voice them. The play begins as Dionysus, god of wine and fertility, returns to his hometown of Thebes, angry and ready to wreak revenge. His mother was the Theban princess Semele, daughter of Cadmus, and his father Zeus. While pregnant with Dionysus, Semele is killed by thunderbolts when Zeus reveals himself to her in his true form. Semele's sisters, including Agave, Pentheus's mother, lie to Cadmus and say that the child is not Zeus's. Because of this impiety, Dionysus has possessed the women of Thebes and set them dancing. Dionysus is also offended by his cousin Pentheus, now king of Thebes, since Pentheus has discouraged his worship.

The play begins with a thunderclap as Dionysus accounts for his anger against those who have offended him; his impassioned speech is followed by a dithyrambic outburst from the Bacchae (in Ian Johnston's translation):

The land flows with milk,
the land flows with wine,
the land flows with honey from the bees.
He holds the torch high,
our leader, the Bacchic One. . . .
As he dances, he runs,
here and there,
rousing the stragglers,

stirring them with his cries,
thick hair rippling in the breeze.
Among the Maenads' shouts
his voice reverberates:
"On Bacchants, on!
With the glitter of Tmolus,
which flows with gold,
chant songs to Dionysus,
to the loud beat of our drums.
Celebrate the god of joy
with your own joy,
with Phrygian cries and shouts! . . . "
Then the bacchanalian woman
is filled with total joy—
like a foal in pasture
right beside her mother—
her swift feet skip in playful dance.

Dionysus persuades Pentheus to dress himself like one of the Bacchae that he may pry into their sacred mysteries. Then, disguised as a stranger, he leads him to the mountains and delivers him into the hands of the Bacchae, who tear him limb from limb.

Along the way, there are transformations, reversals, and discontinuities that would be laughable in a play by a later tragedian such as O'Neill or Tennessee Williams. But as Charles Segal points out in *Dionysiac Poetics and Euripides' Bacchae,* Euripides constructs his play around a character who crosses the boundaries between god, man, and beast, between reality and imagination, art and madness. As Whitman will do centuries later, the playwright employs a poetics that not only permits logical contradictions but celebrates them.

The dithyrambic tradition continues in the six Poetical Books of the Old Testament (Job, Psalms, Proverbs, Ecclesiastes, Song of Solomon, and Lamentations) and the prophetic poems of William Blake, such as *The Marriage of Heaven and Hell, Milton,* and *Jerusalem,* as well as T. S. Eliot's "The Waste Land" (there is also a dithyrambic chorus in *Murder in the Cathedral*), Pound's *Cantos,* and Hart Crane's *The Bridge.* Ginsberg's *Howl,* of course, is a contemporary dithyramb, as are the poetry of Yevgeny Yevtushenko, the long poems of Diane Wakoski, and much of Anne Waldman (see *Helping the Dreamer: Selected Poems 1966–1988*). In fact, the most popular poetry of the moment is dithyrambic: the spoken-word pieces of such authors as African American writer Paul Beatty, performance artist Tracie Morris, and the poets of the Nuyorican Café as well as the Def Poetry Jam performances on television and the countless poetry slams taking place every night in clubs all over the world. And in addition to the poets, there are any number of dithyrambic prose writers: Melville, Dostoevsky, Nietzsche, Céline, Henry Miller, and the two novelists who influenced Ginsberg more than any poet, even Whitman, Jack Kerouac and William Burroughs.

Within the dithyrambic tradition, Whitman connects most solidly with the poets of the Old Testament. This is actually a subject I've spoken on excitedly to more than one skeptical businessman who has sat next to me at a terminal gate and, on finding out that I'm a poet, asks me why poetry doesn't rhyme any more. Over time, I tell them, most poetry hasn't rhymed. Oh, sure, there were a few hundred years there, from roughly Elizabeth's reign through Victoria's, when a handful of highly accomplished poets wrote reams of accentual-syllabic verse with complex rhyme schemes, but for the greatest part of our common Western history, the poetry was, though quite formal, entirely unrhymed. Those were the days, I tell my listener. People paid careful attention to poetry back then and memorized great chunks of it. And almost everybody went to a poetry reading at least once a week. They called it church.

By this time the businessman has drifted to the bar or the newsstand, sorry they ever brought the topic up. However, should one of these unfortunates find himself seated next to me on the flight to Des Moines, say, or Winston-Salem, I go on: there were fifteen hundred years of Hebrew poetry, see, and then the heyday of the accentual-syllabic, and then Walt Whitman came along. What Whitman did was to reach over Tennyson's shoulder, past Keats, past John Donne, and right around the left ear of a startled Sir Philip Sidney to retrieve that whole Hebrew tradition, update it, and make it American.

Hebrew poetry is shaped not by the repetition of sounds and stresses but ideas. And this parallelism takes three forms: it is synonymous when the original and the subsequent thoughts are identical, antithetical when the original and subsequent thoughts contrast, and synthetic when the one is developed or enriched by the other.

Here is an example of synonymous parallelism from Psalms cited in the Scofield Reference Bible introduction to the Poetical Books. Note how the second line says exactly what the first does, only in different language:

The Lord also will be a refuge for the oppressed,
A refuge in times of trouble.

Now here's one from "Song of Myself":

I loafe and invite my soul,
I lean and loafe at my ease observing a spear of summer grass.

The second set of examples are instances of antithetical parallelism; again, the Biblical example is from Psalms. The verse starts in one direction and then turns and goes the other way:

For the Lord knoweth the way of the righteous:
But the way of the ungodly shall perish.

And this is a example of antithetical parallelism from "Song of Myself":

A child said *What is the grass?* fetching it to me with full hands,
How could I answer the child? I do not know what it is any more than he.

Finally, there is synthetic parallelism. The Biblical illustration is from Job this time; the base line serves as a launching pad for lines that enrich and develop its meaning:

And thou shalt be secure, because here is hope;
Yea, thou shalt dig about thee, and thou shalt take thy rest in safety.

And because Whitman was especially fond of synthetic parallelism, I'll give two examples, one from the beginning of "Song":

I celebrate myself, and sing myself,
And what I assume you shall assume,
For every atom belonging to me as good belongs to you.

And one from the end of the poem:

Do I contradict myself?
Very well then I contradict myself,
(I am large, I contain multitudes.)

The businessman is now sleeping contentedly—lulled by the learned recitation, to be sure, but comforted, too, by the knowledge that I, a poet, too, am not the free-verse-spouting anarchist he may have thought I was, a wild-eyed despoiler of traditional poetic forms, but a laborer in the Biblical vineyard. And all thanks to this what's-his-name, this Whitman.

I Pick Out Some Low Person For My Dearest Friend

Yet to identify Whitman as a dithyrambic poet is to run the risk of a second false pigeonholing, one that, like the first—like most, if not all, mistaken categorizations—results from a partial knowledge of the subject. In everything from the deceptive looseness of his lines to his author's photos in beard and slouch hat, Whitman seems like the original coffeehouse loony, a nineteenth-century member of the international wild man tradition who, as an outcast, bypasses and would be ashamed by any sort of parochial loyalty, indeed, any sort of loyalty to anything except the Gilded Age equivalents of sex, drugs, and rock and roll. (Not being familiar with the Bible, most of these miscategorizers would also fail to notice the intensely scriptural quality of Whitman's poems.) Yet Whitman was as intensely parochial as he was cosmopolitan. One may say he was cosmopolitan because he was parochial; in the words of William Carlos Williams, "the poet who writes locally is the agent and maker of all culture."

Part of this miscategorization stems from the assumption that today's America and Whitman's were the same, that if you, as a poet, are fed up with bourgeois values and mainstream politics, so was he. Whitman was fiercely pro-American, though the America he lived in is one that can scarcely be imagined today. One of the best guides to that distant country is David S. Reynolds's invaluable *Walt Whitman's America: A Cultural Biography,* which begins with an imagined evening in the 1850s at Pfaff's, a restaurant and saloon on the corner of Broadway and Bleecker Street in New York's Greenwich Village. Here, Bohemian America was in full sway: actors, artists, comedians, poets, and novelists shouted to one another, told jokes, spilled as much beer as they drank, and filled the air with cigar smoke. If Whitman (for he was a regular) and his friends seemed to cling desperately to the almost-childish innocence of simpler times, says Reynolds, it was because they saw American society becoming increasingly rigid and commercialized, and so the merrymakers laughed and sang as they watched their world come to an end. America was saying goodbye to a largely agrarian world; the Industrial Revolution was moving into its maturity, with an attendant need for the increasingly complex and narrow roles played by workers-turned-specialists. In literature and the arts, now-familiar boundaries between high, middlebrow, and popular culture began to appear, becoming rigid after the Civil War.

Earlier, Shakespeare was performed on the same stage as farces and minstrel shows; political rallies included poetry and musical performances; and popular songs were derived from operatic arias, just as classical compositions incorporated folk music.

Now all of that was changing forever. To illustrate the change, Reynolds compares antebellum utopian life at Brook Farm, depicted in Nathaniel Hawthorne's *The Blithedale Romance* (1852), with the more hierarchical way of life described in Edward Bellamy's novel *Looking Backward* (1888). In the former, people live communally, enjoying poetry readings, concerts, and *tableaux vivants* along with their daily work, whereas in the latter, life is more rigidly ordered, with much of the work done by machines. Tellingly, much is made of the fact that the citizens of Bellamy's utopia don't have to go all the way down to some band shell in a park to hear a concert; instead, live music is piped into their apartments so they can enjoy it alone.

A phrase often used to described the patchwork-quilt country of the young Whitman (for he lived well into the age of homogenization) is "the old, weird America," which is the title of Greil Marcus's book on the so-called Basement Tapes, the recordings made by Bob Dylan and the Band in Saugerties, New York, in 1967. The tapes were not intended for commercial release (although Columbia Records released some of the songs belatedly), and this is Dylan's most mysterious music, rooted historically in a culture that Dylan could only intuit, though Whitman knew it well. The old, weird America is a country of radical individuals, of street preachers, con men, hoboes, frontiersmen, wandering musicians, slaves on the run, Native American shamans and warriors and shape-shifters, folk heroes (Paul Bunyan, John Henry, Johnny Appleseed) and villains (the James brothers, Billy the Kid). You get a sense of the old, weird America on board Melville's *Pequod,* when Ishmael and the pagan Queequeq, who have spent the night cuddling happily in a boarding-house bed, join a polyglot crew to serve maimed Ahab in his vindictive quest. You sense it as well in *The Confidence-Man* as the paddleboat halts in its watery path to let on one group of eccentrics as another disembarks, with hardly a person among them whom he or she seems to be. In Civil War movies, combat units such as the Zouaves, in their faux-Algerian garb, are sometimes shown in uniforms so distinctive as to make it possible to distinguish between friend and foe. In the name of efficiency, modern soldiers are all dressed alike—they can kill better that way.

As with the dithyrambic tradition, that of the old, weird America seems to be, as Shelley once said of poetry itself, "both center and circumference": it's there when you see it, yet even when it seems to be completely dead, it isn't far away. Dithyrambs rise and fall throughout cultural history, and so do Bohemian airs. The literal Bohemia was a Central European kingdom where gypsies supposedly originated and thus it came to stand for a vagabond culture operating outside of bourgeois society. But there will always be resistance to homogenization, and there will always be Bohemias, just as there always have been: in early-twentieth-century New York, for example, where Alfred Stieglitz, Georgia O'Keeffe, Margaret Sanger, and John Reed gathered in shabby saloons along with novelists, artists' models, secretaries, and chess whizzes to argue about Nietzsche as they plowed through mounds of spaghetti and bratwurst and rejected the smug faith that culture was the domain of "the well-born and tasteful," as Christine Stansell observes in *American Moderns: Bohemian New York and the Creation of a New Century* and dug "channels between high and low culture, outsiders and insiders."

The Harlem Renaissance, the Beat Movement, the psychedelic music of the hippie bands, the inchoate thrashings of the punks: each of these is a momentary revolt against the conformity of the times, yet each is a return of the ancient as well. Jonah Raskin opens his book *American Scream: Allen Ginsberg's* Howl *and the Making of the Beat Generation* with a description of the legendary October 7, 1955, reading at the Six Gallery in San Francisco in which he calls the "revolutionary individuality" of work by Ginsberg, Gary Snyder, and the other readers "a quality bypassed in

American poetry since the formulations of Whitman." In those days of the Cold War, of the House Un-American Activities Committee hearings, of unprecedented commercial prosperity yet artistic sterility, "it was as though Dionysus had come back from the dead," writes Raskin. In his own recollections, Ginsberg says he felt like a rabbi reading to his congregation when he read *Howl,* and Raskin notes "indeed, there was something of the Old Testament prophet about him."

Orgiastic Greek poets, prophets fed by crows, Ginsberg's "saintly motorcyclists": you pass each of these on a road that winds through America, one that at times seems like an unpaved lane and at others like a superhighway. And if you drive the whole road, sooner or later you're going to cross over the Walt Whitman Bridge.

I Will Be More To You Than To Any Of The Rest

What you've considered this far, reader, is my attempt to distill some long-held assumptions: that often Whitman is falsely categorized (as American original, as cosmic loony) and that there are better pigeonholes for him (as dithyrambist, as citizen of "the old, weird America"). I'd written these preliminary paragraphs when I was diverted by other writing projects and had to take a break from this essay. One day I found myself facing an LA-to-Atlanta plane trip; since the in-flight movie was *Scooby Doo 2* (shame on you, Delta!), I headed for the bookstore the morning of my trip, browsed the poetry section, and, suddenly recalling the essay I was eager to get back to, grabbed the 485-page Signet Classic *Leaves of Grass* which is based on the ninth or "Death Bed" edition of 1892, the one authorized by Whitman as the final and complete version of his masterpiece. I had a long flight ahead of me, and I figured, how better pass the time than by testing my assumptions about Whitman's poetry?

It wasn't long before I found myself regretting my disparaging comments on the homogenization of culture: the flight was de-layed for four hours, and as I shuffled from gate to gate, watching my fellow travelers prevail or melt down in every possible way, I felt the ghosts of the old, weird America rising around me, and so I sat on the floor and read and waited while the mechanics labored to streamline me to my destination.

I made two columns in my notebook, one headed "Dithy-rambs" and the other "Old, Weird." And the first, almost the only, note in my first column is: "How little there is of this!" Meaning, not of dithyrambic lines (that's all Whitman writes), but of the dithyrambic end, the ecstatic union with the god him-self. The famous section 50 of "Song of Myself" reads:

There is that in me—I do not know what it is—but I know it is in me.

Wrench'd and sweaty—calm and cool then my body becomes,
I sleep—I sleep long.

I do not know it—it is without name—it is a word unsaid,
It is not in any dictionary, utterance, symbol. . . .

Perhaps I might tell more. Outlines! I plead for my brothers and sisters.

Do you not see O my brothers and sisters?
It is not chaos or death—it is form, union, plan—it is eternal life—it is
    Happiness.

All those dashes! And the lack of parallelism: how do "utterance" and "symbol" relate to "dictionary"? In the last stanza, he takes the don't-you-get-it tone that has landed many a husband in the doghouse, the one that says "Can't you understand what I'm fail-ing to explain to you?" The final line has a distinct uh-let's-see quality. And the best the poet can come up with to describe the state of mystical union is "Happiness," which he capitalizes so the reader will know it's more important than mere garden vari-ety small-h "happiness"?

That's the problem with achieving union. Harmony cannot be

expressed because harmony means the sinking of the individual into the whole. But no self, no self-expression.

I'm being facetiously hard on Whitman in my previous paragraph: the seemingly unsuccessful fumblings of section 50 express with unabashed honesty the inability, not to achieve transcendence, but to talk about it. The only way for the poem to end is the way it does, with the lines "If you want me again look for me under your boot-soles" and "Missing me one place search another, I stop somewhere waiting for you." Joy consists of union; poetry consists of the search for union.

A short, seldom-cited poem called "Native Moments" lays out the whole dithyrambic urge in just twelve lines. Here it is:

Native moments—when you come upon me—ah you are here now,
Give me now libidinous joys only,
Give me the drench of my passions, give me life coarse and rank,
Today I go consort with Nature's darlings, to-night too,
I am for those who believe in loose delights. I share the midnight orgies of
    young men,
I dance with the dancers and drink with the drinkers,
The echoes ring with our indecent calls, I pick out some low person for my
    dearest friend,
He shall be lawless, rude, illiterate, he shall be one condemned by the
    others for deeds done,
I will play a part no longer, why should I exile myself from my companions?
O you shunn'd persons, I at least do not shun you,
I come forthwith in your midst, I will be your poet,
I will be more to you than to any of the rest.

Nothing happens in this poem—yet. As my students would say, "Party tonight!" As Robert Louis Stevenson said, "To travel hopefully is a better thing than to arrive, and the true success is to labour." It's not that Whitman fails to express union ("that word unsaid")—no poet can, so what he describes instead and with sweaty, breathy accuracy is his failed quest to do so.

When it comes to the old, weird America, though, there's no need to beat around the bush. The descriptions of that lost country are the best part of Whitman, and who wouldn't rather read about hoboes and blacksmiths and boatmen and streetwalkers than failed attempts at mysticism? In sections 8–10 of "Song of Myself," the poet flips the pages of an album of snapshots almost as fast as he can: he starts with a sleeping baby, two youngsters about to sneak off and have sex, a suicide who has just shot himself in the head. Then a trapper marries a Native American woman, and a runaway slave stops for a bath and a change of clothes before heading north. Section 11 ("Twenty-eight young men bathe by the shore") offers the best-known skinny dipping scene in poetry, and then the poem *really* picks up speed: a butcher-boy, bastard children, an amputee, a "quadroon" as well as a "half-breed," an opium-eater, and the President himself speed past, "a farmer, mechanic, artist, gentleman, sailor, quaker, / Prisoner, fancy-man, rowdy, lawyer, physician, priest."

But even though the poet conjures these disparate figures, he remains separate from them: "I am less the jolly one there," he says in section 37, "and more the silent one with sweat on my twitching lips." In the short poem "Are You the New Person Drawn toward Me?" Whitman issues a distinct *caveat* to his *lector:* "To begin with take warning, I am surely far different from what you suppose" and "Do you think it is so easy to have me become your lover?" And see how emphatic he is about our essential solitariness in "A Song of the Rolling Earth":

Each man to himself and each woman to herself . . .
Not one can acquire for another—not one,
Not one can grow for another—not one.

When Whitman is anthologized briefly, the poems chosen to stand for his entire body of work are usually ones like "There Was a Child Went Forth" and "The Sleepers," three-to-five-page pieces studded with hundreds of specific references to nature and humanity, yet poems in which union is withheld; the latter poem in particular has an almost voyeuristic quality that serves as a counterweight to the image of the poet as shaman. Clearly, the anthologists know what they're doing: these are not only first-rate poems but ones that are representative of what is most characteristic of Whitman's work.

But by the time I'd sat in that terminal for half a day and then flown all the way from Los Angeles to Atlanta, I'd read all of *Leaves of Grass,* and the poem I kept coming back to was "Native Moments," quoted above in its entirety. I tell my students that every literary work contains a built-in tool kit you can use to take that work apart and put it back together again—a key image, a set of repeated words, a quirky syntax—and that, in poetry, they should always look for the minor poem they can use to illuminate the major poems, like one of those pocket-sized Maglite flashlights that can throw a big beam hundreds of feet into the darkness. "Native Moments" is one such poem, which is why I have pillaged it for the title to and subtitles within this essay. The poem promises union, and it says the road to union is not through God or prayer or ritual but someone "lawless, rude, illiterate," a citizen of the old, weird America. And the poem withholds union, not because that state can't be reached, but because it can't be described.

I Will Be Your Poet

Last summer my wife and I drove up to Montgomery to see some plays at the Alabama Shakespeare Festival, which is located in a 266-acre cultural park that features a museum with paintings by Sargent, Hopper, and Rothko as well as the sculpture of local outsider artist Charlie "Tin Man" Lucas, who makes pterodactyls out of car hoods and perches them in the branches of trees. But the museum doesn't have any work by another renegade artist from the area, a lay preacher named W. C.

Rice who maintains a "cross garden" on his property in nearby Prattville. I like to visit Mr. Rice from time to time and survey the hundreds of washers and dryers and air conditioner housings that surround his house, each of which is daubed with a saying like HELL IS HOT HOT HOT HOT and NO SEX WITH MEN ALOUD and NO ICE WATER IN HELL.

Talk about your old, weird America. As well as being an artist, W. C. Rice preaches the gospel, and, his anti-gay bias notwithstanding, I have the feeling that Whitman would have loved him. For one thing, Mr. Rice is severely diabetic, and Whitman's soft spot for the ill and needy is legendary. Mr. Rice isn't well today, so his wife asks me step around to the side of the house and to chat with him through his bedroom window, and soon he's telling me about some visitors he had had the evening before. Mr. Rice is a sort of confessor to a lot of people in the area, and at about eleven o'clock, a woman and her daughter and the daughter's friend came by and knocked, even though Mrs. Rice had already tacked up the cardboard sign that says it's too late to visit and invites the visitor to return the next morning. But the three women were crying hysterically, so Mrs. Rice let them in, and it turns out that the woman's husband, who'd been physically abusive to her their whole time together, had himself been beaten to death that very afternoon by a couple of toughs. What the woman wanted to know was whether Mr. Rice could say where her husband was at the very minute—specifically, was he between this world and heaven, and, if so, could she pray him up there, and if not, could Mr. Rice help? The answer, of course, was no. In Mr. Rice's cosmology, either you're saved or you're not, and no amount of after-the-fact prayer can alter the state of your soul.

No wonder there is nothing by W. C. Rice in the Montgomery Museum of Fine Arts. The local art mavens do a canny job of sanitizing the old, weird America; it's okay for a busload of tourists to see a deer made out of shock absorbers by Charlie "Tin Man" Lucas, but you wouldn't want visitors to pause before a Sargent heiress with her silk habiliments and upswept tresses and Grecian Urn-like guarantees of immortality and then stumble over a rusty Kelvinator on which someone has painted YOU WILL DIE in red house paint. No, the outskirts are the right place right for Mr. Rice, not Art's well-appointed townhouse.

Still, I love Montgomery and its Shakespeare Festival. To stage *Othello* in a town whose other major cultural venue is a racetrack is nostalgic in the best possible way. Shakespeare was like Whitman in his embrace of all cultures. Just as it seems right to have a Rothko painting and a Charlie Lucas sculpture in the same museum or to find a gourmet restaurant and a barbecue joint next to each other in the same strip mall (we ate at both on adjacent days), so it made sense to watch *Romeo and Juliet* at the ASF on a Montgomery evening while James Brown played across town at Jubilee CityFest, the city's outdoor music fair.

It's easy to overlook how important Shakespeare was in Whitman's America. In 1850, an anonymous correspondent for *Literary World* wrote an essay called "Shakspeare [*sic*] in America" that reminds us how culturally vibrant the American interior was in those days. It's easy but wrong to imagine that the hinterlands were populated mainly by grizzly bears, river pirates, and a few hardy pioneers, for, as the writer notes, "we have the plays of Shakspeare every night in scores of theatres in city and country, packet ships, halls, hotels, steamboats. . . ." In the early part of the nineteenth century, play-acting was banned in Puritan Boston and scarcely tolerated in Philadelphia, but out where life was older and weirder, there was plenty of culture; in Louisville alone, there were fifty Shakespearean performances during the first half of the century. (Incidentally, soon this country will be enjoying more Shakespeare, not less, thanks to a program recently announced by Dana Gioia, chair of the National Endowment of the Arts. The NEA will make it possible for six professional companies to stage plays in one hundred small and midsize American cities in all fifty states; the endowment is also seeking additional funding to visit military bases with the Alabama Shakespeare

Festival's version of *Macbeth*. The result, according to Mr. Gioia, will be "the largest tour of Shakespeare in American history." This will be a welcome step—well, backwards. After all, it's a matter not only of reclaiming but improving on a once-rich cultural complexity that has been threatened by television and CDs yet still thrives. Can plays on packet boats be far behind?)

If Whitman's America was ready for Shakespeare, it was because it was the America also of other giants, of Twain and Melville, and the quintessential American book of them all is the biggest: the Bible. *Leaves of Grass*, *The Adventures of Huckleberry Finn*, *Moby-Dick*, the books of the Old Testament: all of these say what *Hamlet* and *King Lear* do. (That Shakespeare's gangs of "sweet wags" were so at home in the world of male friendship described by these authors is the subject of another essay.) Each of these works has a magnificent, vaulting architecture as well as a tragic if necessary incompleteness, and each says what Whitman says in his short poem "The Unexpress'd," another of those short, easily overlooked poems that illuminate the entirety of *Leaves of Grass*:

How dare one say it?
After the cycles, poems, singers, plays,
Vaunted Ionia's, India's—Homer, Shakspere—the long, long times,
    thick dotted roads, areas,
The shining clusters and the Milky Way, of stars—Nature's pulses reap'd,
All retrospective passions, heroes, war, love, adoration,
All ages' plummets dropt to their utmost depths,
All human lives, throats, wishes, brains—all experiences' utterance;
After the countless songs, or long or short, all tongues, all lands,
Still something not yet told in poesy's voice or print—something lacking,
(Who knows? the best yet unexpress'd and lacking.)

Dante, Goethe, Whitman, Shakespeare: each is the national poet of his country. Yet each was a regular guy, in his way; Dante argued with shopkeepers, and while Shakespeare may have written immortal lines in the morning, he totaled up ticket sales at night. Far from being a dreamy bard, Whitman was more involved than any other American writer in the publication of his own work. He chose font styles and type sizes, selected paper, assisted in typesetting, designed bindings, wrote advertising copy, reviewed his own books anonymously, and sold them out of his house. He also managed his own image superbly. An avid seeker of the widest possible readership, he kept poems which stressed homosexual love and political subversiveness out of the public eye—until it was to his advantage to publish them, of course.

When he wasn't pursuing the solitude that is a necessary condition for every writer and that he writes about wistfully in his own work, Whitman had an ability for making connections with others that is described best by Roy Morris, Jr., in *The Better Angel: Walt Whitman in the Civil War.* The war killed Whitman's dream of a world founded on "the blissful love of comrades" and replaced it with the horror of brother killing brother. Deeply depressed, the poet lost himself in "an aimless round of bohemian posturing, late-night roistering, and homosexual cruising." When he learned that his brother George had been wounded at the battle of Fredericksburg, Whitman rushed to find him; George's injury was slight, but in the sufferings of other solders, Whitman found new purpose in life and, eventually, in poetry, culminating in "When Lilacs Last in the Dooryard Bloom'd." To Morris, Whitman was "a great mothering sort of man" who visited the hospitals in and around Washington, D.C., for three years, bringing his charges ice cream, tobacco, brandy, books, magazines, pens, and paper. He wrote letters for those who could not, and more than a few died in his arms. "His long white beard, wine-colored suit, and bulging bag of presents gave him a decided resemblance to Santa Claus," writes Morris. Small wonder that, each time he left, many of the wounded soldiers, some of them still in their teens, called out, "'Walt, Walt, come again!'"

Those young soldiers would not have known that "Song of

Myself" ends with the lines "If you want me again look for me . . . " and "You will hardly know who I am or what I mean."

But Whitman does come again, in Ginsberg's "A Supermarket in California"; in T. R. Hummer's *Walt Whitman in Hell*, in which Whitman strolls through twentieth-century Manhattan; and in Larry Levis's poem "Whitman:," where the awkward colon of the title suggests the inexpressible, "the unexpress'd." Levis's Whitman, like the one I've been writing about in this essay, is everywhere visible and yet never seen:

Across the counter at the beach concession stand,
I sell you hot dogs, Pepsis, cigarettes—
My blond hair long, greasy, & swept back
In a vain old ducktail, deliciously
Out of style.
And no one notices.

It wouldn't bother me if Whitman got the treatment that Shakespeare has and become Everybody's Favorite Poet, became a trademarked and Disneyfied character: that only makes poetry more accessible to a wider audience. And it hurts no one, because these old warhorses can take any amount of punishment dished out by the pop-culture industry and stay just as queer and lawless as they've always been. But it won't happen. As a dithyrambic poet, Whitman is ecstatic. As a poet of the old, weird America, he is eccentric. *Ex stasis, ex centrum:* they amount to the same thing. Whitman is an easy poet to love, but the closer we get to him, the harder he is to see. We'll never merge with Whitman, even though he invites us to; he tells us so in his poetry. Instead, we'll pass right through him. We move from one part of the earth to another, and somebody says, "That was a pretty little bridge back there," and we say, "What bridge?" And then we remember.

An Army Of Chitterlings

When I threw my copy of *Gargantua and Pantagruel* across room 53 of the Hôtel Jeanne d'Arc (twin beds, bath, 95 euros a night), it was because Pantagruel and his friends were about to be attacked by a huge army of . . . chitterlings. I'd endured Rabelais's over-the-top rowdiness as long as I could: Gargantua combing the cannonballs out of his hair after a battle, the pilgrims clinging to his teeth so they aren't washed down in a flood of wine after Gargantua eats them in his salad, the six months that Alcofribas gets paid to sleep all day in the little village he happens upon inside Pantagruel's head. But when the chitterlings lined up to attack, 42,000 strong and flanked by "a large force of game-puddings, stout dumplings, and mounted sausages," I said to myself, enough's enough and let fly.

Then retrieved my book and kept reading, because finally I was understanding France. I had lived in Paris a number of times before: a year in 1977–78, six months in 1998, the summer of 2001, perhaps as many as a dozen shorter visits. Yet I had never asked myself why, which probably means I was enjoying myself; usually we don't examine our pleasures unless they're destructive ones, and even then only if we want to avoid them. Obviously, I wanted to keep coming back. Why, though? Why not someplace warmer and less expensive, a place where I could converse fluently? (Considerable effort notwithstanding, my French seems to be stuck permanently in second gear.)

This time, though, I intended to find out. I meant to discover what it was about France and Paris in particular that kept yanking me back. And I only had eight days to do so; Barbara and I had come to Paris over spring break, and we had to be back in the classroom the following Tuesday. But time, because it was brief, was on my side: in the past, I'd luxuriated thoughtlessly in French *volupté,* and now I meant to use my handful of days to force myself to come up with some answers.

In other words, I didn't have time to make mistakes. But I'd need help. The trip was to be so short that I hadn't even packed a nail clipper, though I did bring two guide books, but not the Fodor or Frommer kind; by now, I know the city too well. No, I brought the Penguin Classics editions of *Gargantua and Pantagruel* and Montaigne's *Essays,* figuring that what I read there, combined with my personal experiences, would lead me to an understanding of the two pillars of French culture: pleasure and reason. This essay is an eight-day diary of my reading and experience, my observations and memories, and as I make my way through the pages of Rabelais and Montaigne as well as the boulevards and back allies of Paris, I promise quick turns and abrupt halts as well as a return trip that culminates, I trust, in a soft landing.

As I figured a Frenchman would, I put pleasure first, and began to read Rabelais while our Air France flight plane was still in line for take-off in Atlanta. And immediately stopped, because when I read translator J. M. Cohen's description of Rabelais as "a man intoxicated by every sort of learning and theory, who had at the same time the earthy commonsense of a peasant," I thought of our friend Claude, whom we would be seeing in Paris. Claude is a lawyer or *avocat,* the equivalent of a solicitor in England, but he is also a stage actor of considerable experience, a folklorist who for many years hosted a Saturday morning radio show in his beloved Vendée, a *caviste* with hundreds of bottles of excellent Bordeaux in his cellar, and an expert on the harvesting, preparation, and consumption of oysters and the other dozen edible crustaceans to be found in the cool Atlantic waters of the Normandy coast.

As both lawyer and actor, Claude, like Rabelais, "plays with words as children do with pebbles," in the words of Anatole France; "he piles them into heaps." Like Rabelais, Claude loves France and is troubled by it enough to view it satirically. In the great protest era of the sixties, I was always too troubled to participate in demonstrations against the Vietnam War and for civil rights; I should have been strong enough to resist, but right-wing fury in the United States is so powerful that it's hard not to think that if you're trying to change your country, you're somehow opposed to it. In France, on the other hand, the almost daily *manifestations* you see in the streets are expressions of patriotism.

During my first long stay in Paris, my son Will went to a preschool where the PTA meetings were highly politicized, with parents actually saying what a good Christian Democrat would do about bathroom breaks. The school was open for half a day on Saturdays, and often the neighborhood communists would be on the corner, welcoming me with their signs ("*Les communistes de votre voisinage vous accueillent*") as well as coffee and pastries, trying to persuade me and the others to see school politics their way. Now try to imagine going into a PTA meeting at Southside Elementary and walking past a sign that says "Your neighborhood communists welcome you." In France, though, politics isn't a matter of being right or wrong; it's what everyone does, and there's something wrong with you if you don't do it. There may be such a thing as a politically neutral person in France, but I haven't met him or her yet.

Rabelais wasn't concerned with individuals, writes Cohen; "he is not sufficient of a Renaissance man for that." Born a generation before Montaigne (around 1494 as opposed to Montaigne's 1533), Rabelais describes enormous egos, but having an ego is not the same as being an individual. The main characters in *Gargantua and Pantagruel* are ensemble players; Friar John, for example, is no more an individual than a midfielder on a soccer team or a cello player in an orchestra. No wonder Mikhail Bakhtin devoted an entire book to Rabelais. In *Rabelais and His World,* the Russian critic emphasizes the carnivalesque, for carnival is rumbustious, lawless, and open to members of every class of society. Katerina Clark and Michael Holquist's biography says that, whereas others argued that they alone owned the meaning of things or that no one did, Bakhtin said, in effect, we all own the meaning.

Carnival is a drunken time; for everyone to own the meaning, it helps if they're all a little tipsy. But though rivers of wine course through his narrative, "for François Rabelais," writes Cohen, "the headiest liquor of all was the liquor of learning." Indeed, the first sentence of "The Author's Prologue" begins "Most noble boozers" and finishes with a reference to Plato's *Symposium*. Both letters and carousing are given equal time in Rabelais's world. Literally: the prologue concludes with the narrator's avowal that he "never spent—or wasted—any more—or other—time in the composing of this lordly book, than that fixed for the taking of my bodily refreshment, that is to say for eating and drinking."

Indeed, the twin notes of literature and booze are struck again in the very first pages of the book proper. As with many an older text, this one claims to have its origin in an accidental discovery: workers opening an Etruscan tomb topped by a goblet find nine flagons, and beneath the middle one is a "great, greasy, grand, grey, pretty, little, mouldy book." Already Rabelais's prose is drunk: how can a book be grand and little and pretty and moldy at the same time? From this nonsense flows more: the whole second chapter is a riddle in verse, and after scratching my head over it, I came to Cohen's footnote, which says "there is very little sense in this riddle. . . . We have not the answer, and probably there never was one." A few chapters later, there is an extended inventory of the young Gargantua's clothing, with a lengthy paragraph apiece on his shirt, doublet, hose, codpiece, shoes, cape, and so on, the details mounting so high that one becomes lost in them and is unable to form any picture at all of the giant. His father, Grandgousier, promises he'll have Gargantua made "a Doctor of Gay Learning," surely the right calling for so exaggerated a creature. Indeed, *Gargantua and Pantagruel* prescribes a curriculum for gay learning, and anyone who finishes it is entitled to claim his or her doctorate in that science.

By now the plane has leveled off over the ocean, and the flight attendants begin to offer beverages and pass around menus. One of the options is a cold express meal for those who wish to "*tra-*

vailler pendant le voyage." I certainly don't want to work during the trip, and to take the express meal would mean to forego the beef that is otherwise promised, and it hardly seems Rabelaisian of me to avoid beef. So I order a Campari and then a little bottle of red wine to go with my *filet de boeuf* and keep reading, alternating sips and sentences, as the master would have advised.

Two seats behind me, a woman begins to talk, first loudly and then more loudly still. The dinner things are cleared, the movie begins, and the woman continues to talk. I'm about a hundred pages into Rabelais now, at the scene where Friar John is smiting his enemies and, again, the details are coming in waves: he beats out the brains of some, breaks the arms and legs of others, demolishes kidneys, slits noses, blackens eyes, dislocates thigh bones, and knocks heads to pieces "along the lambdoidal suture." On and on the woman goes, her voice shrill above the ambient hum of the plane and its passengers. Why doesn't someone seated closer than I am knock her head to pieces along the lambdoidal suture? The movie doesn't interest me, and there will be no sleep as long as the woman yammers the night away, so since I've made a good start with Rabelais's high-calorie prose, I figure it's time to take a counterbalancing dose of Montaigne's more ascetic fare.

The first glimpse we get of the sage of Bordeaux is his reflection in the mirror of his own prose. Montaigne is said to have invented the individual; we know that his essays greatly influenced Shakespeare, and it is hard to imagine a Richard III or Hamlet or Lear in a world in which Montaigne or someone very like him had not lived earlier. "To the Reader" tells us we are about to read a "book whose faith can be trusted, a book which warns you from the start that I have set myself no other end but a private family one. I have not been concerned to serve you nor my reputation; my powers are inadequate for such a design."

Who is he kidding? Like Twain's note at the beginning of *The Adventures of Huckleberry Finn,* warning readers not to read deeply into what has become one of the world's most closely read texts, Montaigne's seeming self-abasement has the opposite effect of its intent, if, in fact, it was intended to be self-abasing at all. "I myself am the subject of my book," he concludes, and therefore "it is not reasonable that you should employ your leisure on a topic so frivolous and so vain." Properly warned, we do the only reasonable thing: we turn the page.

What we find inside is an extended examination of a mind at work. In his essay "On Idleness," Montaigne writes, "Recently I retired to my estates, determined to devote myself as far as I could to spending what little life I have left quietly and privately; it seemed to me then that the greatest favour I could do for my mind was to leave it in total idleness, caring for itself, concerned only with itself, calmly thinking of itself. I hoped it could do that more easily from then on, since with the passage of time it had grown mature and put on weight." Maybe too much weight: on the next page, the mind begins to split hairs at a pulse-pumping rate as it distinguishes between defects due to weakness and defects due to wickedness.

This isn't the first time anyone wrote or thought this way, of course; Aristotle did not begin the tradition of rational materialism in Western philosophy, though he became its best-known proponent over a period of more than two thousand years. But it's the first time anyone has written and thought precisely this way in centuries. When Montaigne begins reasoning in earnest in essays such as the one entitled "To Philosophize Is to Learn How to Die," the reader gets the sense of just how much this rich period in our history is a re-naissance; indeed, the footnotes are studded with references to Seneca, Lucretius, and the Stoic and Epicurean philosophers who not only further the Aristotelian tradition but associate it with pleasure, as Montaigne does in this essay. ("Even in virtue our ultimate aim—no matter what they say—is pleasure," he writes.) Small wonder that Shakespeare, that ardent sensualist, finds a soul mate in this master of reason; even the simplest electronic search gins up thousands of web pages, articles, and books linking the two authors.

By now it is almost six in the morning, and faint sunlight begins to make its way around the edges of the closed windows as the flight attendants creep down the aisle. Soon the interior lights come on, and the breakfast cart appears. I glance back at the woman who has been talking all night. Her husband is wearing an appliance in each ear; fortunately for him, if not for us, he is deaf.

♦

We make our way into the city and soon find ourselves in our hotel in that exhausted, exhilarated in-between state that travelers know well. At one point in Pantagruel's wanderings, his friend Panurge falls in love with a great Parisian lady and offers to show her "Master John Thursday, who will play you a jig that you'll feel in the very marrow of your bones. He's a sprightly fellow, and he is so good at finding all the cracks and quirks and special spots in the carnal trap that after him there is no need of a broom." When I bring up the subject of Master John and his pleasure-giving potential, Barbara gives me a blank stare, and soon we are shouldering our way through the streets on what, in retrospect, turns out to be a three-day binge on all our favorite haunts and a few new ones, at the end of which I more or less clatter to pieces like a poorly maintained Deux Chevaux, the adorable rattletrap of a car that looks as though it's made of leftover aluminum siding.

On Tuesday morning I wake up exhausted, achy, and congested from my kid-in-a-candy-shop behavior of the past seventy-two hours, so I decide to put myself on what Montaigne calls "a diet of reason" and stay in for the day. The quote is from his essay "On Solitude," and, fittingly, Barbara throws herself back into the fray while I curl up with my books and over-the-counter cold medicine. But the intellectual food I eat is Rabelais: reason may keep me in, but I read for pleasure.

One of the pleasures that Rabelais teaches is that you don't have to take anything or anyone seriously, including Rabelais. There's a kind of happy pointlessness to much of *Gargantua and Pantagruel,* and whenever the opportunity arises, he does everything he can to promote one of the great joys of reading the classics: skimming. A number of chapters consist of little more than lists; in "Gargantua's Games," for example, the reader is told the giant played "at Flushes" and "at Primero" and then roughly three hundred other games, all the way through to "Larks" and "Flip-finger." (Here and below, I'll approximate the number of items in the lists; to count them one by one would be for Rabelais to have a laugh, half a millennium after the fact, at my expense.) When Pantagruel goes to Paris to study, the card catalog of books available to him is listed and runs to some 150 nonsense titles covering six pages of text. A variety of languages abound, more than any reader could be expected to know, including German, Italian, Basque, Dutch, Spanish, Danish, Hebrew, Greek, and Latin; the various tongues range from a scholar's French (which is translated "For libentissimily, as soon as there illusces any minutule slither of day" and so on) to three invented languages (*"Al barildim gotfano dech min brin alabo dordin falbroth ringuam albaras"*). Panurge applies about 180 unsavory adjectives to Friar John ("stumpy," "lumpy," "dumpy," and so on—who says Frenchmen can't rap?) and the churchman returns the favor two chapters later with a list of equal length. Soon, Pantagruel and Panurge are ganging up on a fool named Triboulet, whose list of insulting nicknames takes up three double-columned pages.

Everything that can be exaggerated, is: when the great Parisian lady turns down Panurge's invitation to entertain Master John Thursday, the rascal puts a bitch's scent on her robes, and as she walks through town, she is surrounded by, not "dogs" or "a pack of dogs" but "six hundred thousand and fourteen dogs." Everything that can be made sillier, is, often in a *faux* scholarly manner: another lady of Paris sends Pantagruel a ring, which he subjects to a dozen procedures, including those of Messer Francesco di Nianto the Tuscan, Zoroaster, and Calphurnius Bassus, yet the secret message that he searches for in vain turns out to written on the surface of the ring itself.

The diet of reason works, and by Wednesday I'm ready to overindulge again. And it's a good thing, too, because this is the night Claude and his wife, Marie, are coming up to Paris from their house in southwest France to have dinner with us. The best way to explain Claude Mercier is by actual example, so I'll use one from my experience of riding around with him. If, say, you're taking a photo of a car, and you need someone to lie down in front of it and appear to be dead—even, in fact, if you haven't realized that need yet—there's no reason to look further. Don't ask: Claude Mercier's your man. That day, he did a better corpse than most corpses do, and passersby didn't appear to know whether to laugh or call the French equivalent of 911.

Marie, in the best wifely tradition, acts as both sea anchor to Claude's high spirits yet, when necessary, wind to his sails. The four of us end up at L'Ambassade d'Auvergne, a stately old restaurant near Les Halles which specializes in the earthy cuisine of its region, including, of course, chitterlings, which, in honor of my present state of mind, I order. I've ordered chitterlings before in France, and not always successfully: the last time I did, the waiter said, you're American, aren't you? Yes, I am, I reply, Well, 90 percent of Americans who order chitterlings end up leaving them on the plate. Well, I'm the other 10 percent, I say. Having grown up on a farm in Louisiana, I learned to eat everything, which is to say I was a good Rabelaisian before I'd even heard of Rabelais.

One of the great pleasures of the table is to hear someone like Claude go over the wine list with the sommelier. Whereas in America we make fun of wine descriptions ("overtones of lemon, honey, and cheap aftershave, with a hint of cinnamon and old gym shorts"), the French, for the most part, approach wine more religiously than they do religion. Claude takes maybe ten minutes, with a break in the middle to order appetizers, before settling on the right wine. Here, reader, we have a perfect illustration of the marriage of reason and pleasure, of Montaigne's worldview joining hands with that of Rabelais as careful consideration and the assistance of wise counsel leads to the right wine for the right foursome at the right meal.

Now for the pleasure part. The early moments of a great meal are like playing in the calm waters before a waterfall: you splash in the gentle current for a while, then, before you know it, you're heading toward the rapids, and, after that, over the edge. The foie gras and goat-cheese salads appeared, then the chitterlings and capons and leg of lamb, then more cheese, then tarts and creams and ices, all washed down with two bottles of Bordeaux followed by snifters of Armagnac and coffee.

On the street outside, Barbara wants to take a picture of me and Claude standing together, just a normal two-shot of a couple of buddies, but Claude decides it would make a much better photo if it were to look like a drug buy, complete with stagey exchange of money and a mysterious packet (actually a plastic pouch of road maps standing in for a half kilo or so of uncut Burmese heroin). I've never bought from what's sometimes re-ferred to as an outdoor pharmacist, but while he pays the bills by practicing law, Claude is, as I mentioned earlier, a classically trained actor, and the transaction is so authentic that several strollers look alarmed enough, I decide, to alert the gendarmes, so after a hurried embrace, we skedaddle. It's a long walk back to the hotel, but you need a long walk after a meal like that. On the way, we pass several condom machines set into the walls of buildings like ATMs, so that lovers who haven't had too much Bordeaux and Armagnac can deploy Master John Thursday in a safe and enjoyable manner—again, reason marrying pleasure as it never would in puritan America.

Back at the hotel, reason is rearing its head with a vengeance. The pretty young woman at the desk, who has been deferential and even self-effacing for the past four days, scolds me for not having left the key at the desk the day before. Now when I'm wrong and know it, it's my policy to grovel; it saves time, and your accuser will like it. But as I hadn't gone out the day before and had kept the key with me in the room, I suggest that perhaps she is mistaken, that perhaps she had confused me, who is in room 53, with the monsieur staying in room 35. Mademoiselle isn't having any of this: I'd gone out, I'd taken the key with me, confusion and alarm ran through virtually everyone on duty that day, I really needed to be more mindful in the future, and so on. I tried to back away, but she continued to huff until another client arrived and distracted her.

In the end, it was nothing, but try to imagine a desk clerk at a Comfort Inn in Vicksburg or a Courtyard by Marriott in Sacramento lecturing someone in this manner. Mademoiselle was a true Daughter of Reason: there is a way of doing things, and you failed to do them properly, so you better watch it, buster. The most carefree people in the world, the French can turn on a dime and also be the most systematic.

Not that this is a contradiction; rather, I see it as a healthy embrace of extremes (though, in the future, I'd rather not be chewed out for things I didn't do). Culturally, it's a little like the celebrated English bluntness that is the opposite of the celebrated English mannerliness; by practicing the one, you license yourself to practice the other and create a more vibrant culture as well. In the states, we're more middle of the road. Take, for example, our two centrist political parties, one a little right of center and one slightly to the left, as opposed to France's plethora of seven or so parties covering a spectrum from socialists to Greens to the National Front.

Just as American politics are centrist, so, to some extent, are our cultural choices. I am writing this essay in the summer of 2004, just as the presidential campaign is heating up, and it is illuminating to see how cultural choices affect politics. In her *New York Times* column, Maureen Dowd reports that when she asked George Bush what his favorite cultural experience was, he answered, "Baseball," whereas the same question put to John

Kerry elicited a long list of favorite books, films, and musical titles. Bush famously mocked an American reporter who asked a question in French at a joint 2002 news conference with Jacques Chirac; Kerry, in turn, once answered a French reporter in his native tongue and sent his staff into a tizzy as they debated how best to "spin" the incident so as not to make Kerry appear too smart and upset that part of the electorate that distrusts intelligence. The late French president Georges Pompidou once edited a poetry anthology—reader, can you imagine without wincing the reelection chances of an American president after it is learned that he is editing a poetry anthology?

"Learning must not only lodge with us: we must marry her," says Montaigne in one of these essays. To American politicians, learning cannot be the wife, but only because the same is true for part of the electorate; to these people, learning is that girl we dated in high school at the same time we were studying trig or playing volleyball, even though we do neither now.

One morning during our stay, I go down for breakfast at the hotel and pick up a copy of the London *Financial Times,* where I see a headline that says "Chirac Sends Philosopher to Haiti." The piece begins: "France today will revive its tradition of sending philosophers to war zones with the arrival in Haiti of Régis Debray, a leftwing intellectual charged by Jacques Chirac, the French president, with conducting a 'mission of reflection' in the crisis-hit Caribbean island." Reader, can you imagine an American president sending a philosopher anywhere?

◆

With Rabelais and Montaigne as my guides, what I was learning is how willing the French are to embrace opposites: they like to think big, like Rabelais, yet they're as keen to split hairs as Montaigne is. One can do both at the same time, of course: one afternoon we stop at a little shop on the Rue St. Paul so Barbara can look at ex-votos, the little metal body parts that the faithful attach to shrines to effect a cure, and when she can't make up her mind between two different ones, the shopkeeper says that it is all very well for a woman to choose between two art objects, but did I or did I not think it a good idea for a man to have two wives? No, I reply, only one, but a good one. Ah! he says, so each husband should be a specialist, like a scientist with a narrow field that he knows deeply, as opposed to a generalist who flits from one subject to the other? As Barbara dithers, our conversation goes on in this characteristically French way.

Naturally, as overachievers, both of my authors are more than capable of taking things too far. There's no one funnier than Rabelais when he's on a tear, but there's a little too much shit-eating in his prose for my taste. And Montaigne puts me off when he applies his reason to women and uses it to find them inferior. As in books, so in life, too, can pleasure and reason be taken to extremes. The French are smoking themselves to death, as far as I can see. Yet the abuse of reason is far worse, for it can lead, not to individual tragedy, but to cruelty on a heartbreak-ing scale. On our train trip from the airport to the city, one of our stops was Drancy, the camp from which more than seventy thousand French Jews departed on their way to Auschwitz. That morning, fighting the desire to stay in the hotel and sleep, we stopped in at the Patrimoine Photographique museum in the nearby Hôtel de Sully to look at an exhibit of photos taken dur-ing the Algerian war; the one that stays with me is of two grin-ning *harkis* (Algerians who fought on the French side) holding a naked girl by the wrists after they have raped her and just before they shoot her to death.

Wars of every kind are called "barbaric" by political leaders, yet suffering is caused by an excess of reason more often than not. On the morning of March 11, terrorists explode ten bombs in four packed train cars in Madrid, killing and wounding hun-dreds. One of Montaigne's most celebrated essays is "On Cru-elty," especially torture, a practice he loathed yet one which was not widely considered wrong in his day. At present, there are fewer incidents of state-sanctioned torture of individuals, but the cruel are growing in their ability to inflict pain.

Ironically, the day after the Madrid bombings, I see Marco Bellochio's *Buongiorno, Notte,* a film about the kidnapping and execution of former Italian premier Aldo Moro. It's also a study in how reason can distort thinking: some of the kidnappers want to release Moro on human grounds, while others argue that proletariat justice means killing your mother if she's an enemy of the people. One of the reasons I love Paris so much is that it is absolutely the best city for moviegoing; it's so much better than New York, the best city for movie lovers in the states, that the comparison isn't worth making. Whenever I am in Paris, however briefly, I always make sure to see at least a couple of films that I know I won't see in the states.

Other than illustrating the danger of excessive reason, though, the Bellochio movie isn't that successful. European movie makers often defend their work as human portraits or character studies as opposed to the more action-driven films made in the states, so here we don't see Moro's kidnapping or execution or the capture of the kidnappers; instead, the majority of the film consists of conversations among the four Red Brigade members and their victim inside the apartment where he was held for fifty-five days. The problem with detailing human nature is that it tends to be unchanging; we know that some kidnappers will soften after a while, just as, once Moro accepts his death sentence stoically, we know it won't be long before he begins to plead for his life. A well-turned plot, however, is never predictable.

That doesn't mean that one shouldn't see as many movies from as many countries as possible. Cinema in Paris represents the perfect marriage of reason and pleasure; every day, thousands of producers, directors, actors, technicians of all kinds, manufacturers, distributors, schedulers, theater owners, ticket sellers, ushers, and, in recent years, even popcorn makers are working around the clock to make sure that you can start as early as 9:00 a.m. to see movies from Norway, Mali, Afghanistan, Korea, South Africa, even France and the United States.

Paris is many things to me, including a dark room with a screen at one end. I recall that, one day during an earlier visit, it wasn't even dinnertime, yet I was tipsy—from too many movies, not too much merlot. I'd seen four films that Sunday, and as I made my way toward our apartment, the characters I'd watched all day made the trip with me: gigolos and jewel thieves jostled each other on the sidewalk, and Italian peasants rubbed shoulders on the *métro* with mad Bavarian kings. Like others, I go to Paris for food and museums and the beauty of the city, but one of my several Parises is about thirty yards long and ten yards wide and it has a big white screen at the far end—okay, a little white screen, because the average movie auditorium in that city is about the size of the family room in your typical American ranch house.

Yet Parisians get the most out of those little screens: the tiny Accatone movie house on the Rue Cujas has only two screening rooms, but in a typical week, as many as twenty-nine films are shown there. And when the weekly entertainment guide *Pariscope* appears every Wednesday, its cover always boasts of the city's "*300 films de la semaine.*"

Some movies never seem to leave, and the ones that have some kind of permanent status in Paris movie houses often seem odd choices. When I lived in Paris in 1998, I saw *Moonfleet,* a pirate movie with Stewart Granger and Vivica Lindfors, as well as *Party Girl,* a story about the Chicago mob starring Robert Taylor and Cyd Charisse. When I came back three years later, the same two movies were still being shown, despite the actors' middling reputations. Why? Easy: the first film is directed by Fritz Lang and the second by Nicholas Ray. In film terms, Paris is a director's city.

The permanence of some films suggests something else about Paris, which is that new audiences are always showing up: whereas a city with a more stable population brings films to viewers, diehard film buffs are constantly heading to Paris to see movies because they know they won't be able to find more in any other city in the world.

One of those diehards is me. Besides having been an avid fan from childhood forward, I refer to film a lot in my writing. During one Paris stay, I needed to see *Straw Dogs* for a piece I was doing. Thirty years after its making, it's not a movie one would expect to find easily, but I grabbed my *Pariscope* anyway, and, sure enough, Sam Peckinpah's bloody revenge tragedy was showing that afternoon at the Action Ecoles, just a short bus ride away.

In fact, one of the best features of Paris moviegoing is the elegant treatment given to classic American films. Theaters like the Action Christine often have extended mini-festivals of one kind or another; during this stay, there was a film noir festival there featuring *This Gun for Hire* and *The Glass Key* and *The Blue Dahlia*. It would be hard enough to find one of these movies on an American screen, much less all three.

When it comes to films in languages besides English, France is way ahead of other countries in making content accessible. Most foreign films that are shown are original versions that have been subtitled, whereas in Italy and Spain, films are invariably dubbed. Film is primarily a visual medium, so even if you know only a little French, you can follow a French film with a bit of effort, and movies from other countries are quite easy to understand with the help of French subtitles. In Paris I've seen Senegalese movies as well as ones in Danish, Greek, and the major Asian tongues. It was as though the Tower of Babel contained a multiplex on the first floor, and while I'm sure I missed a few subtleties, I had no problem figuring out what was going on.

Another key difference between Paris and other cities is that, in the French capital, movies start showing early in the morning and continue until the last *métro* stops. The day I set my personal record of four movies, I began with three shorter films: Luis Buñuel's *Un Chien Andalou*, then Pier Paolo Pasolini's *La Ricotta* and Roman Polanski's *River of Diamonds*. I ended with Luchino Visconti's recently restored *Ludwig*, nearly four hours in length.

To soak up this much cinematic pleasure, I had to spend a good part of the previous day deploying my powers of reason in service of a strategy that would have made Napoleon proud. Between the first three films and the last, I even found time to eat a *confit de canard* at a sidewalk café. I only drank mineral water with the meal, though. If you love movies, they're intoxication enough. And in Paris, there are more than enough movies to make your head spin.

◆

In my excess of moviegoing, I'd like to think I honored the one quality that Rabelais and Montaigne have in common: excess. Pantagruel's companion Friar John says, "If I don't perform some heroic deed every day, I can't sleep at night." Montaigne writes: "No powerful mind stops within itself: it is always stretching out and exceeding its capacities. It makes sorties which go beyond what it can achieve: it is only half-alive if it is not advancing, pressing forward, getting driven into a corner and coming to blows." These two Frenchmen, dead three hundred years and more, make me a better American today.

Shortly after we returned to Tallahassee, and reluctant to let go of our recent experience, I invited some French and Francophile friends over and prepared a *dégustation* menu for them. In the *dégustation* tradition, there were many courses, each accompanied by its own wine. And I emphasize regional cuisine in my choice of dishes: often, you hear people say, "Come on over, we're cooking Italian" or "Should we have Chinese or Thai tonight?" but no French cook would offer to prepare you an American meal, and I wasn't about to make the same mistake by cooking up a mess of chitterlings in the Auvernois manner.

So here's what we ate and drank that night: roasted Georgia pecans and champagne; fried Appalachicola oysters and cheese grits with a sauvignon blanc; grilled country sausages and black-eyed peas accompanied by a cabernet; wilted spinach salad with bacon and cane-syrup vinaigrette; bread pudding with bourbon sauce and a sauterne; candied orange and grapefruit rinds with coffee. It might have been a bit much for Montaigne, though I'd like to think Rabelais would have lined up for seconds.

As our two masters teach us, the joys of the belly are most abundant when they are met and matched by the joys of the brain. Each of our guests that night is a world-class conversationalist, as good eaters and drinkers tend to be; those who cleave to plain fare are not avoiding calories so much as hedonism itself, including the enjoyment of witty talk.

The playwright Terence urged moderation in all things, but there are two ways to achieve that balance, each with its own risks and rewards. One is to sit quietly at the center of experience; you're unlikely to injure yourself, even though your life may not be the most exciting. The other is to recognize the extremes and travel the road between them; you may stub your toe, but there'll be a thrill around every bend.

Once, when we were visiting Claude and Marie at their home near France's southern coast, we drove out to Montaigne's farm, the place where his mind worked best, away from the huggermugger of the city; this is where he composed his essay "On Idleness." Even on the farm he practiced isolation: there is a tower where he worked in solitude, and, as with a number of cultural sites in the provinces, one can walk right in with a dismaying lack of supervision. In his asceticism and fierce insistence on morality, Montaigne would seem the less likely of our two masters to counsel anything other than strict virtue. But he knew about the extremes of human nature and recognized their value to the fully evolved person: there is a faded painting on the wall of one room of the tower that shows Saint Michael crushing the serpent, and beneath it, Montaigne wrote, "If necessary I would happily carry a candle to St. Michael, and another to his snake."

"Why Does It Always Have To Be A Boy Baby?"

After "Here's your syllabus" and "Take a look at that stain on the carpet and you'll see why you can't bring food into the study center," the first thing I'll tell my students in Florence this fall is that we're going to be looking at a lot of madonnas and bambinos in the next four months. And when I say a lot, I mean plenty, a ton, a whole heap of pretty Nazarene mommies and their bouncing baby boys; the Uffizi alone contains hundreds of them.

Every time I teach in Florence, where my university has a year-round study center, the issue of religion comes up. In Italy, of course, this is like saying the issue of pasta comes up. And then there's the little matter of red wine as well as the whole subject of the Italians speaking that weird language of theirs. But our study center is what's known as an "island campus," in that we import our faculty and students from the states so they can get the benefit of foreign exposure, which means that the students don't really speak Italian anyway (they're required to study it, but the locals are eager to practice their English), although they've already had a certain exposure to *spaghetti alla carbonara* and *Chianti classico* and are looking forward to more.

When it comes to religion, though, that's where things tend to break down, where the center cannot hold and mere anarchy is loosed upon the mind of Josh and Heather. At home in Tallahassee, there's a typically broad student base, meaning lots of working-class students, kids from rural communities, and so on—in other words, youngsters from the very demographics on which the rock of religion is founded, the kind who are likely to leave a truck with a bumper sticker that says "My Boss Is a Jewish Carpenter" in my space in the faculty lot. The study-abroad students, on the other hand, tend to be upper-middle-class (at least) and, as socially aggressive extroverts, they really like to party. This doesn't mean they're bad students; to the contrary, they're the kind who want to get ahead in life, and, with a little push from me and my colleagues, most of them are pretty good about channeling a lot of that energy into their academic work.

Religiously, though, they tend to be loosely wrapped. I've never taken a survey, but I'll bet those kids in Florence fall more or less evenly into these categories: regular churchgoers, Christmas and Easter Catholics, non-Christians, atheists, agnostics, and the group I'll call nothings, which means the group that never thinks of religion at all. If I'm right, this means a good two-thirds of my students in Florence either don't know who Jesus and Mary are or do but don't care. I've taught in Florence five times now, and the most devout student I had there was a Jehovah's Witness, but she had issues with graven images and was clearly nervous with the religious aspect of art history. In other words, like most students there, she, too, did not float in religion's mainstream, though that was because she was all the way over on the other bank rather than sitting on the majority side.

Here's a story about our students and religion that another instructor told me. In the Uffizi, two students are looking at a Giotto Madonna and Child, say, or a Cimabue. The first says, in a tone of unmistakable annoyance, "Why does it always have to be a boy baby?" In a tone of unmistakable incredulity, her friend says, "It's Jesus, you moron!" The first girl says, "Oh, see, I don't know anything about all that—I'm Jewish." Slowly pivoting her head in disbelief, the friend says, "So am I, but I've *heard* of Jesus. You've *heard* of Jesus, haven't you? I mean, you do know who he *is?*"

I want to get my students ready for all this iconography, so, cribbing freely from Jack Miles's *God: A Biography,* I ask them to see the story in human terms. Look, there's a brand-new mommy. Now look closely at her expression; what does it say? She may be the mother of God, but she's thinking what any mother would: "Oh, how pretty my little boy is, and how I love him! Even though he's just a baby, already he seems so smart! I know he'll be a great man some day: a doctor, a teacher, maybe even a rabbi. But he's so tiny still, so fragile. What if he doesn't grow up to be strong and healthy? Or what if he does and people want to hurt him, maybe kill him? Oh, what will happen to my beautiful baby?"

And then I tell the students that, as their mothers dandled them on their knees and wiped the spit-up off their chins with a clean diaper, *their mothers had exactly the same thoughts,* and so did their fathers, once they came in off the golf course. (Just as the baby is invariably a boy, I say, the parent is always a woman—while Masaccio or Masolino or Filippo Lippi was painting the portrait, Joseph was stuck in the sand trap on the thirteenth hole.) And many of you young women will be mothers yourselves one day, I tell them, and some of you young men will be fathers as well as scratch golfers. And you, too, will look at your adorable child and say to yourself what Mary said two thousand years ago.

Taken together, the story involving the two students and Jack Miles's casting of the Madonna and Child story in secular terms manage to touch on almost everything that one can say about religion in these times. Most obvious is the sacred element: it's not *a* mother and child but *the* mother and child. Second, there's the psychological aspect, which means reversing (without canceling) the first proposition: even though it's *the* mother and child, it's still *a* mother and child. And, finally, there is the luminous Know-Nothingism of the student who wouldn't know Christ if he came down from the cross and proselytized her personally, a Valley Girlishness available to all and so innocent in its obliviousness as to amount, almost, to a kind of wisdom. Of the two stories, though, the one most pertinent to this essay is Jack Miles's explanation of this iconic image in secular language,

because if it heals the split between the faithful and the unbeliev-
ers, it also dramatizes that split.

◆

That there is a divide in this country between churchgoers and
stay-at-homes is not news, at least to readers of Nicholas D.
Kristof's biweekly columns in the *New York Times.* In an August 15, 2003, piece, for example, Kristof points out that, while
83 percent of Americans believe in the virgin birth of Jesus, only
28 percent believe in evolution. This fervor is just part of what he
refers to as "another religious Great Awakening," referring to the
widespread religious revivals in the eighteenth and nineteenth
centuries in this country.

If you're reading this essay, chances are you're a present or
former college student and thus somewhat more likely to be
indifferent to religion than otherwise. Kristof points out in an
April 25, 2004, column that there is an odd lack of intellectual
curiosity about the religious right on the part of the secular left
that prides itself in being informed. It's easier to find people on
campus who can discuss *The Upanishads,* he says, than Tim La-
Haye and Jerry B. Jenkins's best-selling *Left Behind* novels.

As I write this, the May 24, 2004, issue of *Newsweek* has just
appeared with LaHaye and Jenkins on the cover behind a cap-
tion which reads "The New Prophets of Revelation: Why Their
Biblical 'Left Behind' Novels Have Sold 62 Million Copies—
And Counting." Among the several sidebars within the story
is one noting that "74% of Americans believe that Satan exists.
Among evangelical, the number increases to 93%." Another survey, a Gallop poll cited in Alice K. Turner's *The History of Hell,*
reports that 60 percent of Americans believe in Hell, though
only 4 percent think they're likely to go there; to modify Sartre's
statement slightly, Hell is for other people.

Kristof's personal gauge for the change in climate is his grandfather, a devoutly religious man who believed steadfastly in evo-

lution and regarded the Virgin Birth as a leap in faith, a view shared by such theologians as Hans Küng, who points out that the Christian version is but an echo of the virgin myths that figure in many ancient religions. But mainline Christians like the grandfather are disappearing, says Kristof. In fact, rational religionists are vanishing from every culture. If, in this country, the number of Pentecostalists has quadrupled since 1960 as the number of Episcopalians has been nearly halved, the Islamic world today is in crisis "in large part because of a similar drift away from a rich intellectual tradition and toward the mystical."

Don't get him wrong: Kristof is no Bible (or Koran) thumper. It's just that, as he says in subsequent columns, there's going to be more trouble than there is already if those on either side of the split don't learn to talk to each other. Yet it's not as though the two camps have everything in common *except* religion. Recently, when I asked Louis Menand, the Pulitzer Prize–winning author of *The Metaphysical Club,* about the gap between the religious and the non-, especially in academe, he responded by saying that he'd been told that 90 percent of people in the United States believed in God, the highest percentage of any nation except Malta. The problem, Menand continued, is that the U.S. university as we know it was founded in the nineteenth century on the German scientific model. (*The Metaphysical Club* offers considerably more information on the history of American higher education, and Menand is working on a study of liberal arts education in this country that will extend his ideas further.) The result is a tension between Us and Them that is illustrated by, for example, the evolution versus creationism debate, though that conflict is only a tiny marker of the much larger problem.

Internationally, the war between reason and faith goes back millennia. In books such as Jennifer Michael Hecht's *Doubt: A History* and Charles Freeman's *The Closing of the Western Mind,* the case is made for there always being doubters and believers; it's simply a matter of who is in ascendance at a particular historical moment. The ancient Greeks emphasized reason, for example, and laid the groundwork for modern science and mathematics. In the first decades of Christianity, all viewpoints were possible. But by 200 AD, the church of Rome began to take a leading role among the diverse sects that had proliferated since Christ's death. Suddenly, nonconformist views were heretical; for example, the church father Irenaeus argued that those who promoted teachings outside of the New Testament should be expelled. The conversion of Constantine in the fourth century began the process by which church and state would eventually become one, and it was not until the Renaissance and the rediscovery of Greek thought that secular reason flourished again.

In this country, the separation of church and state is constitutionally mandated. On the other hand, a 2003 Gallup poll found that 40 percent of Americans considered themselves not merely Christians but evangelicals or born-again Christians, and these included the president, the attorney general, the speaker of the House, and the House majority leader, to restrict the count to national political leaders only. In his book *Lessons from a Father to His Son,* then–Attorney General John Ashcroft described how he anointed himself in the manner of the kings of Israel before both terms as Missouri governor and then again following his successful 1995 Senate campaign. But there are key differences between the ancient ceremony and Ashcroft's recent versions. One is that David and Saul did not anoint themselves but were anointed by the prophet Samuel. Another is that the oil used for the anointing in the ancient ceremony was the sacred oil whose manufacture is described in Exodus 30:22–29, whereas Attorney General Ashcroft used Crisco.

◆

In 2002, I was teaching at my university's study center in London, and one day I read that there would be a memorial concert for George Harrison in the Royal Albert Hall. The first day that tickets went on sale, I called the box office, listened to the hold music for two hours, and then was told that the concert had completely sold out. I rebounded from my gloom a few minutes later with Plan B, which would be to get an assignment from an American newspaper and wangle a press pass. Sure enough, within a few hours, I had a commission from the *Christian Science Monitor*. Not that it did any good; no doubt the Royal Albert Hall press office had pass requests from representatives of every village newspaper in England, Europe, and Asia, none of which they granted. But something positive did come of my attempt to get a midlife start in the journalism business. It turned out that the newspaper didn't have a regular arts correspondent in the United Kingdom at that time, so I became the *Monitor*'s boy in London.

This impressed the students no end, though I found out that some of the more secular ones were perplexed by the paper's historic affiliation with a non-mainstream religion. Most had heard of Christian Science, though only a few of them had heard of the *Christian Science Monitor* and knew that it wasn't a church bulletin but a respected newspaper. As one student told me, some of my charges were speculating that I had become an evangelical Christian, while others thought I'd converted to Scientology. The first group was concerned that I might start proselytizing them. So was the second, though they were more willing to put up with it given what they saw as my association with such celebrity Scientologists as John Travolta and Tom Cruise.

As an erstwhile journalist, I learned quickly what everybody, newspaper correspondent or not, already knows: steer clear of politics and religion. You can make the most provocative statements about music or theater, and your readership will be so silent that you'll wonder if you even have one. But say something pro or con about Richard Nixon or Jehovah and you can expect to see your in-box light up like a badly wired slot machine. I never even tried writing about sports, so I certainly never made the error of treating religion, politics, and sports in the same piece. To have done so would have risked more than a tripled fury, I think, because of the singular overlap that often occurs in these three areas.

I'll describe this overlap by means of a concrete example: my mother-in-law, whom I love dearly, even though we agree on little except our mutual affection for each other. In religion, she is a Southern Baptist; in politics, a conservative Republican; in sports, a die-hard football fan. Reader, does this description sound familiar? Don't you know someone, or more than one person, who is a Protestant Evangelical Right-Wing Sports Fanatic? Of course you do; this is an American type as ubiquitous as the Midriffed Mall Honey or the Bling-Encrusted Rapper or, closer to home, the Tweedy Pipe-Puffer.

But whereas these other types identify themselves mainly through the semiotics of their tribal gear, the Protestant right-leaning sports fan is defined by a single ideological bent, one explained to me by *Tampa Tribune* sports writer Rick Wilber. I met Rick on the Florida writers conference circuit after my return from London and, in the course of our conversation, happened to mention my mother-in-law. Rick says, "She sounds like my father." "Okay," I say, "then maybe you can explain why, if you're either a Protestant fundamentalist or a political right-winger or a football nut, you're very likely to be the other two as well."

"It's Manichaeism," says Rick. "Everything is either good or it isn't: you're saved or you're not, you're right or you aren't, either you won or you lost. There's no middle ground, no gray area: the score may be 40–39, but if you're the one with 39 points, you still lose. Purgatory's for liberals. Purgatory's one big nuance, and Manichaeans aren't interested in nuances: if you aren't going to heaven, you're going to hell."

The preachings of Mani, a Persian born around 215 in a Jewish-Christian community in Assyria, gained a substantial following "for at least a thousand years in the West," says Alice K. Turner in *The History of Hell*, "and much longer in the East, possibly into the twentieth century in China." According to Manichaeism, opposing spirits of good and evil compete for control of the world. On the one hand, there is the God of Light, who creates Adam in his image; on the other is Satan, who is associated with fire, smoke, demons, bad weather, and women, including Eve.

As opposed to other religions of the time, Turner says, Manichaeism had the advantage of being "a rather easy-to-understand system." Too, Manichaeans get to enjoy the delicious two-fold pleasure of knowing that, if they're right, the other fellow is not only wrong but damned. The phrase "abominable fancy," attributed by D. P. Walker in *The Decline of Hell* to nineteenth-century preacher F. W. Farrar, describes the centuries-old Christian idea that the rapture of the heavenly few is enhanced by their being able to see and enjoy the eternal torments of the damned, as though Heaven and Hell were connected by closed-circuit television.

In his sympathetic account *The Faith of George W. Bush,* Stephen Mansfield reports that, following Bush's successful gubernatorial campaign in 1998, Republican leaders began to sound out the possibility of a presidential candidacy. Bush is skeptical. One Sunday, though, at the Highland Park Methodist Church in Dallas with his mother, Bush hears Pastor Mark Craig preach on Moses' doubts about his own leadership ability. It looks as though the Israelites are just going to have to remain in bondage: "Sorry, God, I'm busy," Pastor Craig has Moses saying. "I've got a family. I've got sheep to tend. I've got a life."

From William Bradford forward, there is a four-hundred-year-old tradition equating Americans with the Israelites. Notwithstanding the slaughter of a native population and the African slave trade, Americans are, when it is expedient, re-presented as innocents who need to be saved from Pharaoh or, in the case of the 2000 presidential election, Al Gore. And Pastor Craig is not about to miss his chance: Americans are "starved for leadership," he says, "for leaders who have ethical and moral courage." Somebody's got to step up, even though it's not always easy or convenient to do so. "Remember," says the pastor, "even Moses had doubts."

According to Stephen Mansfield, Barbara Bush then says to her son, "He was talking to you." It's unclear whether the pronoun refers to Pastor Craig or a higher authority, a "he" or a "He." Regardless, Bush tells some friends, "I feel like God wants me to run for president. I can't explain it, but I sense my country is going to need me. Something is going to happen and, at that time, my country is going to need me. I know it won't be easy on me or my family, but God wants me to do it."

The objections to religion are numerous and familiar: it's a crutch, it's irrational, it's the opium of the masses, it distracts from real-world problems, it encourages people to ring my doorbell while I'm still asleep and shove at me those tracts with the grade-school prose and the god-awful cartoons of sinners roasting in hellfire. Historically, though, there is one objection that preempts all others, and that is that religion is used as a justification for political actions that include war, cruelty, and oppression of all kinds.

The current battle over gay marriage is an example; it's easier to say that homosexuality is prohibited in Leviticus (along with tattooing and wearing garments made of different fibers) than to admit to squeamishness at the sight of men holding hands with men or women kissing each other. The Crusades, the Inquisition, the English and French civil wars, the Salem witch trials, the Hindu and Muslim massacres during the struggle for Indian independence, the Mideast conflict, the Catholic and Protestant conflict in Northern Island, the September 11 attacks: the history of bloodshed is in large part a religious history. According to Jonathan Kirsch's *God against the Gods: The History of the War between Monotheism and Polytheism,* religious intolerance, persecution, and warfare are largely a product of religions that worship a single deity of the kind most Americans say they believe in.

Even clashes that are primarily ethnic in nature are often couched in religious terms. The Israelis are the new Israelites;

unfortunately, so is everybody else. To say "We want someone else's land or oil" is too reasonable; to say "God wants us to invade them" is a lot more compelling, especially if you're addressing a nation in which a lot of people see God the way you do: as an Old Testament, old-school, hear-me-and-obey patriarch who calls them as he sees them and doesn't beat around the bush, burning or otherwise. Far from the Deists' concept of a God who wound up the world like a pocket watch and is content to watch it tick away the eons, this God is very hands-on, a micromanager who likes a good war, knows which way to vote, and favors one team over the other in the Super Bowl, which is why those wide receivers kneel and acknowledge Him every time they scamper into the end zone.

As George W. Bush once said to Senator Joe Biden, "I don't do nuance."

◆

Then what is good about religion? As with the complaints against it, you can quickly rack up religion's plusses. Religion consoles. It provides moral structure. It encourages positive social change—is the American civil rights movement imaginable outside of black churches? Religion even prolongs life: it's hard to pick up a newspaper these days without stumbling across yet another article on how membership in social groups (a bowling league, an adult Sunday school class) keeps old-timers healthy.

But there's even more good news. Three recent texts argue that religious belief has positively changed human history so radically that a quality of life taken for granted by everyone, including even the most impious, would not exist were it not for religion. In *The Gift of the Jews,* Thomas Cahill observes that Judaism replaced the pessimistic idea of endless life cycles with the concept of progress and possibility; further, it did it in so pervasive a matter that secular thought changed for the better. Ancient Middle Eastern religions and philosophies saw life as an endless cycle of birth and death that turned ceaselessly, like a wheel, says Cahill. For the Jews, though, time had a beginning, a middle, and a triumphant end that would come in the future. From this idea comes a belief in progress, that tomorrow can be better than today, as well as a new conception of men and women as individuals with unique destinies, a conception that would inform, among other modern texts, the Declaration of Independence.

It has also been argued recently that, throughout recorded history, Christianity has been an indispensable spur to excellence in science and art. Charles Murray writes in *Human Accomplishment: The Pursuit of Excellence in the Arts and Sciences, 800 B.C. to 1950* that Christianity nurtured intellectual independence and drive. According to Murray, Thomas Aquinas argued that intelligence is a gift from God and therefore to use one's intelligence to understand the world is pleasing to Him. This viewpoint prevailed from the Renaissance through the Enlightenment, with attendant advances in art and science. Murray is a controversial author whose book *The Bell Curve,* coauthored with Richard J. Herrnstein, argued that there were genetically differences in black and white intelligence. This new book, too, will ruffle feathers with its seeming promotion of Christianity as a superior religion. Murray describes himself as an agnostic libertarian, though one drawn to Christianity's coherent moral vision. With it, he says, you get *Macbeth;* without it, you get the *Kill Bill* movies.

Everybody knows that religion has a profound effect on the otherworldly pursuits of music, painting, and literature, but did you know that belief in the afterlife—especially Hell—can make you rich? Analyzing data collected in fifty-nine countries between 1981 and 1999, Harvard scientists Robert J. Barro and Rachel M. McCleary assert in a paper entitled "Religion and Economic Growth across Countries," which appeared in the October 2003 issue of *American Sociological Review,* that religious belief affects marketplace behavior. If this sounds like an update of Max Weber's classic *The Protestant Ethic and the Spirit of Capitalism,* which argued that Protestantism transformed feudal European economics and made capitalism triumphant in the West, it is, though Barro and McCleary make their point using amounts of data and sophisticated analytical techniques that would have been unavailable to Weber. Among their findings are that countries such as Malaysia, Singapore, and South Korea have experienced both rapid economic growth and the spread of Christianity, whereas the former East Germany, for example, experienced low levels of growth in both religion and wealth during the years they analyzed.

Taken together, Cahill, Murray, and Barro and McCleary seem to be telling us that religion is so tonic that everyone should embrace it whether they believe in it or not. Or, as Victorian specialist David Parker put it in a recent e-mail to me, "religion is nonsense, but communities that have it are more successful, and individuals who can subscribe to it are fit to survive and flourish in such communities. More and more I take the view of ancient Greek and Chinese sages who, more wistful than anything else, declared it impossible to believe in the gods, but essential for the good of society to behave as if they did."

Yet none of these three arguments for religion's tonic qualities is without nuance; for example, Murray doesn't point out that rationalist Aquinas was a big fan of the abominable fancy (the *Summa Theologica* reports that "in order that the happiness of the saints may be more delightful to them and that they may render more copious thanks to God for it, they are allowed to see perfectly the sufferings of the damned"). And other studies of the relation between religion and economics support many of Barro and McCleary's points while pointing out that, the more religious people are, the less tolerant they are of other races and nationalities and the more negative they are in their attitudes toward women.

Optimistic, cultured, wealthy, bigoted: is this what it means to be religious?

•

In the end, arguing for or against religion, especially on the basis of whether it is good or bad for us, is like arguing for or against automobiles or ice cream or sex. Just because they know it's the right thing to do doesn't mean people are going to trade in their SUVs for goat carts or end every meal with a crunchy apple or drive out to Inspiration Point for the sole purpose of exchanging a series of vigorous handshakes. And they aren't going to go to church or synagogue or temple less (or more) because of an argument. Religion is best taken, not as an idea, but as an appetite. And while I have the kind of doubts about SUVs that only someone can who is the proud owner of a 1985 Toyota Corolla, I like my ice cream and my cuddle time as much the next person, which means that I can't really object to the gratification of the religious appetite, either. If one had to choose among overdosing on big cars or fast food or wife-swapping or prayer, the choice should be obvious.

To me, a better question than "Is religion good or bad for you?" is "Why has there always been religion?" Despite the absence of the slightest shred of scientific proof of God's existence, why have people always believed in God? As much as I prefer the rational scientism of Freud to the murkier speculations of Jung, it is the latter who explains the allure of religion best. As a humanist and a student of art and archeology, Freud saw the appeal of religion, which is why he is almost wistful in his denial of it, as though he is saying, "Let us put away childish things." Jung, on the other hand, is enthusiastic, not about watered-down organized religion, but about the psychological and mythological richness of religious thought. Jung's notion of the archetype, the resonant symbol that appeals to us in spite (or because) of the fact that it transcends precise meaning, is at the heart of every religion. God, the Mother, the Child, the cross, even the Christmas tree: all of these are archetypes, which is why every religious faith (or at least the theistic ones) has some version of them.

"Archetypes speak the language of high rhetoric," writes Jung in *Memories, Dreams, Reflections,* "even bombast," and we have such an appetite for bombast that, when we cannot find it, we'll look for it until we do. Our everyday lives are humdrum, or at least we hope they are: we want the cashier to be in her place at the supermarket, the mechanic on duty in his garage, our doctor available (or at least pageable) when our heart flutters, and so, as part of this vast unwritten contract, we, too, must be at our post when we should be. We are rewarded monetarily, yet we use our money mainly to buy security—food, car repair, medical treatment—and so trade the tedium of the workplace for the tedium of domesticity until it's time to go back to work.

Across these gray skies must flash lightning. Let there be bombast! Religion is as action-packed as a shelf full of Louis L'Amour novels: there are good guys and bad guys, devils and angels, virgins and loose women, salvation and damnation, Heaven and Hell, and, best of all, miracles. There aren't any miracles at the Shop-Rite or Action Auto Repair or your job; you might get a second can of creamed corn for free or learn that your tires just need to be rotated rather than replaced or that your boss decided not to move the factory to Mexico after all, but this isn't the stuff of scripture. Jesus didn't use the Heimlich maneuver on Lazarus; he raised him from the dead. Religion is so seductive that its most basic terms appeal even to the irreligious; anyone who thoughtlessly sighs "Thank god!" or tells the umpire to go to hell is buying in.

A righteous old hullabaloo has long been associated with religion, as in the Medieval mystery plays with their fire-breathing hell mouths and demons capering through the audience. And even today, smart religions will keep topping up their Bombast Quotient. In *The Transformation of American Religion: How We Actually Live Our Faith,* Alan Wolfe describes a church service in Los Angeles in which four mud-covered men leap onto a stage and wash themselves off to reveal that each is of a different race. And even though the Mosaic Church is located in Southern California and sports a trendy New Age name, Wolfe points out that it is a Baptist Church—Southern Baptist, no less.

◆

In *Memories, Dreams, Reflections,* Jung points to another positive effect of religion. He tells us that any secret society is an intermediate stage in the process of individuation, that there is "no better means of intensifying the treasured feeling of individuality than the possession of a secret which the individual is pledged to guard." Membership means "the individual is still relying on a collective organization to effect his differentiation for him; that is, he has not yet recognized that it is really the individual's task to differentiate himself from all the others and stand on his own feet." That, clearly, should be the individual's goal, because "collective identities are crutches for the lame, shields for the timid, beds for the lazy, nurseries for the irresponsible. "On the other hand, there is a positive aspect to collective identities, for they "are equally shelters for the poor and weak, a home port for the shipwrecked, the bosom of a family for orphans, a land of promise for disillusioned vagrants and weary pilgrims, a herd and a safe fold for lost sheep, and a mother providing nourishment and growth."

Many use collective identities as way stations on the road to individuality. Most of my friends, like me, passed through a religious phase when they were growing up yet are no longer observant. A number of my students have surrendered their personal identities to such fringe groups as the Moonies and the Hare Krishnas as a way of distancing themselves from their parents (and their parents' religions) and then become individuals again, strengthened by the collective experience and able at last to live with what Jung calls our "inner multiplicity."

Even if it were not used this way, religion will always be with us for the two reasons Jung gives: the lazy and irresponsible will need it, but so will the weak, the weary, and those seeking the nourishment religion offers. So what choice is there for the rest of us, we who are not called?

If you ask educated middle- and upper-class people who aren't religious what their stance toward religion is, many will tell you that they have substituted some activity that is larger than they are and to which they can give themselves over, that is, that they can approach as one might one's faith. They might take up po-

etry, for example, or long-distance running. Or capital formation; God is a deity, but so is Mammon. But while substituting
something else for religion might result in more sestinas or better
race times or bigger bank accounts, it fails to address the principal concern of this essay, that religion must be engaged, even
by the nonreligious.

As I see it, the latter group has three choices. The first option
is the simplest and very likely the one many readers of this essay
have already chosen: do nothing. Let others tithe, pray, listen to
badly written sermons, avoid pork and alcohol if they want to;
I'll leave them alone if they'll do the same for me.

The problem is that you can ignore religion, but it won't ignore you. You can't pick up a newspaper or turn on the television or read your e-mail without encountering religion. You can't
change the channels on your car radio or overhear a supermarket
conversation or drive past a church marquee and not recognize
that religion is everywhere. Religious people figure in politics,
entertainment, and every other aspect of our culture, and their
numbers are growing. To attempt indifference is to fail; to dis-
dain religion in the twenty-first century is like disdaining hy-
drogen. Ignorance is no excuse. Who wants to be the girl who
wanted to know, "Why does it always have to be a boy baby?"

The second choice is to join up. Even if you don't believe,
there are compelling reasons for religious affiliation, such as the
health benefits. Or for purposes of community: a friend told me
she started to send her son and daughter to church because they
had a hard time fitting in at the school they attended, where
the other children wanted to know "what they were." When my
father-in-law died recently in Hawai'i, my brother-in-law and
his family were given full-fare airplane tickets by their church,
whereas the secular siblings had to pay for transportation from
the mainland.

Here the difficulty is that just as religion gives, so, too, does it
take, and it's hard to imagine anyone embracing faith rationally
and being very comfortable for long. The spiritual allegiance that

religion demands is mother's milk to the faithful; it won't work if you try to get along without or, worse, fake it. Jesus had a thing about hypocrites, and, sooner or later, you'll be found out, not least by yourself. So use your credit card if you have to travel, and if you want to lower your blood pressure, there's always city-league softball.

The third possibility is to study religion, learn from it, take the best that religion has to offer, and use it as a truly religious person would, which is to say in daily practice. It doesn't hurt to be compassionate; compassion is a key idea in every religion. It's a good idea to forgive; being angry at someone else won't do them harm, but it'll hurt you. And lose the ego if you want a healthy blood pressure and fewer wars.

Karen Armstrong, a former nun who is now a distinguished scholar of Islam as well as author of the spiritual memoir *The Spiral Staircase,* notes that Jung says a great deal of religion shields us from religious experience. An example she gives is that much of the conflict in the world today is due to the conviction that one God is better than another, an idea that, according to the scripture of virtually every religion, is blasphemous.

Maybe the best thing the irreligious can do is be religious.

The Goat Paths Of Italy

DANTE'S SEARCH FOR BEATRICE

Before mass transport and the automobile, writers didn't have much choice except to go economy, that is, by foot, rarely choosing business class (mule or horse) and almost never traveling in first class (carriage). Necessity aside, though, there is a connection between walking and intellectual production: "My wit will not budge if my legs are not moving," writes Montaigne.

Keats often walked as many as twelve miles a day, even when his consumption was raging. Dickens trod the streets of London all night "to still my beating mind," as he said (quoting Prospero in *The Tempest*). Wallace Stevens famously composed his poems as he walked to work at the Hartford Accident and Indemnity Company every morning, jotting phrases on tiny scraps he'd give to his secretary, who would type them up for his collection when he left in the evening; as a younger man, he'd often go out with a single phrase of Verlaine in his head and turn it over in his mind as he walked from New York to Connecticut or New Jersey and back in a single day. He boasted that he could cover forty-five miles in a round trip, but those of us who've exhausted ourselves on a twenty-mile hike can't be blamed for doubting him. (Suffice it to say that, as the poems prove, it's quality that counts rather than quantity.)

And before the Dante of *The Divine Comedy* walked through the Inferno on his way to Purgatory and Paradise, the real-life Dante Alighieri navigated some byways that might have made Hell's highways look positively inviting by comparison.

"The roads Alighieri walked often gave way to overgrown paths, dense with briars, thick with trees hiding thieves," writes Harriet Rubin in *Dante in Love: The World's Greatest Poem and How It Changed History*. "The paths led to swamps, where travelers would sicken and die in hours." For five years following his exile from Florence in 1302, Dante was a wanderer; the Russian poet Osip Mandelstam asked, "How many pairs of sandals did he wear out on the goat paths of Italy?"

As Dante wandered, his great poem formed in his mind. The terza rima rhyme scheme that he invented, in which the middle rhyme in every three-line stanza becomes the main rhyme in the next, is a sort of walker's pace: two steps forward, one back, two forward again.

A prior (or sort of senator) belonging to the White Guelf party, Dante had gone to Rome on a diplomatic mission but was exiled as part of Pope Boniface VIII's effort to procure power for the Black Guelfs and Florence for himself. Along with his fellow Whites, Dante takes refuge in Siena, Florence's great rival, and they plot their response to the Pope's actions. But when no one can agree on a plan, Dante splits off from the rest and begins walking.

And poetry changes forever. Scholars have long debated the dates of composition of a poem written around seven hundred years ago, but there is some evidence that he may have written the first two cantos of *The Inferno* before his exile; certainly these cantos are mild-mannered and sensible, and it is only in Canto 3, when Dante and his guide, Virgil, pass the Gate of Hell, on which is written "ABANDON ALL HOPE YOU WHO EN-TER HERE," that the poet begins to write with that mixture of horrified pity and cold vindictiveness that became his signature style.

Fourteen thousand two hundred thirty-three lines later, fol-lowing a long slog through *The Purgatorio,* Dante enters God's presence in *The Paradiso.* Sadly, Virgil has had to leave Dante midway through Purgatory and return to Limbo, where the Vir-tuous Pagans dwell; as a non-Christian, the ancient Roman poet cannot go on to paradise. And throughout, Dante has had only occasional glimpses of his feminine ideal, the Beatrice whom the real-life poet fell in love with when they were children yet who figures only sporadically in his life until she dies in her early twenties.

·

There is a Casa di Dante in the Via Dante Alighieri in Florence where he is said to have been born, though that may be only a scheme to get tourists through the door; many scholars think he was born down the street in a building long since demolished. Certainly the Casa di Dante is worth a visit, as it is an impressive building in thirteenth-century style and contains an array of portraits and wooden models as well as illustrations from various editions of the *Comedy*.

Far more moving is the so-called Chiesa di Dante in Via Santa Margherita, which runs by the side of Dante's house. Actually the Church of Santa Margherita de' Cerchi, this is one of those little churches that can get under your skin, though you have to meet it halfway. Whereas most of the churches of Florence fall into two categories, monumental treasure troves like the Duomo and Santa Maria Novella as well as drab parish churches with no art or history to speak of, Santa Margherita belongs to a third category, the churches whose features either provoke a yawn or make your heart leap into your mouth, depending on which aisle you're in.

There is, for example, a beautiful altarpiece by Neri di Bicci of the Madonna surrounded by Saint Margaret and three other female saints. But there are also two contemporary paintings, one silly and the other merely cheesy if, in a strange way, affecting. The silly painting is a huge canvas of Dante meeting Beatrice in the street; there is nothing about Beatrice that suggests she is anything other than pretty in a vapid way, and indeed Dante is looking at her as though she is less his beloved and more someone who owes him money after a late-night card game. The other painting shows Beatrice coming out of the church on the arm of her bridegroom. As the wedding guests cheer the newlyweds, a figure in red scurries away, downcast. It is Dante as he is always depicted, in his prior's robe, and anyone who has ever been shown the door by the person he loves most knows exactly how he feels.

In its haphazard design, Santa Margherita de' Cerchi may remind American visitors of some liberal Protestant churches they have seen in the United States with their blend of standard ecclesiastical interior and what I think of as Minister's Wife Art: there is the crucifix, the stone baptismal font, and the stained-glass window, but also a gaudy knitted work, say, or splashy "modern" portrait of Christ that can only have been placed there by a well-meaning amateur. Yet each of the two contemporary paintings in Santa Margherita de' Cerchi corresponds to one of the two most emotionally charged passages in the *Vita Nuova*, the masterpiece of Dante's youth and a work he wrote perhaps fifteen years before he began the *Comedy*,

The first passage is Dante's extraordinary description of his sighting of Beatrice when he was eighteen. Here he makes clear how visceral the reaction of this spiritual poet was to the physical presence of the woman he loved above all others. Even when he had seen her as a child, he writes, "the spirit of life, which hath its dwelling in the secretest chamber of the heart, began to tremble so violently that the least pulses of my body shook therewith." Now he is a man and approaching the height of his physical and artistic powers, and when she greets him, he writes, "I came into such sweetness that I parted thence as one intoxicated" and goes back to his room and falls to sleep dreaming of Beatrice, whereupon he has a "marvellous vision":

There appeared to be in my room a mist of the colour of fire, within the which I discerned the figure of a lord of terrible aspect to such as should gaze upon him, but who seemed therewithal to rejoice inwardly that it was a marvel to see. Speaking he said many things, among the which I could understand but few; and of these, this: *Ego dominus tuus* [I am your master]. In his arms it seemed to me that a person was sleeping, covered only with a blood-coloured cloth; upon whom looking very attentively, I knew that it was the lady of the salutation who had deigned the day before to salute me. And he who held her held also in his hands a thing that was burning in flames; and he said to me, *Vide cor tuum* [Behold your heart]. But when he had remained with me a little while, I thought that he set himself to awaken her that slept; after the which he made her to eat that thing which flamed in his hand; and she ate as one fearing. Then, having waited again a space, all his joy was turned into most bitter weeping; and as he wept he gathered the lady into his arms, and it seemed to me that he went with her up towards heaven; whereby . . . a great anguish came upon me.

A passion of this immensity is terrifying. If Dante seems a reluctant suitor—if he was as wooden before Beatrice as he appears in the silly contemporary painting in Santa Margherita de' Cerchi—that is because the custom of the day didn't permit him to be otherwise. Yet other lovers flouted the rules and pursued fair ladies hotly, so if Dante kept his distance, it may have been because he realized he was looking at the woman who would one day devour his heart.

◆

Not many pages later in the *Vita Nuova,* there is another passage that ranks as one of the greatest failed cover-ups in the history of erotic literature. Here Dante pretends to describe, not the wedding of Beatrice to Simone de' Bardi that is depicted in the second painting in Santa Margherita de' Cerchi, but that of "a gentlewoman who was given in marriage that day." Neither here nor anywhere else in the *Vita Nuova* is Beatrice's marriage mentioned, though the language he uses to describe his behavior on this day is as tremulous and anguished as that of the earlier passage. As casually as though he were accepting an invitation to go out for a drink, he agrees to go with a friend to the house of the newlyweds and "do honour" there to the ladies who make up the wedding party.

But as soon as I had thus resolved, I began to feel a faintness and a throbbing at my left side, which soon took possession of my whole body. Whereupon I remember that I covertly leaned my back unto a painting that ran round the walls of that house; and being fearful lest my trembling should be discerned by them, I lifted mine eyes to look on these ladies, and then first perceived among them the excellent Beatrice. And when I perceived her, all my senses were overpowered by the great lordship that Love obtained, finding himself so near unto that most gracious being, until nothing but the spirits of sight remained to me, and even these remained driven out of their own instruments, because Love entered in that honoured place of theirs, so that he might the better behold her. . . . Many of her friends, having discerned my confusion, began to wonder; and together with myself, kept whispering of me and mocking me. Whereupon my friend, who knew not what to conceive, took me by the hands, and drawing me forth from them, required to know what ailed me. Then, having first held me at quiet for a space until my perceptions were come back to me, I made answer to my friend: "Of a surety I have now set my feet on that point of life, beyond the which he must not pass who would return."

What is Dante talking about here? Obviously it is Beatrice's wedding. If not, he's simply reporting that he felt dizzy one day; if so, why doesn't he just say that instead? One of Freud's discoveries that may apply in this case is that of the "screen memory" or memory of an event that never occurred and which functions to cover up a real memory too terrible to recall. An example might be someone insisting that he had been abducted by aliens and in this way screening a memory of childhood abuse, since it's easier to admit that one has been seized by Martians rather than facing a recollection of sexual and physical abuse at the hands of one's relatives. Dante's account of his trauma on the day of the wedding is totally unself-conscious, as it could only be in a pre-Freudian day when one's bombastic reactions might seem the work of otherworldy powers and thus beyond one's control rather than evidence of a shameful weakness. Yet Dante admits to a hysterical paralysis here, one that leads him to the brink of blindness. The bride is not named, yet who other than Beatrice was capable of inflicting so crippling a neurosis with a tilt of the chin, a turn of the head, a glance toward the poet and then, forever, away?

Yet this story may have a sequel that was never recorded. Dante was nothing if not self-reflective, and he had plenty of time on his hands during his years of exile. Surely he looked back at this moment, at this "point of life, beyond the which he must not pass who would return," and realized that the start of his great story had fallen into his lap. A man with a story to tell needs a goal, and if it's a long story, that goal had better be elusive. And here, in a narrow street in Florence, was the most elusive goal of all: the woman he would chase through the afterlife and, if he's really lucky, never catch.

◆

The church of Santa Margherita de' Cerchi is poorly lit and gloomy and becomes even more stygian when one thinks of poor Beatrice, dead when she was just a few years out of her teens, and thinks, too, of the terrible journey that begins at its door, a journey no less awful for being a fiction. Compared to the statues in the nearby Bargello and the paintings only slightly farther away in the Uffizi, the art in Santa Margherita de' Cerchi is negligible. But if, as you face the high altar, you look to your left, you'll see another, smaller altar just under the high-relief depiction of the Madonna freeing some slaves. Below this smaller altar, and you'll have to stoop to see them, are these words: "SOTTO QUESTO ALTARE / FOLCO PORTINARI / COSTRUI LA TOMBA /

DI FAMIGLIA / L'OTTO GIUGNO 1291 / VI FU SEPOLTA / BEATRICE PORTINARI" ("Under this altar / Folco Portinari / built the tomb / of his family / On 8 June 1291 / Here was buried / Beatrice Portinari") and then, just below them, "PIETRO TOMBALE DI BEATRICE PORTINARI" ("Tombstone of Beatrice Portinari").

Every old church in Italy can boast that it contains the remains of at least one celebrity, and the more important the church, the more glamorous its necropolis. Santa Croce, for example, which is just a few city blocks to the east, features the tombs of Michelangelo, Machiavelli, and Galileo, among others. The older and the more legendary the corpse, the less certain its existence. Yes, Saint Peter is buried beneath the dome of his church in Rome, and the transfer of Saint Mark's body from Alexandria to the Basilica di San Marco in Venice is well documented (he was smuggled out of Egypt in a barrel of pork, his handlers certain that no Muslim would take a second look at a container full of unclean meat). On the other hand, one can't be blamed for asking whether the centurion Longinus, having converted to Christianity at the feet of the crucified Christ, really made it all the way to northern Italy before dying in Mantua and being buried there in the Basilica di Sant'Andrea, where his tomb may be seen today.

Yet it's certain that the bones of Beatrice are there just under the stone in Santa Margherita de' Cerchi; scholars do not argue this point the way they dispute the location of Dante's birthplace. And while one might hesitate to pass one's hand over the tomb of one of the severe fathers of the church, as though he might, even in death, pull away and cast a disapproving glance at the person audacious enough to disturb his eternal sleep, it is hard, as one kneels there under the little altar, not to put one's hands on Beatrice's dusty stone, as though something of her force might come through.

That force was given to her entirely by Dante, of course; of Beatrice herself we know next to nothing. Actually, the most important thing we know about Beatrice is that Dante turned her into a figure with godlike powers. In this respect, Harriet Rubin speculates that Dante may have been influenced by the beautiful Pietro Cavallini mosaics in the church of Santa Maria in Trastevere; the poet "would likely have" seen them when he went to Rome for his fateful meeting with the pope. (I both love and mistrust that phrase in quotation marks, one that I have often used myself when I couldn't be sure of a fact yet wanted it to be true.) If so, Dante saw what a twenty-first-century visitor can still see today, a huge image soaring above the altar of Mary and Jesus sitting together as equals, like a Roman *dominus* and *domina*.

When I visited Santa Maria in Trastevere and saw this couple, I had two thoughts in quick succession. First, I wondered "Who is that woman with Jesus?" and then "Is that Jesus?" Because as he is always represented by artists of every time using every medium, Jesus has a way of commanding the foreground so decisively that everyone else in the scene comes across as a hanger-on; he's like Elvis with his retinue or a good boy who went away to medical school and came home a doctor, adored by his mother (and everyone else) because he is smarter, richer, better than the others. Even in Caravaggio's *Vocation of Saint Matthew* across the Tiber in the church of San Luigi dei Francesi, the shadowy Christ who beckons the evangelist from the corner of the painting is made central by the gazes of the other figures, especially that of the foppish boy at the physical (yet false) center of the painting and whose face beams at Jesus like a searchlight. But here in the Cavallini mosaic, Christ not only shares the stage with Mary, *he has his arm around her.* It's as though he's saying, "This is my mother, folks. No mother, no son—no Mary, no Jesus."

And no Beatrice, no Dante. Beatrice sits at the heart of the *Comedy* like an engine that drives its lines forward. She inspired its author as no other muse, mortal or divine, ever inspired any poet. Though it is many things to many readers—epic adventure,

buddy movie, political tract, sci-fi extravaganza, horror tale, poetry manual—the *Comedy* was, in Dante's mind, a religious essay
as well. In this sense, Beatrice was not a sweetheart or heartthrob
or Poe-esque beautiful dead woman. She was much, much more.
Beatrice was to be chased but never caught, and in that sense, she
was, to use a word Dante wouldn't, a goddess.

◆

As a goddess, Beatrice fits right into the Christian pantheon. The
Greek and Roman gods chattered, flirted, and quarreled: they
were like us. But in the Christian bible, Jesus says little, God
less, the Virgin almost nothing. The essence of Christianity is the
pursuit of the unworldly; "my kingdom is not of this world," said
Jesus, and a good Christian could not imagine talking to a god
who boasted of his affairs with mortals, complained about his
wife's stubbornness, and gossiped about his colleagues on Olym-
pus. To a good Christian, the only divinity worth pursuing is a
silent one.

And Beatrice is largely silent throughout *The Inferno* and most
of *The Purgatorio.* Yet she becomes a regular talking machine in
The Paradiso, which is one reason why that part of the *Comedy* is
the least successful. Here she goes on about the errors in Platonic
thought and the nature of free will, for example, and her final
words to Dante, in Canto 30, are not a grand statement about
love but a denunciation of his enemy, Pope Boniface VIII. For
the great poem to be written, Dante needs to chase Beatrice, not
catch her.

Dante's biographers point to various sites that may have suggested to him an entrance to the underworld; high on the list is
the volcanic plain of Solfatara, near Naples, which the ancient
Romans spoke of as the entrance to Hades and that is visitable
today, its soil still hot to the touch. But his journey can really
be said to start here in the little church of Santa Margherita de'
Cerchi in Florence: it was here that Beatrice was buried into a
marriage to Simone de' Bardi, here she was buried out of this

world and into the next. In the dream the eighteen-year-old Dante has following his encounter with Beatrice, the "lord of terrible aspect" speaks to the poet yet conceals more than he reveals: "Speaking he said many things, among the which I could understand but few." Everyone who has recounted a dream to someone else knows that often the dream itself is of extremely short duration, though the recounting can take a long time indeed as one remembers (or invents) additional details and realizes the provenance and meaning of those details and elaborates on them. Could it be that the "lord of terrible aspect," who seems as much Satan as he is God, tells Dante the story that becomes the *Comedy*? Remember, Dante is still a teenager and hasn't grown into the physical and artistic maturity he will need before setting out on the road that leads through Hell and Purgatory to Paradise. Are the "many things" of which the just-wakened Dante remembers "but few" the themes of his terrible journey, the one he won't be ready to take for years? The details of the trip are the poet's invention, but his obsession with Beatrice had already led him to the ideas he would struggle with in his great poem: love, loss, sorrow, salvation.

The bad news is that Beatrice died when she was still young and Dante still loved her; the good news takes the form of the *Comedy* itself. For, though the poet says in the first lines of *The Inferno* that our trip is through "a gloomy wood," one that is "wild and rough and tortured," the main point of his poem is not to describe the darkness but to relate "all the good" he draws from his time on the road. Dante was looking for Beatrice on the journey that he undertook down the goat paths of Italy, but he knew he wouldn't find her there.

◆

Meanwhile, he had a lot of territory to cover before he could join his beloved in Paradise. Exile, friendlessness, heartbreak: this is the food on which Dante dined, which made him a poet whose only rival is Shakespeare. No wonder the great modern artists of renunciation—Nathaniel Hawthorne, Henry James, George Eliot, T. S. Eliot, Sigmund Freud—were drawn to him. "Shakespeare gives the greatest *width* of human passion," wrote Eliot the poet, "Dante the greatest altitude and greatest depth." Dante, and these others, are each "a stranger to the world," to use Harriet Rubin's expression, certain that perfection is not here but just ahead.

Yet, like Shakespeare, Dante was a rock star in his own age as well as ours. The story is told of Dante passing a smithy one day and hearing the blacksmith chanting lines from the *Comedy* with more enthusiasm than accuracy, whereupon the poet goes in and begins tossing the blacksmith's tools into the street. "Why are you tossing my instruments into the street?" says the smith. "You have ruined my business," says the poet; "take no offense if I should ruin yours!"

Popular enough to be misquoted then, popular enough to be misquoted now, though this time deliberately: as I write this essay, I walk one day down the busy Via Vincenzo Gioberti, which cuts through our working-class neighborhood, past a restaurant where I see posted a handwritten poem that begins "*Nel mezzo del cammin di Via Gioberti*" and goes on to promise that travelers who find themselves, not before the entrance of Hell, but at the door to Osteria Cocotrippone, will find within, not salvation, but hearty Tuscan food and drink.

Of course, Dante was also very much a man of his own time, and the greatest strength of Harriet Rubin's book is that it shows how he embodied so much of what we know call the High Middle Ages. Rubin argues how his life parallels that of Saint Francis of Assisi, for example, who preceded Dante into exile a hundred years earlier and whose story Dante would have discussed with his friend Giotto, whose murals of the saint's life can still be seen today just a few streets away in the church of Santa Croce.

Dante may have also based the architecture of his masterpiece on the method of Saint Thomas Aquinas. "The Thomist method was to think up orders of images with inscriptions on them, memorized in the order of a carefully articulated argument," writes Rubin, just as Dante and Virgil walk through the Gate of Hell with its chilling words and enter a cosmos consisting of hundreds of levels, each with its distinctive habitats for the damned and the saved, yet all of which is, in the end, a single unified whole.

His wanderings took Dante to Paris, and the Gothic cathedrals he saw in France, with their buttresses and gargoyles and side chapels and crypts, must have reminded him of his own construction. "Eighty magnificent cathedrals were built in France between 1180 and 1270," according to Rubin, "and they were models of the *Comedy:* books in stone."

Led by Virgil, the poet of ancient Rome and therefore the father of all literature yet a character who becomes a personal father figure to Dante as their acquaintance deepens, Dante enters a Hell that, says Rubin, has "more in common with the Marquis de Sade than with the Gospel of John." Here Dante learns that "everything wrong with a person's vision has to do with energy wasted on the wrong or diverse passions," that "genius is not found in desires, but in the choice of one desire, pursued against all else."

That one right desire is for God, of course, but Heaven is a long way from Hell. Fortunately, there's a zone called Purgatory that connects the two territories, and Rubin points out how taken the rising bourgeois class was with this middle-class middle ground. Purgatory offers a second chance, an opportunity to be neither permanently damned nor saved but to move from one extreme to another. In contrast to Hell, Purgatory represents the viewpoint of nurturing women, not that of stern judges. Here, Beatrice, who briefly flits through Canto 2 of *The Inferno* and then disappears before her hem could be sullied by the ashes of Hell, returns to give Dante several brisk pep talks which are designed to move him on to the next level, where she will talk his ear off.

◆

And eventually Dante arrives at—oh, dear—Paradise. Everyone knows that a story without villainy is no story at all; it's a commonplace that, for example, Satan is the most interesting (attractive, appealing, seductive—choose your own adjective) character in Milton's *Paradise Lost*. Part of the problem is that Dante had to send Virgil back to Limbo, which means the one great source of snappy dialogue is now gone. Without a buddy, the buddy movie turns into a loner's quest for virtue, and who wants to see a person who's pretty good already strive to become perfect? Dante the character is going for the Best Actor award, but he has lost his companion in the Best Supporting Actor category, and a story about one person is no story at all. He gets the girl, of course, but he wasn't supposed to, and the work suffers.

As contrasted to the sweaty sinners in the Inferno who remind us of ourselves, the angels in Paradise are uniform and chilly. Maybe that's what it's really like up there. But "it's not poetry," says contemporary poet Mark Strand, and thus *The Paradiso* contrasts starkly with *The Inferno,* the sci-fi/adventure/horror story that is laced with political/literary/religious elements and is, in the words of Harriet Rubin's subtitle, the world's greatest poem.

Available translations of *The Inferno* are now in the dozens; I'd recommend the one by John Ciardi among the standard renderings as well as the new version by Irish poet Ciaran Carson, who blends eighteenth-century ballad rhythms with Dante's much older measures. Any translation will leave Dante by himself in the dark wood again, for *The Divine Comedy* ends as it begins, with Dante a mere mortal. He hasn't become perfect, after all; the genius of Dante the poet is that Dante the character doesn't disappear into the light but comes back wiser, chastened, and ready to tell us what he has learned on his strange journey.

And he comes back solitary as well. In Paradise he finds the goddess he has pursued down the goat paths of Italy and through Hell and Purgatory, but he doesn't stay with her. Their parting is astoundingly casual. One moment they are walking and talking, and the next, Saint Bernard has taken her place. Dante cries out after her, but Beatrice smiles and disappears, as though she knows what he doesn't: that he needed to look for her more than he needed to find her.

Besides, Dante has a job to finish. After his long sojourn in the afterlife, the world's greatest wanderer returns alone to this world, to this life, and he begins to write.

Looking For Leonardo

This fall I am academic director at my university's study center in Florence. But my direction is honored more in the breach than in the observance: thanks to a weak dollar and a fear of terrorism, there are only sixteen students (as opposed to the usual fifty or more), and since they spend most of their spare time traveling, I have very little to do. Sometimes I pretend to be my own secretary and, in a mock-Southern accent, say things like "The directuh will see you now" and "Why, yes, ah do believe the directuh is in—can you wait a moment while ah check?" Besides, Barbara is in Italian class every day from nine to one, which means I've got a lot of time on my hands. After three or four trips apiece to the Uffizi and the Bargello, I start taking buses out to the end of the line and walking back. Or I try to buy something from every stall in the Mercato Centrale. Or to use my fancy title to talk my way into some of the private art collections with which the city abounds, which proves to be a whole lot harder than buying something from every stall in the Mercato Centrale.

And then one day I decide to go looking for Leonardo. Over time, I've dogged the steps of Dante and Michelangelo and Machiavelli in Italy and come away with a sense of who they were and what they meant to their time as well as ours. But Leonardo da Vinci has always eluded me. The weather's uncharacteristically cool and dry, and time's not a problem, so why not try to find Leonardo now?

I begin with his birthplace, catching the train from Florence to Empoli and the bus from Empoli to Vinci. From there, it's a bit of a hike, since the house Leonardo was born in is a couple of kilometers outside of town. There's nothing special about the building I finally find, though. Stone walls, beamed ceilings, terra cotta floors: it could be anybody's house, and, in fact, some spoilsport experts say he may not have been born there at all. So

I putter around, try to imagine the young Leonardo playing in the woods and avoiding the ancestors of the bees who buzz me at every turn, clumsy flying machines who are said to be too poorly designed to sustain flight.

After a while, I return to Florence by foot, bus, and train, having been on one of those outings that gives one the sense of accomplishment that follows a huge expenditure of physical energy rather than the gaining of an artistic or cultural or historical insight. Leonardo has meant so many things to so many people. Who was he—where is he? There is nothing of him in the sunny piazzas of Vinci; if Leonardo is anywhere, he will be in the shadows.

So my first step is a misstep, though later, as my search takes me up a steep trail in the foothills of the Apennines and down a foul-smelling canal in Venice, it makes sense that, at the moment I start seeking him, it's as though Leonardo wants to show me just how good he is at hiding.

◆

Part of Leonardo's invisibility is his lack of identification with something other than a dark, hard-to-figure painting tucked away behind bulletproof glass in the Louvre. Dante is equated with the *Divine Comedy,* Michelangelo with the statue of David, and Machiavelli with *The Prince,* but Leonardo is known to most people as the creator of one enigmatic painting and, after that, as a world-class procrastinator. Indeed, given his legendary inability to finish projects, would Leonardo da Vinci have gotten tenure at an American university? The answer is yes, since he certainly finished enough to meet any university's minimum requirements. It's doubtful, though, that he ever would have become a full professor, instead languishing permanently among the unpromotable associates who have job security but can't bring themselves to do enough of the safe, predictable work that will advance them beyond the middle rank.

He did paint the *Mona Lisa,* of course. At the same time, he became the poster boy for goof-offs; anybody who wants to leave the lawn half mowed can always point out that Leonardo didn't finish *The Adoration of the Magi* for the monastery of San Donato a Scopeto. Interest in Leonardo's inability to follow through begins with Freud's 1910 attempt to see the artist's many unfinished projects as a sign of sexual frustration and peaks in the current era of what Joyce Carol Oates calls "pathography" or the rewriting of the lives of great people to show that they are just as flawed and pathetic as we mere underlings.

Often, though, our mistaken view of others is based on the assumption that they want the same things we do. The more I learn about Leonardo, the less I think that he was interested in the kind of résumé building that most of us take for granted. The early-twentieth-century stage actress Mrs. Patrick Campbell said that success is the ability to go from failure to failure without losing your enthusiasm, and if Leonardo didn't complete everything he started, maybe that was because he was more interested in the journey than the results—in other words, maybe he wouldn't have wanted the Renaissance equivalent of tenure in the court of one nobleman or another.

Of the many books and essays I read on Leonardo, the most helpful is Martin Kemp's recent study (called simply *Leonardo*), an insight-packed, no-frills book that also happens to be just the right size for a hiker's shoulder bag. If Kemp's book is as widely read and discussed as it deserves to be, a third and definitive Leonardo will supplant the earlier images of the one-off genius and the indecisive polymath. This new Leonardo will be seen as a consummate quester, one whose curiosity took him everywhere. True, he didn't leave as many finished works as Michelangelo and Raphael. But his career was radically different from theirs— indeed, from that of any artist of any time. Shakespeare can be compared to Marlowe and Galileo to Kepler and Brahe, but Leonardo didn't have any real competition. The term "Renaissance man" can be applied to a number of contemporaries who could brag about achievements in more than one field, but no one was as accomplished across the full range of human activity as he.

So why the reputation as a do-little? To begin with the simplest reason, Leonardo didn't really have to hustle commissions the way many of his peers did. Like that tenured professor, from his earliest days he usually had a regular job, thanks to the influence of the father who, as a procurator for the government and also a notary for an order of monks, made sure that the young Leonardo had regular work. In fact, more than once he failed to finish a job because a better-paying (or more powerful) patron called him away on another project.

True, he was a meticulous planner. Or overly so, some might say: after he received the commission for *The Adoration of the Magi,* he drew sketch after sketch of his master plan, which was to include more than sixty figures arranged according to a complex perspectival scheme. But his ideas never really came together, and eventually he went to Milan to take up another project, leaving the job unfinished.

Too, Leonardo's options were extraordinarily broad, since he was unique among his peers for being an engineer as well as an artist. And his options went well beyond these two choices: on the one hand, his paymasters often asked him to make such simple devices as locks, tongs, jacks, and candlesticks, and, on the other, to stage such spectacles as a celebration of the wedding of Gian Galeazzo Sforza to Isabella of Aragon that featured a representation of "the mobile heavens complete with luminous stars."

In sum, says Kemp, Leonardo "did not sustain himself and his household primarily through the delivery of paintings," especially given the growing importance of his "general courtly duties as impresario of visual events, as consulting engineer and architect, and as a producer of utilitarian and decorative items." And in the end, Kemp points out, Leonardo may have dragged his feet deliberately; like business people of every era, the nobility of his day often tried to pay as little and as late as possible and still get the product they desired.

◆

With so little to do as academic director, I spend a lot of my time thinking about climbing Monte Ceceri, where Leonardo planned to launch one of his flying machines. One sunny October morning, I get an e-mail out of the blue from friends who have planned to meet us in Florence for months and who, as it turns out, are arriving the following week and want to know if I have found a hotel room for them yet. So I run down to reserve at the nearest hotel, which looks like the kind of place where brigands would stay, though ones who wouldn't necessarily practice their brigandage on the other guests; it's a low-ceilinged, shadowy place where one might comfortably sharpen one's knives, consult maps, and do whatever brigands do as they plan their outrages.

But it's near our apartment and it's cheap; even better, there's exactly one available room. By the time I reserve it and find myself on the sidewalk again, I realize I'm right by the bus stop and, without planning it out in detail, have already started the journey up Leonardo's mountain that I've been thinking about for days. So I catch the #6 bus to Piazza San Marco and the #7 bus from there to Fiesole, a lovely ride that quickly leaves the city's grimy suburbs behind and winds for fifteen minutes or so to the little hilltop town. Armed with a fuzzy memory of a guidebook map, I take the Via Giuseppe Verdi out of right side of the main piazza. I'm lightly dressed, but the wind is blowing hard, and most of the Fiesolani I pass are wearing nylon windbreakers that they've zipped to the neck.

After five minutes or so of walking uphill, I'm wringing wet. Fortunately, the terrain levels off by the time I reach a fork in the road and take the street to the left, which bears the encouraging name of Via Monte Ceceri. Ten minutes later, I start seeing signs for the Parco di Monte Ceceri. From here everything is easy, because the trails are well-marked, though the climb is steep. Soon I'm passing old stone quarries, and there are informational exhibits in Italian and English to urge me on.

After numerous pauses to wheeze and catch my breath, finally I reach the so-called Piazzale Leonardo at the top of this low mountain (okay, it's a hill, but if the Italians are going to call it a *monte,* then I'll say it's a mountain). Since the main piazzale in Florence is the Piazzale Michelangelo that overlooks the city from the Arno's far side and that is filled day and night with tour buses, tchotchke vendors, unself-conscious Italian teenagers sticking their tongues in each others' mouths, and enough foreigners to fill the Tower of Babel and then some, I'm slightly taken aback by the empty grassy hilltop that is the Piazzale Leonardo. There is another informational exhibit, a couple of benches, and not much else.

And then you see it—off to one side, a waist-high rock that is the monument marking the site of Leonardo's launch. Engraved on the rock is the poem Leonardo wrote in 1505 in his "Codex on the Flight of Birds," the notebook in which he planned the flight from Monte Ceceri that is also known as the Codex Turin (and this is proof that I made it all the way to the top, folks, because you can't get this off the internet):

Piglierà il primo volo
il grande uccello
sopra del dosso
del suo magno cecero
empiendo l'universo
di stupore
empiendo di sua fama
tutte le scritture.
E gloria eterna
al logo dove nacque.

Here's my somewhat free translation:

The great bird
will lift in first flight
from the top
of mighty Cecero, ·
filling the universe
with wonder,
filling all the histories
with its fame.
Thus glory eternal
to the place that gave it birth.

Alas, it was not to be. Or if the flight did take place, we know nothing of it. In the aptly-named *Leonardo da Vinci: Flights of the Mind,* Charles Nicholl writes of the event, "no letter-writer or diarist . . . mentions it: either it was a well-kept secret or it never happened." Certain it is from the Codex Turin that Leonardo was serious about making the attempt; we see as much in his poem, which Nicholl calls a "fairground-barker proclamation." The notebook evidence suggests that Leonardo thought of everything, even down to recommending that the flight be attempted over water rather than the harsh Tuscan countryside. And it's not as though other questers hadn't made the attempt in recent years; an engineer named Giovan Battista Danti, known, perhaps ironically, as "Daedalus," crashed his machine onto a church roof in 1503.

If Leonardo himself hadn't tried out his airplane, perhaps someone else did; one candidate is his mercurial associate Tomasso Masini da Peretola, nicknamed Zoroastro, who was himself an engineer of sorts as well as an alchemist but who seems, from our modern perspective, more like one of Shakespeare's fools than anything else, a jester who kept his position by saying and doing what other, more sycophantic followers dared not. Some authorities think (though "hope" or "like to imagine" might be more accurate) that Zoroastro took the apparatus without Leonardo's permission, leaped from the peak of Monte Ceceri, fell to the rocks below, and limped into hiding to avoid his master's censure. Forty-five years later, Girolamo Cardano, whose father was a friend of Leonardo, wrote of the polymath that "He tried to fly but in vain. However, he was an excellent painter." This was in 1550, though; Cardano does not say that the attempt was made from Monte Ceceri, and there is no reason to think that he was any more knowledgeable (or wishful) than modern scholars.

My guess is that, if anyone tried to fly from Monte Ceceri, it wasn't Leonardo. He was ambitious, but in keeping with his reputation for procrastination, he was also cautious. To put it another way, he didn't test his flying machine because he knew it would fail.

❖

From the Piazzale Leonardo, it's a no-brainer to retrace one's steps back to Fiesole, but there's also another path leading downhill in the opposite direction. What would Leonardo do, I ask myself, and take the other path. By now, it's cold again: Monte Ceceri isn't part of the Alps, exactly, but it's the highest spot around, and the wind is brisk.

Flapping my arms for warmth, I make my way down, but it isn't long before I realize I'm not alone on the path, because I hear a voice below me and see movement through the tree branches. This is not an especially scary part of the world except in the sense that one is always a little apprehensive about meeting strangers (how many? are they armed? drunk?) when one is far from shops and people and police cars. In the Middle Ages, real brigands lived in run-down castles in these hills, men with names like Guido Guerra and Guido Bevisangue (Guido War and Guido Blood-Drinker), warlords who were a law unto themselves.

As it turns out, there's nothing to worry about. Less than nothing, actually: to my relief (because I'm happy not to be murdered) and then dismay (because, up to that point, I was feeling pretty macho about conquering Leonardo's "mountain"), it is a sixtyish woman with an upswept hairdo wearing makeup, jewelry, and a couple of thousand dollars worth of designer pants and jacket. Even worse, she has with her one of those dogs that looks as though it's the love child of a mosquito and a carpet brush, the type of dog who can only walk ten paces or so before it has to be picked up and carried. This one is limping and looking miserable and is clearly signaling that it's time for a ride.

I give the lady a hearty *"Buon giorno!"* that she returns tentatively; a candy-ass in my own eyes, I suppose I look capable of mischief to someone like her. Then the dog does something peculiar: he comes to life and begins to sniff and circle and wriggle as though in search of something he can't find, much in the manner of the contraband-sniffing beagles you see around luggage carousels in airports.

I keep moving, and ten minutes later I meet another walker with another dog. I'm glad I didn't meet him first: this one *is* a murderous-looking fellow, wild-haired and muscular, though this time he is the one who offers the cordial greeting. He has a dog to match, a big bear cub of a mutt, though this one, too, begins to bark and sniff and search.

By the time I encounter my third human/dog pair and witness the same puzzling canine behavior, I can't resist asking what's going on with the dogs. *"Che succede con il cane?"* I ask the elderly gentleman with the newspaper under his arm as his terrier runs circles around me, yipping in bewilderment. In the way educated Europeans always do, the man sizes me up instantly and, realizing his English is much better than my Italian, says: "HE WANT TO KNOW WHERE IS YOUR DOG!" *"Ah, scusi?"* I say. "ALWAYS WHEN HE MEET SOMEONE HE HAVE A DOG SO HE LOOK FOR YOUR DOG!" "Oh, well," I say, "I don't have a dog," feeling somewhat embarrassed, as though I've shown up at a black-tie affair in my gym clothes.

Edging downhill, I find myself in a few minutes on the road I had taken up to Fiesole several hours earlier. On the other side is the stop for the bus back down to Florence, but as I'm quite warm again and it's only noon, I wait on my side of the road for the bus that will take me back up to Fiesole again. Because I've got another piece of business to take care of, one I've been thinking about ever since I arrived in Italy.

In one of the classes I'm teaching this fall, we're reading Michael Ondaatje's *The English Patient*. A few months earlier, I met Ondaatje in Toronto, where I'd been flown by the Griffin Prize Trust because I was one of the finalists for a poetry award. I didn't win. But Michael Ondaatje was one of the trustees, and I asked him if he had a personal story for me about the writing of *The English Patient* that I could wow my students with. "Sure!" he said unhesitatingly. "When they made the movie, the convent where the film was shot got so much attention that the authorities found out the nuns hadn't been paying their taxes, so on Italian TV they showed these nuns being led away in handcuffs!"

Hmm. Having been manhandled by their fellow Italians for not rendering unto Caesar what was rightfully his, I doubt that the holy sisters will welcome an interloper like me with open arms. Still, Ondaatje had told me where the convent was, so I figure I'll give them their opportunity. Thus, when I find myself in the main piazza in Fiesole again, this time I take a left instead of a right and head down the Via Vecchia Fiesolana. In just a few merciful minutes (the wind is blowing again, and once more my sweaty shirt feels like an icy rag across the shoulders of one of Melville's foretopmen), I am standing before a heavy gate to one side of which is a sign that says "Villa San Girolamo."

There's the usual intercom below the sign, so I push the button with the usual results: nothing. I pause a minute or so and ring again; again, nothing. So I walk around the walls of the villa until I reach a place where I can climb up and look over, where I see just about exactly what you'd hope to find behind convent walls: olive trees, some rose bushes (but not so many or so luxurious as to distract the heaven-bound soul), a well or two, pebbled paths. For a moment I think about dropping over the wall for a quick look-see, but then I remember Michael Ondaatje's story about the cops and the handcuffs.

So I start back to the piazza where I'll catch the bus down to Florence again. On the way, though, I figure, what the hell and ring the bell at the convent gate one more time. Only now I hear a scratchy *"Chi è?"* and so quickly ask if I can visit the convent's church, which is of some historical importance. No, it's being restored, says the voice. Okay, thanks! I reply. But then I run back and ring again and when the voice says *"Sì?"* I ask when the church will be open again and the voice says, When the restoration's finished!

As with the trip to Vinci, I didn't find Leonardo on Monte Ceceri, either. But I did freeze, climb a mountain, swelter, learn something about dog behavior, freeze and swelter and freeze again, and almost scale a convent wall and get myself arrested. I did all of it by myself and most of it without much second-guessing. In the weeks before the climb, I put a lot into the planning, yet I set out on my hike more or less spontaneously. I was flexible when I needed to be, though I never let myself be distracted by the unforeseen. And in the end, I failed, since I never found what I was looking for.

The novelist Robert Stone says the world will come for you if you don't go out and get it, and I've always believed that, not so much as a philosophical maxim as a call to action. On the path up Monte Ceceri, I learned that, if you're going to go out to get the world, it's a good idea to take Leonardo with you in spirit; with his combination of energy, inquisitiveness, and flexibility, there's no better traveling companion. Forget about succeeding and failing: f you're trying to live a full life, chances are you're going to spend a lot of it being Leonardesque.

◆

Much of what Leonardo knew has been superseded. But when I lived in Florence earlier, in the fall of 1992, the Arno rose higher in its banks that it had at any time since the disastrous flood of

1966 that inundated the city, and it was clear that, over time, little had changed in this area of knowledge since Leonardo's day. At night I stood on bridges and listened to the old timers compare this flood to others they remembered as the water rose to within inches of our feet and entire trees hurtled downstream and crashed against the bridge foundations, shaking them as though they'd been hit by artillery fire. The problem, as I remember, is that someone up river had failed to open a gate that would have diverted the water and weakened its flow, so that Florence was getting the full brunt of nature at its most powerful.

Leonardo, where were you that night? Designated a Master of Water by authorities in both Florence and Venice, he would have known "it was better to work with water than against it," says Martin Kemp, giving the example of a house on a river bank that was in danger of being undermined and for which Leonardo recommended, not "straightforward shoring up of the banks, knowing that the remorseless nature of erosion was such that the problem would return," but instead "a weir upstream to cajole the water into a different flow pattern, so that it would exercise its erosive force somewhere else."

◆

One day our group of faculty and students sets out on a weekend trip to Venice. On the way into Italy's most watery city, I ask our art historian if Venice is doomed. "Oh, yes!" she says brightly, and then, perhaps in response to my downcast look, "Well, not in the next ten years." The authorities are building a complicated system of "flap-gates" between the Adriatic and the Lagoon, barriers that will open when tides exceed forty inches and keep high water from flooding the city; as with any attempt to save anything in Italy, there are as many against the measure as there are for it, and, again, as is always the case, the opponents say the new measure will not only not make things better but guarantee that they will become much worse.

At the church of San Stae, there's an exhibit of machines built from the drawings in Leonardo's codices. But on my way there, I remember I haven't called a restaurant to book a table for that evening, so I stop by a bar that has the familiar logo of the red phone receiver against a gray background. I've also had to go to the bathroom for a couple of hours, but since I have my scruples about doing that when I haven't spent any money in the establishment proper, I order a large mineral water.

When I ask where the phone is, the burly young woman behind the bar says "No phone," and when I look over my shoulder toward the sign we'd be able to see if there weren't a wall in the way, she says they just haven't had time to take the sign down yet. "Okay," I say, because now I *really* have to go to the bathroom, "then can I use the bathroom?" She looks at me for a second and says, "Do you understand Italian?" "I do!" I respond with more enthusiasm than veracity. "Then you can use the bathroom if you promise two things. We're having trouble with the plumbing, so you have to one, *fare solo pipi.* And two, if you use any paper at all, you have to throw it in the trash, not in the toilet."

Reflecting that this is the first time I've ever had this conversation with a tavern keeper, I solemnly give my vow to make nothing but *pipi,* even as I realize I must have an honest face; someone who's just washed down too many fried calamari with a bottle of sour wine is liable to swear anything and then unleash such an abomination in the squalid, phonebooth-sized bathroom in which I cheerfully (and relievedly) make *pipi* as would cause every toilet in the city to back up. Doomed city, doomed plumbing: on every scale, things large and small need fixing.

The exhibit of Leonardo's machines would make a great show for kids. Actually, a good show: even though the sign outside promise "visitors can touch and handle the models," most of them are labeled with don't-touch signs in Italian, German, and English. Still, children would have connected better with Leonardo's machines than many adults. After all, as Freud wrote in 1910, "Indeed, the great Leonardo remained like a child for the whole part of his life in more than one way; it is said that all great men are bound to retain some infantile part. Even as an adult he continued to play, and this was another reason he often appeared uncanny and incomprehensible to his colleagues."

Two of these untouchable models relate to my topic of flight; they are *Glider with Manoverable [sic] Wing Extremities* and *Flying Machine*. Made of canvas, string, and unisex doll figures, they'd make great toys—if only the infantile part of me were allowed to send them flapping around the gray columns of this tiny Baroque church! ("San Stae" is Venetian dialect for Sant'Eustachio or Saint Eustace, the patron of hunters, though the church has been deconsecrated and is used now for expositions.) As art for grownups, they're a bust; there's no way a cloth-and-wood model can do justice to the fine lines, the shading, the exquisite detail of the drawings on which they are based.

I discover this when I look into Frank Zöllner's monumental *Leonardo da Vinci: The Complete Paintings and Drawings,* several copies of which (like the hands-off signs, in three languages) are displayed on giant rostrums and are the best thing in the show. Zöllner uses the Freud quotation above as the epigraph to his first chapter, so it sets the tone for the entire book.

In Zöllner's chapter on flight, I find nearly thirty pages of drawings with titles like "Vertically Standing Bird's-Winged Flying Machine, 1487–1490" and "Bird's-Winged Apparatus with Partly Rigid Wings, c. 1488–1490 (?)." The closer he gets to the launch from Monte Ceceri, though, the more Leonardo slows down, moving in reverse, as it were, to do the sorts of preliminary sketches you'd think he might have started out with: "Studies on the Speed of Objects, 1505," for example, and "Notes on the Material Strength of Poles and Ropes, 1505." As the date approaches, more and more pages refer to avian flight: "Notes on the Influence of Gusts of Wind on the Flight of Birds, 1505," "Notes on the Composition of Bird's Wings, 1505," "Notes on the Physical Strength of Birds and a Comparison with the Strength of Man, 1505."

Where Leonardo really differs from all other artists is in the manuscripts he left, a body of work that is "utterly exceptional," says Martin Kemp in his book. "Not one of his predecessors or contemporaries produced anything comparable in range, speculative brilliance, and visual intensity. And we know of nothing really comparable over succeeding centuries." His drawings were often accompanied by texts, his writings were usually illustrated; working up his ideas in both sketch and paragraph, the highly visual Leonardo scorned abstraction and rendered his ideas as concretely as possible. If he couldn't "see" it, it wasn't worth doing, though clearly he needed to "see" in the double sense of "to look at" and "to understand." The plate which shows the mechanisms of the hand, with ten drawings and hundreds of words in a minute script, alone suffices to demonstrate the master's thoroughness. Of the paintings Leonardo undertook, perhaps fifteen survive; his real legacy consists of the approximately four thousand works on paper.

What the hand illustration has in common with sketches of a fetus in the womb, a jack, a giant crossbow, wigs for an artist's model, and a hundred other subjects is the idea of proportion, an understanding of which reveals the inner unity that connects everything created by both God and humanity. Leonardo "never looked at anything without thinking of something else," says Kemp, and makes his point with a passage in which the master draws an analogy between water and hair, noting that the latter "has two motions, one of which responds to the weight of the strands of the hair and the other to the direction of the curls," just as flowing water makes eddies that go against the current.

◆

If Leonardo never flew, the monumental record he left, with its detailed analyses of the mechanics of flight and its sketches and formulae detailing the physics of wind resistance and the effects of air currents, suggests it wasn't because he planned wrong or didn't plan enough. Nor does distraction or procrastination or any of the other sins laid at his feet seem responsible for his inability to follow through. No, the real reason for Leonardo's "failure" is his ambition. After all, he was designing an airplane, something that wouldn't become a reality for another five hundred years. If he had worked on a new type of chair or camp bed or stepladder and hadn't followed through, okay; that'd be adequate justification for a scolding. In referring to somebody who's not too bright, it's often said that so-and-so is no rocket scientist. But that's exactly the point: Leonardo *was* a rocket scientist.

And no less a rocket scientist for being, as Freud said a hundred years ago, a child. Holland Cotter writes in the *New York Times* that Leonardo was "an artist who always preferred to dream and draw rather than to do, who remained at some level a venturesome child controlling his world by taking it apart, piece by piece, to see how the whole thing worked."

When told that Leonardo was experimenting with recipes for the perfect varnish at a time when he was supposed to have been painting, Pope Leo X said, "Alas! This man will never do anything, for he begins thinking about the end before the beginning of the work." Whenever I waste eight dollars on a bad movie or hear of some vast piece of wilderness lost to environmental destruction or read the latest headlines about the latest ethnic conflict, it makes me wish there were more Leonardos. As Cotter says, "by thinking big, Leonardo became big; illusions sometimes work that way. And the neat thing is that in his company, we get to think big, too."

What I learned from my walks and web searches and books and boat rides and bar visits is that Leonardo is neither painter nor procrastinator so much as he is seeker. No wonder I couldn't find him: he was always around the next bend in the path or canal, always one piazza over from the one where I stood. Leonardo never halted in his quest to know everything, even though he knew that everything couldn't be known, and with that attitude, he learned more about the world around and inside him than anyone else of his day, and, in some areas, ours as well. Martin Kemp points out that when engineers tried to replicate

Leonardo's giant crossbow for a television program, they had to change the design when they realized that the sliding laminations originally conceived to allow the bow's arms to bend without breaking were based on a knowledge of wood no longer available. And when they tried to cock the weapon, it broke.

The Naturalist And The Narrative

Over cocktails, the celebrated naturalist is telling me a story so sad it brings tears to my eyes. It seems the government had cut funding for a project to teach chimpanzees sign language, so the hapless chimps were shipped off to a medical lab where they would be subjected to painful experiments. "But since they could sign," the naturalist says, "the chimps would beg for mercy and use their hands to say 'Please don't do this to me' when the scientists came at them with their needles."

It's a story that would melt anyone's heart; fortunately, it's not true. The naturalist gave me the title of a book about the incident, but what I found there was that, first, the chimpanzees were not in any way abused, since the administrators followed the guidelines governing the ethical treatment of lab animals. The big revelation, though, was that the chimps' ability to sign disappeared almost immediately. One or two of the more aggressive animals kept signing for "More fruit!" for day or two. But without constant reinforcement from the trainers who taught them to sign in the first place, most of the chimps stopped, and even the gluttons gave up when it became obvious that their new masters didn't understand them.

So why had the naturalist told me the story that had me dabbing at my eyes with my sleeve while other partygoers came and went among the finger sandwiches and crudités? That's not easily explained, but just as there have always been stories in our culture, there has always been, at least in recent history, no shortage of experts to tell us why are stories are told.

On this subject, two new books by Jerome Bruner and Francis Spufford couldn't possibly be more different. In *Making Stories: Law, Literature, Life,* the distinguished educator Jerome Bruner, who has taught at Harvard and Oxford and published seminal works on cognition, comes across as a patient uncle you'd meet at the coffee shop on Saturday mornings to share his lifetime of experience in studying how the mind works; he tells you about the scientists he has worked with over four decades, punctuates his lessons with references to the classics of fiction and drama, and pauses often to rephrase and sum up, making sure you come as close as you can to grasping everything he knows.

Bruner begins (and ends) with one big idea, that a story contains a sudden reversal that must be recognized, understood, and dealt with. Aristotle called this peripeteia; rhetorician Kenneth Burke calls it Trouble with a Capital T. No matter what term you use, it amounts to the same thing: a mild-mannered atomic scientist turns out to be leaking secrets to the Russians, or God taps Abraham on the shoulder and orders him to kill his son Isaac. What to do? You take measures, sure, but in doing so, you write a story.

The same is true in the legal realm; while Bruner's law studies are less interesting (at least to non-lawyers) than his literary ones, he makes some of the same points tellingly. In discussing peripeteia, for example, he asks you to imagine you have a swimming pool that you associate with family fun and healthy exercise. Then your neighbor has it classified as an "attractive nuisance" and compels you to build a fence around it, and there you are in court, listening to someone conjure images of death and heartbreak, of a small body floating face down. . . .

No wonder Plato banned poets from his republic. A story signals the loss of innocence, and thus storytellers are troublemakers. Not that that's all bad: maybe you didn't want to build the fence, but nobody's drowned so far. Historically, storytellers have often stirred up trouble that needed to be stirred up: Bruner points out that *Uncle Tom's Cabin* was a rallying point for the War of Emancipation, and the poems, stories, and novels of the Harlem Renaissance humanized the plight of African Americans and made possible the landmark civil rights legislation of the 1950s and '60s.

The same is true at the other end of the spectrum, of course: Bruner doesn't say so, but *The Turner Diaries* still gives heart to white supremacists, just as the new forty-one-part dramatization of *The Protocols of the Elders of Zion* on Arab television is promoting anti-Semitism in Muslim countries. But even these negative examples support Bruner's contention that, "for all that narrative is one of our evident delights, it is serious business," a point that can be hard to argue if you're trying to justify an arts budget to the city commission or explain to your parents why you want to be a poet. In either case, you could do worse than support your argument with Bruner's observations on the relation between storytelling and evolution and his conclusion that "culture is as much a prod to the development of human cognition as human cognition is to the development of culture." As individuals, we're being advised these days to work the crossword puzzle and sign up for night classes so we don't lose a step mentally as we grow older. As a culture, we should encourage the production of challenging art works for the same reason. Great dramas—or "awesome breaches in ordinariness," as Bruner calls them—may be big box-office, but they're also the way to big brains.

In contrast to Bruner's wise uncle who sits calmly with you in the coffee shop, happy to explain and even take little breaks as you go for refills, Francis Spufford is an excitable chatterbox who throws open the door to *The Child That Books Built: A Life in Reading* and rushes past you, hoping you'll keep up with his pell-mell pace but much more interested in his own pronouncements than anything else. A young but already much-heralded British writer, he hopes here to teach some of the lessons that Bruner does, though through self-revelation rather than impartial study. *The Child That Books Built* is a dense yet swift-moving account that is probably entirely too personal to appeal to every reader, though it's hard to be critical of a book that offers a wonderful insight every twenty pages or so.

Spufford's project here is to go back and reread all the books he adored in his youth, from baby stories through the science fiction novels of his teens. Without being terribly systematic about it, he identifies three types of readers. The first is the omnivore (my term, not his) who has always read, who always will read, and who reads everything, from airport thrillers to the classics. The second might be called the purely literary, and these are the readers who only began to read as teenagers and who read the best books—Spufford mentions Flaubert and Proust—rather than all books. And the third group consists of that small group of readers who fixate on one book only; with no apparent irony, Spufford calls these readers lone gunmen, citing Mark David Chapman and John Hinckley, who had in common not only homicidal tendencies but also an obsessive love for *The Catcher in the Rye.*

Spufford is clearly an omnivore, and it can be interesting to watch him cycle through the books of his past, spinning off the odd insight or engaging riddle. (Question: What do a soap opera, a Jane Austen novel, and your immediate social group have in common? Answer: They all consist of between ten and thirty people; fewer means you're a hermit, and more hints at superficiality.) And it's obvious that he would agree with Bruner that, by bringing characters to life, authors bring *us* to life.

So why did the celebrated naturalist tell me that story that was untrue? Well, partially untrue, because he had started with a true story and then distorted the facts to achieve an extraordinary effect, an editing job which anyone who has ever spun a tale can understand. But he had also told me where to go to verify the tale. Now that could mean that he had forgotten how much he had changed the story. Or maybe he was more cunning than that; maybe he thought that the book title would serve as an authentication of the story, one that would keep me from checking on it. Or—wait a minute here—it could mean he *wanted* to get caught. (The book, by the way, is Eugene Linden's *Silent Partners,* though the naturalist told me its title was *Poor Relations.*)

Obviously, there is no single answer to this question. But Bruner, citing Freud's little-known book *Delusion and Dream,* points out that each of us contains an entire cast of characters,

like those in a novel or play. So it isn't so much a case of a naturalist telling a story to a poet as it is one of many voices speaking to many listeners. And even if these performers only half-
understood what was happening, neither could resist narrative's
irresistible spell.

I Brake For Richard Petty

BLACK WATER AND BOREDOM
IN THE TALLADEGA INFIELD

Talladega, Alabama—If you ever have to buy groceries for the NASA space shuttle, you should call me: one day this spring I bought enough provisions to sustain human life forms (five of them, all guys) for a five-day trip to the Talladega Superspeedway on a race weekend, and I can tell you exactly what to take with you in the recreational vehicle and what to leave on the shelf at Publix. Three of the travelers shared a barber and NASCAR fan named Howard, who told each of us in the course of our pretrip trims that "you can't take too much with you," but the first time I inspected the no-frills vehicle we'd rented, it looked like a phone booth on wheels.

So I shopped accordingly. Energy bars, pasta, dried beans: anything that didn't require much preparation or that would expand to several times its size when cooked automatically went on the shopping list. Steaks and chicken were included to boost variety and morale. Vegetables take up a lot of space, but I did bring a couple of packages of prewashed salads and a big bag each of carrots, apples, and onions. We traveled like astronauts, if astronauts take carrots with them into space. We probably took a lot more beer than astronauts take, and there was a box of cigars on board as well.

By the time everything was stowed, the RV was looking pretty homey and not nearly as primitive as it first seemed. But after a leisurely six-hour drive, it turned out that the infield was closed and that we had arrived at the Talladega Superspeedway a day early—well, not really, because the idea was to get in line with what I estimate was easily another four hundred oversized vehicles of every type, all primed to tear into the stadium the next morning. So we settled in for a night in the purgatory of the parking lot before being admitted to the paradise of the infield.

As my traveling companions were not only writers and professors but also first-time race attendees, like myself, I was eager to start meeting authentic NASCAR fans as soon as I could. Actually, my first one, Bill, an oil-rig construction worker who lived in Texas, came after me as I was setting up our grill the first evening: he boiled out of his RV to pump my hand and ask if it was okay to open a sliding extension that would increase his interior space and encroach (but only slightly) on our cooking area.

If a lust for the racing circuit is to enter my blood and turn me into a speedway rat, I hope to travel the way Bill does, since his RV made ours look like a real tin can—after seeing his extension extend itself and glancing in later to see Bill and his entire family sitting around chairs watching a television bigger than the one I have at home, I went back to my original low opinion of our vehicle. (The only way for us to increase our cramped space was to open the door and walk outside.) When I complimented Bill on his accommodations, though, he said, "Aw, this ain't nothin'! Richard Petty has an RV that costs 3.5 million dollars!"

Bill did have one modestly proportioned possession, and that was his Yorkshire terrier Chelsea. (That was just the name on her papers, though, because the American Kennel Club, in a baffling resistance to traditional canine terminology, refused to accept her real name: Miss Bitch.) Chelsea, as it turned out, represented a NASCAR standard of sorts. Among a demographic you'd expect to bristle with rottweilers and Rhodesian ridgebacks, I saw more cute little fluffy dogs than I'd expect to see at a flower show. If I'd drunk a Budweiser every time I saw a tattooed, bandanna-wearing three-hundred-pounder cradling a chihuahua in his muscular arms, I'd either be in the Betty Ford Center now or sporting the "Rehab Is For Quitters" tee that seems to be popular among NASCAR fans.

That night I grilled chicken and tossed a salad; I'd managed to squeeze a couple of containers of Häagen-Dazs into the freezer, so we celebrated our successful trip-thus-far by spooning up ice cream when dessert time rolled around. After dinner, we strolled around the encampment, puffing on our cigars and coughing and returning to the RV to chip away at our beer supply. In the course of the walk I talked to Ursula, a track paramedic with a charming Germanic-Southern accent (she'd married a G.I. but has lived in the U.S. for the last twenty-six years), and when I asked her if she'd ever seen Richard Petty's RV, she said, "Oh, ja, darlin'! Dot's a home away from home for dose guys! You spend all dot time on da road, you gotta have one of dose, sugah!"

Sleep wasn't *entirely* impossible, either that first night or the next four, though it goes without saying that men who drink beer all day have to make more trips to the bathroom than otherwise. Also, (1) every guy snored except me, (2) every morning, every guy accused every other guy of snoring, and (3) I don't snore, though see items 1 and 2, above.

In the gray light of early day, unshaven men wearing sleep masks look like prisoners of war in a Goya sketch. Coffee quickly restored my friends to the good humor of the previous day, though, and before long the RV rang with the helpless laughter that tends to recur among men in close quarters, as when one fellow was trying to figure out how to prime the sewage system and another warned that we should do everything in our power not to anger "Spewy the Toilet Fairy."

A console in our RV warned us about levels in two tanks, one labeled "gray water" (shower drainage) and "black water" (best left unexplained). Clean water, especially the hot kind, was at a premium, and eventually we had to give up showers for quick splash-and-shave sessions. In a sense, our greatest achievement during our five-day trek was not coming down with typhus or some skin disease that hasn't been seen in the West since the end of trench warfare.

On a race day, the Talladega Superspeedway looks like a combination of Mardi Gras and a Boy Scout Jamboree as administered by the Italian Post Office. At 5:00 a.m., staffers banged on RV windows so that everybody would wake up and get in line, and promptly at 6:00, we took off in a stampede that must have resembled the Oklahoma land rush. As some of us were writing for print media, we had to get credentials, but finding out where to do that became a part-time job. The passes we ended up with turned out to be "cold passes," which meant we could go into the pits as long as there was no movement on the track. There were also "hot passes," which allowed access during races as well as "hard cards" that, from the way people were talking about them, could probably get you into the papal apartments in the Vatican.

Bringing a variety of cereals and several gallons of milk would have been a gigantic space-sucker, so I encouraged the guys to eat English muffins with Canadian bacon and cheese for breakfast. There were energy bars and fruit for snacks, though I couldn't convince anybody to eat a carrot. I'd loaded up on sliced ham and turkey, so a variation on the breakfast blueprint made for a hearty lunch, though nobody added the lettuce and tomatoes I'd squandered precious space on to their sandwiches, either. Haven't these guys heard about the five-to-nine servings rule?

The infield is studded with overpriced coke-and-burger shacks that make one feel even smugger than before about over-the-top RV provisioning. But as one works one's way up the ladder at a NASCAR track, the food becomes more sophisticated. The pit crews I strolled among were wolfing down hot dogs and tacos, food you can shovel in with one hand while cranking a torque wrench with the other. The drivers, of course, get to eat whatever they want, though my conversations with the cooks in the pits suggest that what drivers want tends to be not that much different from what any well-heeled, hard-working guy young enough not to fixate on his blood lipids might go for: a quick breakfast of cereal or bagels; grilled chicken and hamburgers for lunch; grilled ribs and steaks for dinner. One cook I talked to said that every driver was different, though most were meat and potato guys, with the exception of Jeff Gordon ("lasagna, lasagna, lasagna").

Side dishes tended toward the portable and dense: slaw, corn, pasta salad. I never heard the words "mesclun" and "coulis" even once during my time in the pits. On the other hand, I never saw a single potato chip; you can imagine the chip storm that would ensue as forty cars tore past at speeds of 180-plus miles an hour. Some of the pits featured lavish dessert buffets, though by the end of the day, those cakes and pies looked as though somebody had smashed them with tire irons.

Asking drivers about their drinking habits seemed to me about as polite as putting the same question to airline pilots, so I assume that, while it's understandable that drivers might unwind with a chilled adult beverage or two after a blistering race, they do their serious recreational consumption, if any, in the off-season. In the soft drinks department, I noticed that more than one driver's hand seemed permanently welded to a can of Mountain Dew, the most highly caffeinated of carbonated potables. Incidentally, some of the NASCAR drivers *are* pilots and fly into the track du jour on race day in their own planes.

One pleasant aspect of infield life is that most of the essential services you require are brought right to your doorstep by the squadrons of little trucks that slowly patrol the gravel paths that separate each row of trailers from the next. Ice, water, and newspapers are available at all hours of the day. What surprised me was that there were no mobile food vendors. If the board of directors of the Domino's corporation doesn't think a rolling pizza oven could make money at the Talladega Superspeedway faster than the U.S. mint prints it in Philadelphia, then I've got some excellent free advice for them.

The first day, I was convinced we'd have plenty to eat as long as everybody's last couple of meals consisted of a pound of carrots, four sugar cubes, a slice of provolone, and twelve beers. But it turned out that we had plenty of food, thanks to the advice of Howard the barber. The chicken and steaks were no-brainers; just grill and serve. Pasta is easy to boil, coat with a premium sauce like Paul Newman's, top with some grated cheese, and nestle onto a plate next to a salad. Another surprisingly good astronaut meal is vegetarian chili, which can be found in any health food store; you just add water to a box of powdered mix and then two cans of kidney beans and one of diced tomatoes, though I threw in a lot of black pepper and a fistful of chopped garlic sautéed in several lashings of good-quality olive oil. You could probably add carrots, but I didn't. The "meat" is really textured soy protein, but it looks and tastes like ground turkey, and your tablemates should be allowed to think that it is—in the history of dining, no one has ever cried, "Hey, this textured soy protein is really delicious!"

◆

A lot of race watching is waiting. One police officer I talked to was wielding a Buck knife with impressive skill as he leaned against the credentials trailer, and when I asked him what he was doing, he showed me: whittling baskets out of peach pits. "I just give 'em to the ladies," he said with a grin. If you've ever passed a road crew and seen one guy digging a ditch while half a dozen others look on, hands stuffed into jean pockets or else lazily caressing ample bellies, you'll feel right at home at Talladega: the one who's busy is usually turning something on a charcoal grill or trying to pick up a favorite race on a scanner as the others wait patiently for food or high-speed intelligence from a car going so fast they can barely see it.

An infield is a gadget lover's paradise. There are generators, grills of every type, better TVs and systems than most people (with the almost certain exception of these people) have in their homes. A NASCAR track offers the kind of environment where, when someone tries to sell you a motorized bar stool that can reach a top speed of thirty miles per an hour and costs only $1,950 for the standard model (the tandem edition is a little more), you find yourself thinking, "You know, that vacation to the Keys last year cost a lot more than that." As I watched other campers fiddle with their high-tech gear, I was afraid to look at my friends for fear I'd discover that we were all nervously smoothing our grass skirts and fingering our lip plugs as gods from distant lands dazzled us with their sorcery.

On the other hand, watching guys fool with stuff can be awfully entertaining when there's nothing else to do. And then there's always plenty of excitement and usually when you least expect it. During the Saturday race, our gang was watching the straggler who seemed a turn or two away from being lapped by the leaders, and it was just as one optimist had said, "Look, Wallace Stevens didn't publish his first book until he was in his late forties" that a multicar pileup went off like a mortar attack and so close to us that I couldn't help instinctively flinging my arm over my face.

The wreck had driver Casey Mears skidding several hundred yards on the roof of his car yet emerging not only unscathed but also fully capable, from what I could hear on our scanner, of chewing out other drivers that he blamed for causing the wreck. It's easy to understand how that's possible once you wander through the pits and stick your head through a car window or two and see the cocoon-like cushioning that protects the drivers from impact, including the head restraint that became mandatory in every car following the death of NASCAR legend Dale Earnhardt in 1999. That's the promise of NASCAR: you get to drive like a maniac and even crash, yet you live to drive another day.

♦

I've been writing about the infield as though it were a preserve for hungover males with a beta carotene deficiency, but the fastest-growing group of NASCAR fans over the past decade has been women ages eighteen to thirty-four, and I talked to more than one woman at Talladega who had introduced her husband to auto racing. But fan populations only explode thanks to aggressive marketing, and marketing works best when the faces the public sees are movie-star handsome. There's a lot of eye candy in the driver's seat these days, such as Carl Edwards and Jeff Gordon, the California wonder boy who is largely responsible for the new youth trend in racing.

What may be less apparent to the casual observer is how personable almost all of the drivers are. Whereas it's virtually a given that pro athletes are arrogant or, at best, aloof, the NASCAR drivers I met at Talladega mixed with their public, not only signing cap brims and tee shirts but taking time out just to shoot the breeze. Veteran driver Kenny Wallace singled me out of a crowd of media people because of my Western hat, shouting, "Who's this cowboy here?" Taking my questions, Wallace all but sat in my lap and ruffled my hair, and he charmed others as well with his folksy, slightly manic jokiness.

Why? Probably because race teams rely on corporate sponsorship in ways that other types of sports teams don't. Like hockey players and third basemen, good drivers start young, but while other athletes are likely to be pampered darlings catered to by parents, teachers, and coaches, teenaged drivers who want to be successful need to polish their social skills to impress companies that make car parts and breakfast cereal.

The new female demographic among NASCAR fans means changes in corporate sponsorship, and while you still see main endorsements from auto-parts companies—Wix Filters, Penske Shocks—the first car I saw on my first visit to the pits had "Vassarette / Sexy Fun Lingerie" emblazoned across its hood, thus endorsing a chic hedonistic lifestyle while simultaneously managing to smuggle the name of a historically female college before the view of millions of racing fans. (As a surely unintended complement to Vassarette, the Pfizer Corporation sponsors the blue-and-white "Viagra" car that is driven by a sentimental favorite, forty-six-year-old Mark Martin.)

While "Boudreaux's Butt Paste" sports a decidedly downmarket name, the product itself is a salve for diaper rash, which is about as family-oriented as a product can get. And though the "Army," "Navy," "Marine," and "National Guard" cars advertise in English only, the car that says "Coast Guard" on one side says "Guarda Costas" on the other in deference to the bilingual population (and potential NASCAR fans) of the California and Florida shore lines.

All this new interest is not surprising; in a way, car racing is the ideal sport. On one level, a four-year-old can follow it: cars drive around in circles, and the one that goes the fastest wins. On another level, the amount of minutiae to be mastered is enormous, not only because of the competitors' performances but also the equipment they use. Most baseball fans don't really care about, say, bat handle width, whereas a high-tech racing machine with thousands of parts is a weekend tinkerer's fantasy. Like all hard-core sports fans, diehard NASCAR nuts love minutiae not for their own sake but because details are the glue of their conversation with other devotees. Within twenty-four hours of our arrival in the infield, three separate fans wearing caps sporting the logos of their drivers gave me their version of the key to a successful racing career: "It's the tires," each said, holding his hands a palm's width apart and pumping them slightly in an unmistakable it's-the-tires gesture.

Too, NASCAR racing is driving as it exists only in one's dreams. Far from being merely tolerated, furious speed is encouraged, just as tailgating, cutting drivers off, and other lapses in manners are applauded. And if you've recently spent a morning getting your tires changed, you have only to watch a pit crew do the same thing to realize that's how it should be. During one at Talladega, Jeff Gordon's car was refueled and all four tires changed in a little less than fifteen seconds.

Many of the fans I talked to during my five days in the infield were there to meet family or friends and had been doing so for years. It'd be hard to imagine a friendlier group of people: my gang of writers and professors (and first-time RV renters) was not the most mechanically adept group, and as soon as we began to set up our camp, veteran race fans of both sexes all but ran over to help us to set up the tent, wrangle the roof ladder, and assemble the grill on which we'd soon be cooking our chicken.

Karl Marx himself couldn't have designed a better system for a collective society: as the firefighters and police officers camped out next to us began to slather sauce on their steaks and ribs, they let us know in no uncertain terms that the only way we could irritate them was if we asked before we helped ourselves to anything they had. I watched Thomas, a psychology professor who'd recently won a Guggenheim, talking baseball and bonding over Polish sausage with Jim, a DEA agent, and I couldn't help thinking I belonged to a high-tech version of the world Walt Whitman dreamed of. (Whitman himself was crazy about the technology of his day, predicting in "Passage to India" that the transatlantic cable would lead to "the marriage of continents.")

Sure, there were a lot of Confederate flags in view, though my conversations with the owners suggest that theirs was more a don't-tell-me-what-to-do attitude than a racist one. As far as the semiotics of rebelliousness goes, there were almost as many pirate flags at Talladega, and I didn't notice any of their owners putting port towns to the torch or flogging their enemies to ribbons. (A surer sign that we were in the South, as one of my friends pointed out, is when people walk by your window and you hear somebody say "Beaver!" and somebody else say "Don't be disrespectful!")

In the past decade, NASCAR has opened new tracks in Florida, Texas, Nevada, California, Kansas, and Illinois and has just announced that it has bought land for a track on Staten Island and intends to build one in Seattle as well. Executives have also signed ten Mexican drivers and have begun to sponsor races south of the border. Hemingway wrote that "there are only three real sports: mountain climbing, bullfighting, and automobile racing." But in a day when a sport isn't really a sport unless it's heavily sponsored and televised, that leaves only racing. Climbing is too slow and hard and to catch on camera. Bullfighting has all the color and drama that drew Hemingway to it in the first place, but it's as hard to imagine millions of Americans watching an animal being slowly killed on TV as it is to think of the matador trading in his traditional *traje de luces* for the driver's suit made of Nomex (a fire-retardant material) and festooned with ads for Advil and Preparation H. Still, with the expansion of the NASCAR franchise into Mexico, that puts at least two of what Hemingway claims are the only real sports in a single country.

◆

On our last day at Talladega, I took one more stroll through the pits. Led by the nose (literally), I was heading toward the Weber Grill tent when I realized I was being passed on my left by none other than racing legend Richard Petty himself, whose look is uncounterfeitable: caterpillar mustache, sunglasses, Stetson hat with trademark feather-from-no-bird-that-ever-lived-on-this-planet hatband. I'd never have the nerve to hail Sylvester Stallone or Bruce Willis by their first names, but presuming on NASCAR drivers' renowned affability and seeing as how we were both headed in the same direction, I said, "Richard, what are you having for lunch?"

"I'm going to get me a steak," he replied; "come on, let's get in line." "Think that'd be okay?" I asked. "It's not okay," he growled, "but nobody'll ask," thus neatly summarizing the credo that has gotten many a good old boy into and out of hot water for millennia.

You don't get anywhere in the racing business by standing still, so I wasn't surprised when Richard Petty toodle-oo'ed and walked away, eating his steak with his fingers. My friends may be right in their dietary choices: Richard Petty looks as though he's never eaten a carrot in his life. The whole thing was over in about as much time as it takes a pit crew to change four tires and refuel, but for a few shining seconds, I can say truthfully that I had a steak with Richard Petty.

In the end, we didn't run out of either food or beer. The black water tank never hemorrhaged and unleashed an Old Testament plague on the infield. We saw a couple of great races, and we made it home alive. Will I return to the infield at Talladega?

Not likely. Even if they didn't eat their carrots, I like my buddies more than ever, but men weren't made to spend five days together in an RV that, now that I'm out of it, has gone back to looking lilliputian.

Besides, how can you go back to dining with mere fans once you've had a steak with Richard Petty?

Bang The Drum All Day

[The lyrics that begin each section are from the Todd Rundgren song whose title is also the title of this essay.]

◆

Ever since I was a tiny boy
I don't want no candy
I don't need no toy
I took a stick and an old coffee can
I bang on that thing 'til I got
Blisters on my hand. . . .

"If you don't put that thing down right now," Barbara says, "I'll divorce you." I look at the drum in my hand. Divorce? I've heard of marriages going off the tracks for cruelty, abandonment, and a dozen other reasons, but never drumming. I love my baby, though, so, hey, I put the damned thing down.

This is at the house of our friends Steve and Marsha. Steve's the kind of guy who is always going to have a lot of guy stuff around: athletic equipment, a motorcycle, and, here and there, the odd percussion instrument, one of which, following dinner and a good many drinks, I have just picked up. On the other hand, Marsha, like Barbara, still refers to herself as a "girl." That is, both women think of themselves as sexy, funny, fun, even though neither brooks any nonsense about who's who, what's what, where the lines are, and how people should behave, especially in public. Come to think of it, I'd never seen Steven play his own drum.

But it won't do to speculate along gender lines or investigate the unwritten codicils of the marital contract: thou shalt do thy half of the housework, thou shalt not grouse about thy wife's shopping, thou shalt not drum. Yes, most of the drummers you see in the Piazza di Spagna in Rome or on the steps of Sacré Coeur in Paris or a curb on New York's Seventh Avenue are male. A band teacher told me that all middle-school boys want to be drummers, and it's a mark of a teacher's skill to be able to persuade them to take up the trombone or viola.

On the other hand, the best-known percussionist in the world right now is Scottish superstar Evelyn Glennie. All children drum—on their high-chair tray, their crib bars, an empty cardboard box—and it's this preverbal love of and ability to create rhythm that sets drumming apart from every other form of musical expression. "Genius is childhood recaptured at will," said Baudelaire, and no act recaptures childhood like drumming. No kid likes piano practice. Every kid wants to bang the drum all day. Played well, a cello or a clarinet makes music; played well or even badly, a drum makes music *and* noise and is the only instrument to do so. Drumming is an equal opportunity nuisance, a chance to wake the neighbors, annoy the boss, delight any four-year-old in earshot. No, I'll guess that my wife looked askance at my drumming aspirations because, in fact, I'm not a very good drummer. It's like what they say about tasteless jokes; all this means is that the jokes aren't funny enough, because if people are laughing, they're not noticing whose toes are stepped on, their own included.

Like me, Barbara likes a lot of different kinds of music. She's also from Hawai'i, and it was while we were visiting her parents there once that I went to my first all-percussion concert. This was a taiko or Japanese drum concert featuring Seiichi Tanaka, Kenny Endo, and other masters playing a variety of instruments, including the *kotsuzumi* or hourglass-shaped drum that's about a foot long and ten inches in diameter—about the size and shape of the one Steve owns, come to think of it—as well as the *shime-daiko* or two-headed drum that's hit with *bachi* or drumsticks. The biggest drum is the *odaiko*.

According to legend, the original *odaiko* came from the gods. The sun goddess Ameterasu got so angry at her brother's teasing that she barricaded herself in a cave and vowed never to come out. The other gods threatened, pleaded, and tried to roll back the stone in front of the cave, but Ameterasu stayed put, and the world lay in darkness. At last, another goddess, a wily trickster named Uzume, opened a sake barrel, poured out the contents, and began a wild dance on the head. The other gods laughed as she sang and danced and pounded the barrel; after a while, Ameterasu couldn't resist the fun, and that's how sunlight returned to the world.

In comparison, the *odaiko* on stage that night made a sake barrel look like a sake bottle. The drum that we all came for, the one that was featured in all the ads, the drum that got everyone off the beach and into their seats at Blaisdell Concert Hall that evening, the big drum, the howitzer, the kahuna, the be-all and end all of drums, the omega to the alpha of every other drum in the world combined, the *odaiko* is made from a single piece of wood that comes from a centuries-old (it has to be that old to be that big) tree. Some *odaikos* are seven feet long, weigh 350 pounds, and require eight people to lift them onto their stand. The one in use that evening was so far off the ground that the top of it was a good three feet over the head of the tallest performer. Like the smaller *shime-daiko,* the *odaiko* had two heads, and it lay on its side, which meant that it could be struck by one, two or more drummers. When they hit the *odaiko,* the world, or at least the part I occupied, shivered on its axis.

Writing about music is like dancing about architecture, as Elvis Costello said, and there is no point in trying to describe the delicious pandemonium we saw on stage that night. The final piece was called "Tsunami," and it began with an *uchiwa* or fan drum and climaxed in a crescendo of *odaiko* solos that almost lifted the audience out of their seats. If you've seen Philip Kaufman's movie *Rising Sun,* you saw the San Francisco Taiko Dojo performing "Tsunami" near the film's start; since the camera cuts between the taiko concert and a sex scene that turns into a murder, it's not exactly a pure musical experience, but the drumming part does capture some of the excitement that concert goers feel. "Tsunami" means "tidal wave," but teasing metaphors out of musical compositions is a pointless task; the piece could have been titled "Big Bang Theory" or "The Battle of Verdun," and either would have made as much sense as "Tsunami."

As with all music, the point is not the meaning but the sound, although the sound a drum makes is not the same as that made by a violin or a clarinet. It's elemental; no toddler ever fashioned a string or wind instrument out of everyday materials, yet every child has dragged pots and spoons onto the kitchen floor and created his own percussion section, like the boy in the Todd Rundgren song.

By the way, half the drummers at the taiko concert that night were women.

◆

When I get older they think I'm a fool
The teacher told me I should stay after school
She caught me pounding on the desk with my hands
But my licks was so hot
I made the teacher wanna dance. . . .

At some point, making music either stops being private entertainment and becomes a way to delight or, if you're a punk band like the Sex Pistols, annoy others, though this will happen only if the musician is good or (again, if you're a Sex Pistol) bad enough. Guys strum their guitars in the quad in hopes that others will sit and listen. Women hum tunes as they walk down the hall; as they pass open doors, men look up from their desks and think, "How pretty" or "She couldn't carry a tune in a bucket."

I was a junior in high school at the height of the folk music craze. As David Hajdu points out in *Positively Fourth Street,* the folk movement took root in the culture in a way that no other musical phenomenon ever would, even rock; after all, it's lot easier to learn three chords on an acoustic guitar and call yourself a folk singer than it is to staff and equip an electrified band.

The biggest of the groups was the Kingston Trio, accomplished musicians and also savvy marketers who maintained a boyish look that allowed them to peddle a blend of pop songs and genuinely subversive music to mainstream audiences, a strategy adopted by the Beatles a few years later. Their release of "Tom Dooley" in 1958 started a folk music revival of immeasurable proportions. Within days of the appearance of the Trio's *Close Up* in 1961, my friends Al Edwards, Bob Spain, and I decided that the road to glory was paved with guitar picks and banjo strings.

Bob was a talented guitarist already. Al was one of those musicians who can see a new instrument, wonder aloud how it works, and, within five minutes, be playing "St. James Infirmary" or "Satin Doll"; since he already owned a banjo, though, that took care of that slot. Which left me. I knew maybe ten chords and could play rhythm guitar if someone else tuned the instrument, but since Bob was a much better player (he could even read music, which I didn't think was quite fair), it was decided that I'd be the rhythm section, playing slap bass and bongos.

Now the bass was a problem, since it's not the kind of instrument that's priced for a teenager's budget. Our school had one, and Mr. Daigle, the music teacher, let me use it for practice. One day, I got up my nerve to ask him if I could borrow the instrument. Having been exasperated by musical incompetents for decades, Mr. Daigle had the stereotypical short temper of his breed, and as he contemplated my effrontery in silence, it seemed to me that his face grew even more purple than usual.

Finally, Mr. Daigle spoke. Yes, he said, I could borrow the bass, but I had to help him out with a problem. It seemed that the music department needed a new piano yet couldn't have one as long as the old piano still worked, however cacophonously. More hints were dropped, and before long, I was given to understand that, if I and my friends would dispose of the old piano, I could borrow the bass any time it wasn't being used for a school concert.

Bob and Al were aghast at the plan; Al in particular had had brushes with the law and was not about to add Grand Theft

Piano to his rap sheet. So we turned to our friend Bertrand, the closest real-life equivalent to Tom Sawyer that I know and someone who would have been incensed *not* to have this opportunity for glory and possible incarceration.

Bertrand even asked to borrow Mr. Daigle's pickup truck, and, early one Saturday morning, he and I drove to school, where we found the door to the music room left open, and rolled the piano out and away. After driving around for a couple of hours, we tipped the piano out into a field in North Baton Rouge, where it rolled a couple of times, making a glorious noise, before coming to rest on its side. The part of town we chose for the drop-off was suitably disreputable, and I've always hoped that a few of nature's noblemen of the type that I'd seen warming their hands over blazing barrels decided to right the thing and, until the elements destroyed it, bang out a few tunes.

Now that we had our bass, we needed only a set of bongos, so I talked my mother into an early birthday present of as beautiful a set as of drums as I've ever seen, then and now. The veneer of both small and large bongo was a pearly blue of the kind used as exterior paint on some of the sleazier dragsters I'd see around town, and the drum heads themselves were made of a thick white leather that, due to our habit while practicing of snacking on pizza, chips, and other required items in the teen-age diet, quickly became grimy and discolored, i.e., authentic-looking. There was a big key to turn the several tightening posts that surrounded each drum head; after every few songs, I'd put my ear to one head or another, give it an experimental thump, give a post or two a twist or two, and do the same again, eventually announcing I'd restored my instrument to a state of perfect tune, though turning the key one way or the other didn't seem to make all that much difference in the way the bongos sounded. They set my mother back all of seventy-five dollars, which made them, if less fun to get, also a lot less costly than the bass.

Finally, the assistant principal booked us for a show in our school cafeteria, and we had to face our final challenge: naming ourselves. Since the whole point was to sound as much as possible like the Kingston Trio, names like the Folksmen or the U-High Singers came and went, as, eventually, did Bob, Al 'n' Dave, which is who we were during our incubatory stage. No, we had to be the Blank Trio, though the search for the word that would substitute for the Blank kept us up nights and caused more than one practice session to end in slammed cases and huffy exits. The Regency Trio? Too snooty. The Rawlston Trio? This was after a rich kid in our class who, we hoped, would provide us with money for burgers, gas, and broken strings, though the promise of largesse dried up when he, who was an even worse musician than I was, found we had no interest in becoming the Rawlston Quartet.

Three days before the show, we still had no name, and the girl who was making the posters was getting insistent. Al's parents used to vacation on Dauphin Island, off the Alabama shore, and he proposed that we be the Dauphin Trio. "I don't want to be named after no fuckin' fish," said Bob. No, no, said Al: Dauphin, not Dolphin. Like Louis XVI's son? I thought, but said nothing, and the next day, posters everywhere proclaimed "The Dauphin Trio! Wednesday, 7:00, in the Cafeteria! FREE!" It remained only to get our mothers to starch and iron our look-alike shirts, white half-sleeved affairs with blue stripes that appeared to be made out of the cloth usually reserved for window awnings. They were the kinds of shirts worn only by hot dog vendors and folk singers, which means they were the kind the Kingston Trio would have worn had they been us.

Of course, the Kingston Trio was never referred to as "the Kingston Trio." Folk music had a well-scrubbed side, but the movement was culturally, if not hygienically, aligned with the Beats and their attendant irony, which means that nothing could be referred to by its actual name. "Money" was "bread," "guys" were "cats," and "the Kingston Trio" was "the Triad."

The night we played, we ran through the songs we knew— "Tom Dooley," "Charlie and the MTA," "Long Black Veil,"

"They Call the Wind Maria"—and when, unbelievably, our audience begged for an encore, "Tom Dooley" again, since we had exhausted our entire repertoire.

When the show was over, four of the bustiest girls in our school ran up and squealed, "You sound *exactly* like the Triad!" What were they talking about? None of us could sing at all. Bob and Al should have practiced more and squabbled less. And I tried to mask my incompetent bass-slapping and bongo-thumping with manic "ethnic" shouts of the kind I imagined a gaucho would make while singing beside a campfire on the pampas. The best thing you could say about us is that we didn't forget any of the words and that we more or less began and ended together. Other than that, we were terrible.

I've never been happier in my life.

The Dauphin Trio played another dozen dates or so and actually had a brief flirtation with the commercial side of music. Al's uncle, who was something of a hustler, proposed he take us on the road for the summer; we'd play mainly in the high school gymnasiums of towns so isolated that people who couldn't make it to Vicksburg or Montgomery to hear real musicians might actually pay to hear us. But our mothers said no; they gave no reasons, but I'm guessing they saw us falling into the clutches of hard women, desperate small-town divorcées who'd introduce us to cigarettes, underage drinking, and worse. After a few feeble cries of "Aw, Ma!" we gave up, realizing we really didn't care all that much about being famous and rich. Local girls liked us, and, mainly, we just liked to play. Music was to us as golf is to golfers; it'd nice to be good, but you don't have to be good to enjoy what you're doing, especially if you're the drummer.

Recently I attended a gamelan concert featuring, among others, my student Andrew Jimenez. "Jimenez" is not exactly a Balinese name; nor are "Barton," "Chapman," "Townsend," or any of the twenty-two names of the musicians who played xylophones, chimes, and gongs in this all-percussion orchestra. According to ensemble leader Michael Bakan, probably more than half of these students are music majors, although even they get only one or zero credits for participation, which means these musicians play mainly, in Bakan's words, "for the love of it" or "the curiosity of it" or because "that sounds cool!"

Gamelan has a religious dimension, as does everything in Bali, Bakan tells me. The instruments, performers, audience, and performance space should be consecrated before every show, which he did by sprinkling holy water (according to Bakan, Balinese Hinduism is called Agama Tirta, the "religion of holy water"). During the consecration, someone in the back shouted, "I want my daddy!" This, I found out later, was four-year-old Isaac Bakan, in whose direction his dad tossed an extra spritz of holy water, which rendered Isaac blissed out and silent for the rest of the performance. Even in practice, the proprieties must be observed; for example, should you step over your instrument, this is seen as a sign of disrespect to the gods, and you must kiss the instrument as a sign of deference and to seek forgiveness.

The religious dimension of gamelan is a puzzler for some students; as Andrew says, many players wouldn't endorse prayer in public schools, though they gasp in horror if you step over your instrument. Blessing the instruments with incense before practice or making an offering of fruit to the gods could be seen simply as a sign of respect to another culture, although bowing to deities they don't know or understand is clearly troublesome for some students.

None of this is apparent to the audience, of course, which has no choice but surrender to the fabulous jangly noise of the ensemble as it strikes, bangs, beats, and taps in unison, though I had to take Michael Bakan's word for that: in the style his group uses, tightness is the goal, and the aesthetic end is for a performance to be *incep* and *resik,* words meaning "precise." The opposite way of playing is *matu malablab,* roughly "boiling rock." Bakan says, "Say those words aloud and you'll catch the onomatopoeic correlations," which I did, even though his players sounded a lot more *matu malablab* than *resik* to my untrained ear.

As a Hollywood movie is a dream dreamed for you by Steven

Spielberg or the Coen brothers, so a gamelan concert is a car crash orchestrated by, say I Wayan Beratha, the Beethoven of Bali. ("Actually, the Stravinsky of Bali might be more appropriate," says Michael Bakan, "but everybody knows Beethoven!") It's the only non-rock concert I've ever attended where I needed earplugs.

My seat for the show was a box well forward of the rest of the auditorium, which gave me a chance to appreciate from time to time the visceral, gleeful response of my fellow listeners to the glorious racket that boiled out of the drums, gongs, symbols, bells, and, mainly, the *gangsas,* which are like vibraphones and are struck by tiny hammers. Hunched over their instruments in their matching red t-shirts and black pants, the twenty-two performers looked like nothing so much as dwarves mining the earth for gold.

Amateur musicians, be they the bongo player for the Dauphin Trio or my student Andrew, are one step up from the four-year-old pounding the pans on the floor of his mother's kitchen; they're in it for the elemental fun, for the only noise that becomes music yet stays noise.

Of course, many percussionists have a higher calling. Recently in Tallahassee, I attended a drum concert performed by a Korean troupe called SamulNori. I had little idea of what to expect (my ticket was part of a six-concert artist series package I'd bought months earlier). But my experience told me there were likely to be more surprises in the percussion world than in that of, say, oboes, so I was hardly taken aback when I heard, rather than saw, the seven performers in the lobby as they first blessed the auditorium—you could tell because they used the English word "auditorium"—and then danced down the aisle to the stage, playing their instruments.

I learned from the program that the Korean words "sa" and "mul" mean "four things" and "nori" is "to play," so "SamulNori" means to play four instruments, each of which represents an element: the *kkwaenggwari* or small gong represents lightning, the *jing* or large gong is wind, the *janggo* or hourglass drum is rain, and the *buk* or barrel drum stands for clouds.

From ancient times to the outbreak of the Korean War, wandering entertainers who played these instruments roamed the country, announcing their arrival at the main gate of a village and then making their way to the central courtyard, which they would occupy for several days, performing mask-dance dramas, puppet plays, acrobatics, and shamanistic rituals. Bidding evil spirits to leave and benevolent deities to come, the players invited the villagers to join them in nightlong performances that were part religious ceremony, part revel. After the war, South Korea became more urban and westernized, so SamulNori was formed in 1978 to reclaim a heritage that was in danger of becoming mere legend.

Like the gamelan concert, this one, too, had religious elements. There was a ritual altar on stage displaying fruit, fish, rice wine, and what appeared to be a ceramic pig's head. Audience members were invited to bring their prayers on stage and to light incense, bow, and put money in the pig's mouth, but with the exception of a few Koreans and one or two members of the ethnomusicology faculty, most of us kept our seats; I, for one, had seen too many *National Lampoon Vacation* movies to risk a Chevy Chase moment by tripping and profaning the altar of gods I didn't believe in but who might turn out to be real, after all.

Yet the main impression on this westerner was of consummate showmanship and even athleticism. The entire second half of the program consisted of a single long piece called "Pangut" in which the performers played their instruments while dancing, their movements accentuated by their headgear, the *sangmo* (ribboned hat) and *bubpo* (feathered hat). The choreography was based on military exercises, and indeed the piece was loud, spirited, even scary at times as the performers drummed, leaped, and threw their bodies through the air. Yet the ultimate goal was cosmic harmony: according to the program notes, "with feet treading the earth, ribbons flying upward, and rhythms sounding through the air, the musicians attempt to symbolically consummate the union of heaven, earth, and humankind."

As far as I was concerned, it worked: when the concert was over, I felt pretty much in tune with the whole universe. Of course, it's common to feel a sense of relief and satisfaction at the end of any extended ritual, be it the Catholic mass or a physics lecture. But imagine the priest and altar boys or the physicist and his post-docs leaping, spinning, drumming, shouting, and striking gongs throughout, and you can imagine the heightened sense of harmony I felt.

Actually, the positive health benefits of drumming can be quantified. The Fall/Winter 2003 issue of *Advances in Mind-Body Medicine* reports that a six-week drumming "class" (actually a study) conducted for 112 employees of the Westbury United Methodist Retirement Community Center in Meadville, Pennsylvania, resulted in the subjects reporting more energy and less depression and anger. "We are rhythmical organisms—from our heartbeats to our breathing to our hormonal cycles," said study author Dr. Barry Bittman. "When we create rhythms, it resonates with our bodies."

Pass the bongos, please, the pie tin, sauce pan, soup spoon.

♦

Every day when I get home from work
I feel so frustrated
The boss is a jerk
And I get my sticks and go out to the shed
And I pound on that drum like it was the boss's head. . . .

In this country, religious drumming is restricted largely to Native American rituals. There was an attempt to give drumming spiritual significance within the Men's Movement that developed following the publication of Robert Bly's *Iron John: A Book about Men* in 1990. But after an initial flurry of interest, mainly derisive, in the media, the Men's Movement seems to have largely moved away from drumming, face-painting, and running through the woods toward tamer activities such as monthly discussion groups or else metamorphosed into some version of Promise Keepers, the evangelical Christian men's organization.

Which is as it should be: who wants to drum for a cause? Not that drumming is anarchic, necessarily, but the point I have been making throughout is that the drum is the only musical instrument that has its roots in childhood. Perhaps the best adjective to apply to drumming is Bakhtin's "carnivalesque." In the Renaissance, carnival played a central role in the life of all classes, and cities sometimes devoted as much as three months to carnival festivals. According to Bakhtin, carnival is not the province of one sect or class of specialists. Anyone can play. And carnival isn't a spectator sport: you don't watch it, you do it. Carnival is funny, rowdy, anarchic; best of all, it's democratic. In their biography *Mikhail Bakhtin,* Katerina Clark and Michael Holquist argue that there are three ways of looking at meaning. If you are a personalist, you are saying "I own the meaning." If you are a deconstructionist, your viewpoint is "No one owns the meaning." But Bakhtin would say, "We all own the meaning."

In the midst of writing this essay, one of my colleagues had a book manuscript taken, so I had a few guys over to celebrate. We irrigated our aridity with a fertilizing decoction of strong waters, to use Melville's phrase, then walked down to a neighborhood Indian restaurant for dinner. With all due respect to the culture, Indians cooking has dropped the ball as far as desserts are concerned, so after our chicken tikka and shrimp vindaloo, we came back to my house for strawberry pie, banana pudding, and a few more drinks.

As I was listening to a lot of drum music at the time, I put on *Sokobayashi* by the San Francisco Taiko Dojo. The alcohol was already working, and as we scarfed our pie and our pudding, our heads bobbed in time (or not in time) to the driving rhythms. Before long, one fellow began to wave his spoon as a conductor might, and the evening turned into an impromptu taiko performance conducted by spirited amateurs on table top, lawn chairs, upended flower pots, and the pie tin itself; each of us soloed on air *odaiko* as though there was no tomorrow.

According to the liner notes of the CD I was playing, "Soko" is the old Japanese word for San Francisco, and "bayayashi" means "festival," which is what we had there on my deck. Some of us were balding, and all of us were a few pounds overweight, but we attacked our instruments with the gusto of four big babies laying into their mothers' cookware. In his photos in the Clark and Holquist biography, Bakhtin comes across as rather severe, but had he been there that night, I'd like to think he would have grabbed an *uchiwa* and joined in.

◆

I can bang that drum
Hey, you wanna take a bang at it?
I can do this all day!

When my children were small and I used to drive them to school, for a time one radio station played "Bang the Drum All Day" just before 8:00 a.m. as a battle cry for the two primary groups the song addresses, schoolchildren and working stiffs. I'd call out spelling words—"Banana!" "B-A-N-N- . . . " "No! Banana!"—and dodge other pedestrians and cyclists, and the boys would spell or do math or ask geography questions that I didn't know the answer to ("Dad, is Miami the capital of Minnesota?"), though at any given moment, one, two, or all three of us would be singing along and thumping on the dashboard.

But sometimes the hot-rockin' mutha who played the song would cut it short in order to insert his own inanities, and I'd miss one of my favorite parts, the little bridge which precedes the final verse. "Hey, you wanna take a bang at it?" All day long, I'd think of that Whitmanesque invitation to the listener to drop whatever humdrum task he or she is performing and start whacking that drum.

Curiously, the only time I heard Todd Rundgren perform his hit, it was one of the big disappointments of my musical life. He performed solo, slurring the tempo and singing the words in falsetto as he accompanied himself on, of all things, a ukulele. Now a ukulele, too, I have heard often in my visits to Hawai'i, and a noble instrument it is, whether played with the simple authority of the late Israel Kamakawiwo'ole or the panache of present-day boy wonder Jake Shimabukuro. But an *odaiko* it is not. In New York, maybe, the idea of playing a drum anthem on a ukulele might be regarded as ironic or arch or even postmodern. But we don't buy that kind of crap here in Tallahassee, Florida. An idea may look pretty racy in lower Manhattan, but its actual thinness will become apparent by the time it makes its way to the provinces.

As I write this essay, Todd Rundgren is about to make a return trip to perform here again, but having heard him sully his own creation, none of my friends seem especially interested in seeing him. They'd be better off seeing the Dauphin Trio.

What they'd really rather do is bang the drum all day.

Shrouded In A Fiery Mist

Santa Maria della Vittoria, which houses Bernini's statue *The Ecstasy of Saint Teresa,* is Rome's most sugary church. Its walls and ceiling teem with angels that seem to be made of meringue or perhaps that type of porcelain known as "biscuit," a word that implies both fragility and mouth-feel. One flight of seraphim is tacked to another with garlands of gold. Ribbons of nougat are the only thing that keep the heavenly folk aloft; otherwise they'd slide down columns of licorice, cherry, butter.

The marble is like marzipan; the rock is sawn to reveal the whorls inside that seem ready to shimmer, like clouds of marshmallow floating in grape jelly. You feel that if you drew a finger down a column and looked at it before you popped it in your mouth, it'd be thick with frosting, as though you had swiped it across the top of a cake. For contrast, one need only go two blocks west to view the work of Bernini's great rival Borromini, the church of San Carlo alle Quattro Fontane with its ovoid, all-white interior. After romping through the candy store that is Santa Maria della Vittoria, the visitor to San Carlo steps carefully, certain he is about to crack the shell of a giant white egg.

If you're staying in the center of Rome, you might have to take a cab to Santa Maria della Vittoria, and it doesn't hurt to have a map: our cabbie dropped us off at the wrong church, and it took a while to find the right one. Once there, I realize again that, no matter how many times I've seen it before, nothing prepares one for the beauty of this statue. The saint isn't merely in ecstasy; she is melting.

As she slips into a state of ecstatic abandon, Saint Teresa seems to be falling into a swoon brought on by pleasure that is at once physical and spiritual. The angel who presides over her passion stands at a slight distance from her, smiling down at rather than joining her; he does not touch her at all but only fingers her robe lightly with his free hand. This is Saint Teresa's description of the angelic visitation that Bernini captures in his sculpture:

> Beside me on the left appeared an angel in bodily form. . . . He was not tall but short, and very beautiful; and his face was so aflame that he appeared to be one of the highest ranks of angels, who seem to be all on fire. . . . In his hands I saw a great golden spear, and at the iron tip there appeared to be a point of fire. This he plunged into my heart several times so that it penetrated my entrails. When he pulled it out I felt that he took them with it, and left me utterly consumed by the great love of God. The pain was so severe that it made me utter several moans. The sweetness caused by this intense pain is so extreme that one can not possibly wish it to cease, nor is one's soul content with anything but God.

A few years ago, Barbara took a sketching class, and wherever we go, she's liable to pull out her pad and pencil box and capture something on paper. I like this; on my own, I'm far too likely to take a quick look at a painting or statue, buy a postcard, and move on to the next sight. Spending a half hour or so in front of an art work is good; I may not be sketching, but I'm seeing things I wouldn't see otherwise.

But standing in front of the statue of Saint Teresa and the angel is like standing in traffic in a small town: people cruise by, take a look, comment, glance around, step off. Like a lamp-post, Barbara is in the center of the flow, unmoving. Sometimes there are twenty people around her, and a few minutes later, there are none. As I watch, I think about the lives of the saints, Bernini's life, lunch, Emily Dickinson, the Catholic visionary tradition, my aching metatarsals, lunch again, convent life, the life of Emily Dickinson, the lousy exchange rate, the sex life of Emily Dickinson. Emily Dickinson: how'd she get all the way from her father's house in Amherst, where she prided herself on what she described in a letter to Thomas Wentworth Higginson as a "simple and stern" life, to the Baroque church of Santa Maria della Vittoria with its high-calorie decor?

Both Saint Teresa and Dickinson were female, celibate, and visionary. Beyond that, each was also intensely literary, to the point of logorrhea: Dickinson not only wrote nearly 1,800 poems but also thousands of letters, only a fraction of which have survived, and Saint Teresa's collected works comprise three volumes. If it seems that they parted company when it comes to physical pleasure, that is because Bernini left us with an indelible image of Saint Teresa's ecstasy.

But is what Saint Teresa describes in her autobiography and what Bernini depicts the same as sex? If so, and considering their other similarities, did Dickinson have a sex life, too?

♦

Around 1860, something decisive happened to Dickinson. She began to write like a woman possessed; in his introduction to *A Choice of Emily Dickinson's Verse*, Ted Hughes writes that she had "a conflagration within her that produced just about one thousand poems in six years, more than half her total. In 1862 alone it has been calculated that she wrote 366 poems." Though there are many ways to account for this astonishing output, Hughes notes that "the central themes of the poems have suggested to many readers that the key event was a great and final disappointment in her love for some particular person."

One prominent candidate for this mysterious love object was Samuel Bowles. Dickinson wrote a poem in which she describes a wrenching conversion from carnal love to spiritual and sent it to Bowles. In *The Life of Emily Dickinson*, Richard B. Sewall notes that the poem suggests that Dickinson is both "the imagined wife of Samuel Bowles, a title denied her in reality" (Bowles was already married) and also "the Bride of Christ."

Title divine — is mine!
The Wife — without the Sign!
Acute Degree — conferred on me —
Empress of Calvary!
Royal — all but the Crown!
Betrothed — without the swoon
God sends us Women —
When you — hold — Garnet to Garnet —
Gold — to Gold —
Born — Bridalled — Shrouded —
In a Day —
"My Husband" — women say —
Stroking the Melody —
Is *this* — the way?

Here she puts aside secular passion to embrace spiritual love, which means going into uncharted territory. After all, there are married men walking down every street in Amherst; some are having affairs, as her brother Austin was with Mabel Loomis Todd, who was married herself. On the other hand, no one knows what it's really like to be married to Christ. Characteristically, the poem does not make a statement but asks a question; the last three lines say, "If I can't have an earthly husband like other women, is *this* what I should do?" Note her making of "bridle" into the participle "Bridalled," a homonym for "bridled," so that she is saying "made a bride" but also "reined in." And then "Shrouded"! Is earthly marriage a kind of death, and is that why Dickinson avoided it? Or is she expressing the desire to die into love, into "the swoon / God sends us women?"

When we ask what the idea of sex meant to women like Emily Dickinson and Saint Teresa, we are really asking what it means to us. The question is a loaded one, and the gun that fires it is double-barreled, for nothing is more wonderful than sex and nothing more tawdry, nothing more elevating yet nothing more degrading. We divide it into good sex, usually ours, and bad sex, usually everyone else's, though it could be the other way around. And we make our art, our lives, and our laws accordingly.

What if there were another possibility, though? What if, instead of being divided into good and bad, the choices we make were divided into good, bad, and *really* good? In a notebook, Hawthorne describes an allegory he wanted to write but never did; in it, the Heart is sunny around its Portals, then sinister just inside, but, at its core, a Garden.

•

Before she was a saint, Teresa of Avila was a sensualist. She was always intense: in *Teresa of Avila: The Progress of a Soul,* Cathleen Medwick reports that, following a spiritual crisis as a young nun, she became so paralyzed that "it was eight months before Teresa could move (she still had only the use of her little finger) and three years before she could crawl." And though she's famous for her encounters with God, she seems to have had as many or even more run-ins with the devil, though some of these read more like insect attacks than life-changing events. He tries to make her laugh at inappropriate moments, for example, and one night she complained that she couldn't read because the devil kept landing on her book.

But it wasn't all gods and devils for Teresa, who once said, "There is a time for penance and a time for partridge." Teresa was aware of her charms and knew they affected others: when a gentleman admired her shapely foot, she told him, "Take a good look—this is the last time you'll ever see it."

As a teenager, Teresa recalls she "began to be aware of the natural abilities which the Lord had given me—which people said were considerable." And as an older woman, she was peevish when she recalled how she once looked; when she saw the portrait that Juan de la Miseria painted of her when she was sixty-one and that is often contrasted with Bernini's portrayal of her as a lissome beauty, reportedly she snapped, "God forgive you, Fray

Juan, you've made me a bleary-eyed old hag!" Proud in more ways than one, she also knew she was a world-class visionary and mocked the *abobiamentos* or "silly raptures" of nuns like María del Corro, a charismatic who was forced upon Teresa by powerful friends who insisted she be admitted to the convent.

In other words, Saint Teresa was sexy and she knew it. She knew what sensual pleasure was; more importantly, she knew how to get it at a time when, for a respectable woman, the pursuit of a carnal life meant becoming a wife—in Medwick's words, "consigned to virtual slavery by her husband . . . and the unceasing agony of childbirth" and a possible early death from puerperal fever (Teresa's own mother had died at thirty-three after giving birth to her tenth child).

Thus it would be a mistake to think that the Teresa depicted by Bernini was caught unaware by pleasure, that she was saying her rosary one day when the cherub showed up with his spear. As a beauty, she would have expected pleasure. And as a worldly woman, as well as a keenly observant and critically intelligent one, she would have known its degrees.

Most adults have had two kinds of sex. The first is the quick, uncomplicated kind that leaves you feeling as you would after playing handball or mowing the lawn; yes, another person was involved, but the act is essentially a solitary one. The second kind has a long, slow build-up, a fiery climax, and a dreamy, wonder-filled afterglow—you think, "Did that really happen?"

It goes without saying that this second kind of sex involves someone you're absolutely crazy about. After the first kind of sex, you towel off and go back to your everyday life. After the second, you feel as though you've moved from one world to another, even from one life to a new one; eventually, you go back to being your old self, but for hours, you have a sense of transfiguration. Teresa may have died a virgin, but just as many sexually experienced people have never felt real pleasure, so may a nun know pleasure in all its degrees, including the highest.

Some of the most beautiful passages in Saint Teresa's writings are the ones in which she talks about Christ's gradual revelation of himself to her. During one prolonged visitation, she says she first sees Christ's hands, which are ravishingly beautiful, and then, a few days later, his face, and after that, his body, which shines more brightly than the sun: "It isn't a dazzling radiance but a soft whiteness and infused radiance, which delights the eyes so much, they're never tired by it. . . . This light is so different from what we're used to that the sun's brightness seems very dim by comparison. . . . Afterwards, we don't want to open our eyes again. It's like seeing a very clear stream running over a crystal bed that reflects the sun, and then a very muddy stream, running beneath a clouded sky." She wonders at the slow approach, but then realizes that "His Majesty was catering to my weak nature. May He be blessed forever. A creature as base and vile as I am would not have been able to stand all this glory at once."

In *The Interior Castle,* her extended meditation on the journey the soul takes through a many-chambered crystal palace as it seeks God, she again emphasizes the gradualness of the approach; in Medwick's words, "when the time comes—and not a minute before—God invites the soul into the seventh chamber. Here is where the king lives, the inner sanctum, where He will make the soul his bride." This is the moment of total nakedness, of union. As Saint Teresa says, "Understand that there is the greatest difference between what happens in this chamber and everything that happened before, between spiritual betrothal and spiritual marriage: one occurs between those who are betrothed, and the other between those who can no longer be separated." The two lovers just can't keep their hands off each other.

As a young woman, Emily Dickinson didn't attract passionate overtures from young men, as Teresa of Avila did; photographs show her as thin and plain to the point of sickly-looking. Yet men came to her or tried to, and if they couldn't reach her, that was her choice. Her benefactor, Thomas Wentworth Higginson, wrote "I have the greatest desire to see you, always feeling that if I could once take you by the hand I might be something to you;

but till then you only enshroud yourself in this fiery mist & I cannot reach you." Yet when he finally visits her in Amherst, he wrote his wife, "I never was with any one who drained my nerve power so much. Without touching her, she drew from me. I am glad not to live near her."

Higginson was not the only one to complain of Dickinson's intensity. It may have been that the only way she could meet people was when she was excited; almost everyone who met her gives the impression that her personality was stuck in fast-forward. Like Saint Teresa, though, her approach to divine love was different: calm, at first, then eager, then almost greedily participatory. Here is a poem by Dickinson that is also about the gradual revelation of God's beauty:

He fumbles at your Soul
As Players at the Keys
Before they drop full Music on —
He stuns you by degrees —
Prepares your brittle Nature
For the Ethereal Blow
By fainter Hammers — further heard —
Then nearer — Then so slow
Your Breath has time to straighten —
Your Brain — to bubble Cool —
Deals — One — imperial — Thunderbolt —
That scalps your naked Soul —

When Winds take Forests in the Paws —
The Universe — is still —

The gears shift perceptibly in this poem: "Then nearer — Then so slow." But suddenly it's as though a car careens over a cliff; there's an explosion, the dust settles, and silence returns, though the world's been changed utterly. That gap before the last two lines speaks volumes to me; Dickinson was fond of regular stanzas, especially quatrains, or single long ones. Here, though, she pauses as a composer would before a final chord. One almost hears the inhalation of breath that takes place in the gap between the crash of the thunderbolt and the stillness that follows.

As I read the passage in *The Interior Castle* and the Dickinson poem, I found myself thinking not of religion or sex per se but of something far more mundane; "dating" isn't quite the word I want, though the play between the male and female figures sounds very much like that of two people getting to know each other, first casually and then intimately. One night I was talking to a woman at a party and she used the expression "the third time you meet your lover." I can no longer recall the context, but I know what she meant. The first time, you're nervous: am I pretty enough? Will he like me? The second time is when everything goes smoothly, but the third time is when you feel so at ease that you can let yourself enter the whirlwind. A good lover doesn't rush things but makes it possible for you to be bridalled and bridled and unbridled, to be so filled with desire that you desire feverishly the scalping of your already-naked soul, to relish the paws as well as the pause. For in the midst of all that bright fury, the universe is still.

◆

More than one scholar has commented on the singularity of Dickinson's visionary, nun-like life in a cultural corner where nuns were all but unknown and visionaries would have been frowned on. After all, Saint Teresa is one link in a long chain of religious ecstatics that precede and succeed her; plenty of other nuns had mystical experiences, and, as we shall see, some convents seem to have been home to some rather spirited competitions between sisters trying to outdo one another in both the frequency and intensity of their heavenly visitations.

But Dickinson lived in frosty Puritan New England. Thus Angela Conrad wonders, in *The Wayward Nun of Amherst: Emily Dickinson and Medieval Mystical Women,* if Dickinson "decided to live in the same way as medieval women mystics even though she couldn't have known anything about them." That the answer is clearly "yes" says less about direct influence (or its lack) and more about the common experiences of people who free themselves through self-imprisonment. "Nuns fret not at their convent's narrow room," wrote Wordsworth, "and hermits are contented with their cells." Dickinson's niece Martha reports that her aunt once pretended to lock the door to her bedroom and pocket an imaginary key, saying, "Mattie, here's freedom."

This poem speaks with uncommon directness to Dickinson's decision to find freedom in a "simple and stern" life:

A solemn thing — it was — I said —
A Woman — white — to be —
And wear — if God should count me fit —
Her blameless mystery —

A hallowed thing — to drop a life
Into the mystic well —
Too plummetless — that it come back —
Eternity — until —

I ponder how the bliss would look —
And would it feel as big —
When I could take it in my hand —
As hovering — seen — through fog —

And then — the size of this "small" life —
The Sages — call it small —
Swelled — like Horizons — in my vest —
And I sneered — softly — "small"!

One doesn't think of the unfailingly polite Dickinson "sneering" that much; that she does so here is an indication of her strong feeling about the largeness of a life others think of as tiny. Note, too, her emphatic use of the word "small," said three times in four lines in a disbelieving, are-you-kidding-me? tone. And this from the mistress of slant rhyme, the poet who goes out of her way to avoid echoing a sound, much less repeating one.

As she reinvented poetry, Dickinson reinvented religion in a way that allowed her to be the poet she became. "We too must write Bibles, to unite again the heavens and the earthly world," said Emerson, and Dickinson's collected poems are hers, though the Bible she writes is more a poetry manual than a religious guide; it contains what Judith Farr, in *The Passion of Emily Dickinson,* calls "the captivating songs of the artist" as opposed to "the forbidding stories of the theologian." As Dickinson says:

The Bible is an antique Volume —
Written by faded Men
At the suggestion of Holy Spectres —
Subjects — Bethlehem —
Eden — the ancient Homestead —
Satan — the Brigadier —
Judas — the Great Defaulter —
David — the Troubadour —
Sin — a distinguished Precipice —
Others must resist —
Boys that "believe" are very Lonesome —
Others boys are "lost" —
Had but the Tale a warbling Teller —
All the boys would come —
Orpheus' Sermon captivated —
It did not condemn —

Commenting on earlier versions of the poem (and, obliquely, on Dickinson's habit of tirelessly revising certain poems until they said exactly what she intended), Farr notes that Dickinson chose "warbling" over thirteen other adjectives: "typic," "thrilling," "hearty," "bonnie," "breathless," "spacious," "tropic," "ardent," "friendly," "magic," "pungent," "winning," and "mellow." To Farr, each of these suggests "the humanity (and hence the beauty, energy, sympathy) of art by comparison with the strictures of Scripture." With all these choices, why choose "warbling," then? Beyond the basic writing-workshop truism that a word with sense appeal is always better than an abstraction, only an auditory image can, to use Emerson's phrase, unite the heavens and the earthly world—or, in terms of the Orpheus myth, the afterlife and this one. The Bible's horizons are limited, in Dickinson's view; traditional scripture belongs to "faded Men" and their "Lonesome" adherents. But a song is heard by everyone.

◆

What makes Dickinson and Saint Teresa especially interesting cases is how free they were to do other than what they did; after all, there's no freedom in practicing the only thing you can do. Just as Teresa could have cast her lot with the gallants of Avila who pursued her, so white-habited Emily, who meets the world as a virgin, had opportunities for earthly love. Even late in life: she had a second chance in 1882, when, apparently, Judge Otis Phillips Lord asked her to marry him. Dickinson seems to have genuinely loved Lord, and her letters to him are tender and affectionate, but she turned him down.

This decision made at least one person happy: his niece, Abby Farley, who stood to gain a good deal if Lord remained single, since he was wealthy and had no children. One measure of success in life is the envy we inspire in others, and Farley was bitterly jealous of Dickinson. Long after the poet's death, Farley denounced her thus: "Little hussy—didn't I know her? I should say I did. Loose morals. She was crazy about men. Even tried to get Judge Lord. Insane, too."

Saint Teresa, too, inspired jealousy in her enemies. Her passionate nature was used against her by such rivals as María del Corro, who brought the Inquisition to the convent when she charged that Teresa had had numerous lovers; that one of them liked to dance naked in front of the other nuns; and that at least one other nun, Isabel de San Jerónimo, a favorite of Teresa's, had had sex with devils. Though they stayed many days, the inquisitors decided that the sixty-one-year-old Teresa was behaving herself, that the other nuns had not been corrupted, and that Isabel de San Jerónimo was, at worst, slightly unbalanced.

As she aged, Teresa's ecstasies ceased, which allowed her to devote more time to the serious business of church reform. At the very end, though, her old passion returned in a final, radiant burst. She died in the arms of a nun named Ana de San Bartolomé, who reported that Christ and an angel were in the room. In Medwick's words, Ana reported that Teresa "died in ecstasy, her soul ripped away from her body by the force of God's love. The blood on her sheets, her biographer Yepes wrote, was proof of that holy consummation—and his opinion was borne out years later, when her coffin was reopened and some drops of blood on a cloth that had been buried with her were still fresh."

◆

It is a commonplace that, in Bernini's representation of her, Saint Teresa is having an orgasm. In *Angels and Demons,* Dan Brown, author of the better-known *Da Vinci Code,* has hero Robert Langdon refer to Bernini's work as "pornographic" and reflect that, "though brilliantly rendered, the statue depicted St. Teresa on her back in the throes of a toe-curling orgasm." Overlooking the fact that she isn't on her back and her toes aren't curling, one has to wonder about that "though," which suggests surprise, as though sex is dirty or otherwise unworthy of artistic depiction.

A page later, Langdon reads the famous passage from Saint Teresa's autobiography and thinks, "If that's not a metaphor for some serious sex, I don't know what is." Thus transcendent ecstasy is dumbed down to its lowest common denominator, reduced to the spasms of a quick screw. Langdon's attitude strikes me as no different from that of the middle-aged man I saw in Santa Maria della Vittoria that morning wearing a t-shirt that boasts, "Good boys go to heaven, bad boys go to Amsterdam." His leerings take love out of the equation and turns sex into what it is for the Robert Langdons of the world: a solitary act.

Saint Teresa's partner isn't the angel, of course, who is only the middle man for a force so great that it can't be confronted directly, that is off-stage, out of the frame. The Old Testament warns us against looking God in the face. ("Had'st Thou no Face / That I might look on Thee?" begs Dickinson in one of her poems.) It also tells us that He is everywhere: not just in the tip of a golden spear but everywhere, like a fire that burns away our old lives and leaves us naked as babies. Yet I'm not sure everyone in the church of Santa Maria della Vittoria that day was looking at the statue the way I was, and when another group of smirking backpackers stepped up to get a look at the saint famous for having "some serious sex," I confess I entertained the un-Christian desire to pull out my folding map of Rome and bop them on the head with it.

In the end, what is the secret of Dickinson and Saint Teresa—what do they know that we don't? And if they're not having sex, what *are* they doing? In her introduction to *The Flowering of the Soul: A Book of Prayers by Women,* Lucinda Vardey distinguishes between the prayer of men and that of women by identifying what she calls "five key virtues shared by women who pray": relatedness, perceptiveness, unity, dedication, and care. To accept the implication that women have more of these virtues than men is to run the risk of proclaiming one gender superior; I've known as many perceptive, caring men as I have women who are obtuse and self-centered. But the virtue of unity is essential to an understanding of the ecstasy of the saint and the poet. Vardey quotes the twentieth-century saint Edith Stein as saying "the deepest feminine yearning is to achieve a loving union . . . such yearning is an essential aspect of the eternal destiny of woman. It is not simply a human longing but is specifically feminine." Perhaps so: again, I know men who seek companionship and women who prefer solitude. But Stein's comment on union explains the passion at the heart of the lives and the writing of Dickinson and Saint Teresa. What is clear is that, if, as traditionally represented, God is a man, then women who are heterosexual will unite with Him in ways that are different from those of heterosexual men. This conjecture doesn't examine the prayers of homosexual women as well as the more interesting matter of the prayers of homosexual men, but it does explain the romantic language that these two women use when they write about God, from Dickinson's "Might I but moor — Tonight — / In Thee!" to Saint Teresa's "My Lord, I do not ask you for anything else in life but that You kiss me with the kiss of Your mouth."

It's easy to think of Dickinson as loveless and agoraphobic, a writer whose audience wasn't born yet and thus was isolated and misunderstood. As far as Saint Teresa goes, she was a nun, which, in our secular age, all but amounts to a condemnation; worse, to the casual observer she can come across as a quivering hysteric. Seen fully, though, how complete the lives of both women were—how satisfied they were. Both are associated with religion, with sex, yet what they apparently had was so much greater than either of these.

Ultimately, Emily Dickinson and Saint Teresa of Avila expand our definition of who women are and what they can be. To paraphrase Hawthorne's notebook entry for the allegory he never wrote, think first of the ordinary life that most people choose, a life that is both spiritual and physical in varying degrees. Inside of that, think of the narrower life, the kind that very few people choose: at one extreme, the life of a nun or a cloistered poet, say, and at the other, that of an addict to sex or any other appetite. These two choices, of the quotidian life and the highly specialized one, account for the lives of almost all of us.

Now imagine a third choice, a life in which physicality and spirituality aren't alternated but combined, fused in a way that transcends both states, the self, our physical surroundings—that unites the heavens and the earthly world, as Emerson said. Dickinson calls this third way "the swoon / God sends us women," Saint Teresa a "radiance." Hawthorne calls it Eden, a garden that, for both saint and poet, shimmers like a fiery mist.

Like A Twin Engine Bomber

Florence, December 2004—The sexiest women in the Uffizi are also the chubbiest: Titian's *Venus of Urbino,* for example, and especially his *Flora* with her just-brushed hair and her uncertain neckline, not to mention all those fleshy Judiths, each chortling with pleasure as she saws the head off a blood-spewing Holofernes. One picture calls to another, and soon I am thinking of other nudes in other museums, of paintings and statues by Canova and Ingres and Manet and especially Rubens, whose sea nymphs, in the painting cycle he did for Marie de Médicis that now hangs in the Louvre, look, with their cakey bosoms and their powerful broad bottoms, as though they could hoist a pair of sailing ships onto their shot-putters' shoulders and carry them from a Dutch harbor all the way to the Indies.

And then I come back again to *Flora,* whose model, had she lived in nineteenth-century America, could have found work in another branch of the arts with burlesque queen May Howard, who boasted that her troupe featured no woman who weighed less than 150 pounds, or even the bigger-thinking Billy Watson, manager of Billy Watson's Beef Trust, because you had to weigh in at over 200 to work for Billy. . . .

These last figures are from the recent study *Striptease: The Untold History of the Girlie Show,* which is the definitive treatment of its subject; its author is Rachel Shteir, who teaches drama at DePaul University in Chicago. When Shteir found out that "her otherwise ordinary school friend" Jane had become a stripper, it occurred to her, she writes, that stripping stands for "a possibility that women could reinvent themselves as desirable creatures every night." I've got news for Professor Shteir and Jane both: we men desire you women already. There's no need to get yourselves up like Virginia "Ding Dong" Bell or Evelyn West, The Girl with the $50,000 Chest, or any of the other "peelers" and "torso tossers" whose labors are chronicled in Shteir's book.

Actually, we really, really desire you, and it doesn't take that much to make us pant, which is why classic stripping, as opposed to today's total runway nudity, was, as Shteir points out, pointedly demure. Classic stripping begins with the Jazz Age and ends with the Sexual Revolution, which is about the time that the agonies and ecstasies of puberty were writhing about my limbs the way the sea serpents wound themselves around the arms and legs of Laocoön and his boys. When Judy Higgins dropped her protractor in eighth-grade geometry class and bent over to pick it up, I watched, first curious and then spellbound, as her blouse slowly disengaged from the waistband of her skirt and rose until it revealed a full inch of creamy skin. Today, of course, no self-respecting woman under thirty would dream of leaving her house without baring at least a palm's breadth of tanned midriff.

By the time Judy had retrieved the errant protractor, straightened up, tucked her blouse in hastily, and glanced around red-faced in hopes that no one had seen, I'm sure my face resembled that of Bernini's Saint Teresa just after the smiling angel had plunged his golden spear into her heart. The saint wrote that "the sweetness caused by this intense pain is so extreme that one cannot possibly wish it to cease," but cease it does, and then the sweetness comes back again. It is this seesawing back and forth that is the at heart of striptease, this oscillation between, on the one hand, a desire that blazes so high that it threatens to consume every shred of clothing, every stick of furniture, every thought of job or home or the future and, on the other, a fulfillment that never arrives. Or, as Rachel Shteir says, "as long as the promise of sex is more alluring than the reality, striptease will command our attention."

This paradox has delighted and confounded hedonists, philosophers, artists, and prosecuting attorneys from time immemorial to the present. The illustrations in Shteir's book dramatize the push-pull of allure and abandonment precisely because they are so tame, especially in light of what's available on the internet these days. In a pre-silicone age, all of the women depicted might be described as attractive if, to use Shteir's description of her friend, "otherwise ordinary"; the most one can say about the real bombshells is that they were "pneumatic," a bygone phrase that, when applied to both tires and women, suggests slight over-inflation. On the book's cover, the title is artfully used to conceal the charms of seven smiling women in fancy hats and feather boas before a replica of the Eiffel Tower. The unretouched photo is on page 301, but even here the most enticing element is not the extra flesh but the fact that the cardboard Paris suggested by a few sketchy building fronts is so much smaller than they are, giving the impression that the French capital has been taken over by a squad of good-natured, scantily-clad giantesses.

Happily, Shteir takes no stand on her subject; which is wise; after all, being for or against sex is like being for or against weather. The author's interest lies in examining the way we humans insist on satisfaction and then get cranky when we're satisfied. When Francisque Hutin, the first solo ballerina to appear in New York, let her light silk frock flutter above her waist during her 1827 performance, reformers were scandalized, and for a few weeks, she wore trousers beneath her skirt. But the public had seen something it liked and demanded more, so Mademoiselle Hutin went back to showing her bare legs. And show biz hasn't been the same since.

In the nineteenth century, burlesque shows mixed what we now call high and mass culture, though no one would have made those distinctions then. At a time when it seemed as though art didn't have to be lodged in big cities but could go anywhere, when drama troupes roamed the country putting on both *Macbeth* and *Uncle Tom's Cabin* in frontier towns and riverside hamlets, a typical burlesque revue would consist of skits, parodies, melodramas, classical music, popular songs, poetry, and theater of all kinds. When the British Blondes performed in New York in 1868, one reviewer called them "optically edible," though the voluptuous beauties performed not only cancans and Amazon marches but also a version of the Greek myth of Ixion. Only two years later, though, the theatrical climate had changed, and when the British Blondes returned in 1870, instead of playing to middle-class men and women, they now performed for a mostly working-class all-male audience.

Ping-ponged back and forth in the struggle to decide what is art (not mention what is legal) and what isn't, stripping eventually entered its golden age in the mid–twentieth century, an era dominated by Lili St. Cyr, Tempest Storm, Blaze Starr, Candy Barr, and the incomparable Gypsy Rose Lee. The best of these peelers peeled very slowly; they continued the tradition of 1930s stripper Gladys Clark, whom one reviewer described as "walking around like a queen wondering if the tub is full." Although every stripper's costume was ultimately skimpy or nonexistent (vaudeville performer Eva Tanguay boasted that she could hold her entire Salome outfit in her closed fist), the road to near or total nudity was often a long one. At times, that road took a turn toward the ironic: sometimes a "bust developer," such as Robert Alda, actor Alan Alda's father, stood off-stage and crooned a chaste love song like "The Sweetheart of Sigma Chi" as a shapely lass went through the melancholy motions of unlayering. (Part of the pleasure of Shteir's study is that she retrieves snappy 1930s patter such as "peeler," "torso tosser," and "bust developer," a phrase preferable to its brutally frank equivalent, "tit serenader.")

Sally Rand danced to Chopin and Debussy and gave a lecture at Harvard on "How to Be Intelligent Even Though Educated." Gypsy Rose Lee performed as she sang about her love for the paintings of Van Gogh and Cézanne, the plays of Wilde and Shaw and even Racine. For a time, Lee lived in a Brooklyn boarding house with W. H. Auden, Benjamin Britten, Paul and Jane Bowles, and Richard Wright; visitors included Salvador Dali, Christopher Isherwood, and Aaron Copland, and poet Louis MacNeice recalled trying to concentrate in vain while Britten rehearsed on one side of him and Lee was on the other side "like a whirlwind of laughter and sex."

The other side of demure stripping, of course, was the raucous kind. If some peelers remained veiled and unattainable, like the houris of the Muslim paradise, others, like Georgia Sothern, danced, in the words of one impresario, "just like she had dynamite for lunch." Lili St. Cyr did one number in which she stripped down to a G-string; the house would go dark, and the G-string, which was fluorescent, would fly off into the balcony on a wire to which it had been attached. And Carrie Finnell (of Carrie Finnell and Her Red-Headed Blondes) used what she called her "educated bosom" to astounding effect as she brought tassel twirling to unsurpassable heights. Fellow entertainer Ann Corio likened Finnell's act to the revving up of a military aircraft: "Faster and faster it [the first tassel] would spin while its fellow tassel lay limp and neglected on the other bosom. Then the other tassel would come to life. It would start spinning slowly, while the first tassel was at full speed. Carrie looked like a twin engine bomber."

Alas, not all strippers were as admiring of others as Corio. The big acts were phenomenally successful, and strippers could be as cutthroat as other businesswomen. Rosita Royce trained seven doves to carry off pieces of her evening gown; when someone peppered the birds with a BB gun, all eyes turned toward Tirza the Wine Girl, who may have fretted that her own "wine bath" was not as splendid as Royce's avian extravaganza. The Wine Girl's guilt or innocence may never be known, though it is certain that when Evangeline, the Beautiful Pearl in the Half Shell, became unbearably jealous of Devena the Aqua Tease, who undressed and swam as a mermaid in a 550 gallon tank, she smashed Devena's tank with an ax.

Through "cool eros" or "wisecracking bacchanalian humor" or a combination of the two, then, at their best the women of striptease "sent up desire's inconstancy instead of merely reproducing it," to use Shteir's terms. The great ones knew that sex is a twin engine bomber that is propelled as much by restraint as by promise. In that sense they earned the right to pepper their routines with the names of the great painters and playwrights, for all art, high or low, is a dance of the seven veils, a flirtation, seduction, and abandonment of its audience. Literary theorists love to make much of the Fort-Da game that Freud described in a little boy he observed throwing his toy away and pulling it back with equal satisfaction, first shouting "*Fort!*" or "Away!" and then "*Da!*" or "There!" Every type of art pushes its subject forward and then pulls it back in a performance that doesn't end until the last note dies, the last page is turned, the house lights come up. Shteir quotes Marshall McLuhan as he describes his experience in a topless restaurant, where customers couldn't bring themselves to look at the waitresses as they took orders but gazed at them only as they walked back toward the kitchen, becoming more attractive as they got farther away. McLuhan's right, but so were the Minsky brothers when they built runways that ran out into the audiences of their burlesque theaters; that way, the customers could smell the dancers' flesh and hear their heavy breathing.

What Shteir offers her reader is a wide-ranging social history more than a close look at the lives of individual peelers. If she uses the word "quiddity" once or twice and makes reference to Roland Barthes and Samuel Beckett (whose clowns the best strippers resemble because "they combine the whisper of copious eros with the pathos of missed opportunity"), these are but the spangled bra and panties of academe and soon disappear so that we can see Shteir's subject in all its complicated splendor. She provides valuable context by relating stripping to parallel developments that take place in the world of the sartorially unchallenged: she correlates stripping with jazz, for example, noting that cities associated with the rise of striptease were often Midwestern jazz strongholds like Saint Louis, Chicago, and Kansas City, and with the rise and fall of hemlines (which, for the record, started going up in 1912, reached the knee around 1916, then returned to midcalf for another ten years).

The most important parallel, of course, is between stripping and the law. For the most part, the trial reports excerpted in

Striptease are enough to make you feel sorry for judges and prosecutors; the law might not have always been on the side of the entertainers, but the comic muse always seated herself at the defense table. When Mother Elms, the ninety-three-year-old wardrobe mistress at the Minskys' famed Republic Theater, was asked if she approved of the dances she saw nightly, she replied, "I wish I could do them myself. There was a time when I could," and she neatly side-stepped a prosecutorial trap when asked if Victorian dresses weren't longer than present-day ones by saying, "They could lift them just as high." In another trial involving Ciro's in Los Angeles, the defense lawyer humiliated the arresting officer by establishing that he didn't know the difference between a bump and a grind; when portly Herman Hover, the club's owner, took the stand, he defined a bump as "a pelvic propulsion," and the entire courtroom roared with laughter.

The problem with the law is that it's rational in all its applications but especially so when it comes to the arts. When we try to satisfy other appetites, the road to satisfaction is a one-way street; we want more food, say, or more money. With art, though, we want to see yet not see; this both fulfills and frustrates us, and the fulfillment of our desires is just as liable to leave us frustrated as the frustration of them is liable to leave us strangely satisfied. Following the 2004 presidential election with all its emphasis on the importance of faith-based voting and Red-State morality, an article in the *New York Times* pointed out that some areas of the country that are most conservative have the highest viewership of racy, violent television shows. "We say one thing and do another," said an NBC spokesman. "People compartmentalize about their lives and their entertainment choices." And some don't even bother to compartmentalize: sociologist Herbert Gans notes that "for some people it's a case of 'I am moral, therefore I can watch the most immoral show.'" From Janet Jackson's exposed breast to the apparently naked star of *Desperate Housewives* leaping into the arms of an athlete on *Monday Night Football*, there is always a backlash against televised nudity followed by an insistence on seeing the offending moment again and again, just as Francisque Hutin's 1827 audience first wanted pants under her frock and then wanted them off so her bare legs could be seen once more. A representative of Viacom, which owns CBS and UPN, addresses art's half-conscious appeal when he says that it wouldn't make sense to tinker with the network's offerings: "As soon as you think of something that makes you start putting other things in a show, you change the nature of the show." On the screen or on the runway, art taps areas of the mind where the law can't go.

Given the academy's current fascination with victims, one expects to learn that Shteir's peelers lived tragic lives, but overall they seem not to have suffered more than performers in any other branch of show business. True, Faith Bacon jumped out a window, leaving in her Chicago hotel room a few personal effects and an eighty-five-cent train ticket to Erie, Pennsylvania. And Dixie Evans, "The Marilyn Monroe of Striptease," became destitute after the actress died in 1962 and no one wanted to book her double. But Rose Zelle Rowland married a Belgian baron, while other strippers saved their money, bought one or more clubs of their own, and enjoyed a well-cushioned old age.

By the 1970s striptease was more or less dead, having been replaced by mere "stripping" or "exotic dancing," the goal of which is get naked fast and stay that way. Over time, capitalism takes every phenomenon to its extreme: sex becomes pornography, food becomes fast food, and portions—of everything—become supersized. Worse, when striptease became mere stripping, it lost its sense of humor. From there, the descent is swift into the hellish taxonomy of internet pornography sites, where the twin engine bomber of sex crashes and splinters into a thousand aberrations: "Braces," "Drooling," "Farting," "Insertions," "Mask," "Prison," "Speculum," "Toilet," "Vegetable." I know, it's a free country, but none of this sounds like fun to me, not for the participants and probably not for the vegetables, either. Come on—carrot? cucumber? A porn site is like a Bosch painting without the laughs.

Striptease was outward-looking and smiled at its audience, whereas stripping is self-absorbed and glum. Gone is the coy sophisticate who strolls downstage languidly, pulling off her glove a finger at a time as she sings the praises of Racine, her place taken now by a petulant nude pestering customers for lap dances. Reed-thin yet siliconized, this nymphette is more likely to resemble a boy with breasts than a real woman—I almost said "mature woman" but hesitated because, judging from what's available on porn web sites these days, "mature" means "between thirty and forty," a restrictively youthful age range that doesn't take into account the decades of ripe lusciousness still available to older women and the men who love them.

Growing up in Baton Rouge in the 1950s and '60s, I and my friends would sneak out our windows at night, speed down to New Orleans, and watch the dancers on Bourbon Street go through their routines. I remember seeing Candy Barr, though it may have been Candie Barr, Candy Barre, Candie Barre, Kandy Barr, or Kandy Barre—strippers were shameless in more ways than one, and a hot act was often replicated under a soundalike name.

And then we'd race back down Highway 61 and make it into our beds just before our mothers woke us, their noses wrinkling suspiciously at the lingering scent of cigarette smoke, cheap beer, perhaps even the stale perfume of the half-dressed women who had sashayed past us and who, come to think of it, were probably not much older than our moms. And no less zaftig, either: the strippers of blessed memory wouldn't have qualified for Billy Watson's Beef Trust, but they were older and meatier, like the nudes of the Uffizi and the Louvre. They were like our mothers, in other words, whereas today's women of porn are more like our daughters—Herr Freud, what do you make of that?

In 1969, when the Sexual Revolution was at its peak and the killing was picking up in Vietnam, I got called in for my draft physical, which took place at the Armed Forces Entrance and Examining Station on Canal Street in New Orleans, not far from the French Quarter. After a long day of being poked, probed, and tested, I walked out of AFEES a free man; I had a well-documented history of asthma, which means I didn't have to go to Vietnam and shoot at Asian boys and be shot at by them. The bus back to Baton Rouge wasn't leaving for an hour, so I walked down to Bourbon Street to get a beer and celebrate.

I went into the first bar I came to and asked for a Busch; I'd sweated a lot that day, and there is a big snow-capped mountain on the label of every bottle of Busch, and if you look at that mountain while you drink, it really adds to the pleasure of drinking that cold beer. The bartender puts the bottle on the counter and says, "That'll be a dollar," but as I reach for my wallet, the music comes on, and this bored stripper huffs out onto the runway and begins to gyrate lazily. "Whoops, that'll be four bucks," says the barkeep. "What happened to the dollar?" I say. And he says, "It's four bucks while the entertainment's on." "Keep it," I say, and push the beer back across the bar and leave.

If I'd known an era was ending, I would have stayed.

Poetry, Television, And
The World Wide Web

ART IN A TIME OF TERROR

Each life is a play, lit by the familiar glow of home and office but acted out on a stage built by history. When the curtain went up on the latest act of my personal drama, I had just opened an e-mail message from Will, the elder of my two sons, saying I should call him because he had something important to tell me.

When a twenty-eight-year-old single man says he has an announcement to make, it's usually either "I'm getting married" or "I'm gay," either of which statements I was prepared to meet with paternal approval tinged with the trepidation that accompanies news of any life change. But what he said was he was a finalist for CBS's reality TV show *Big Brother 2* and thought he stood a pretty good chance of being picked. I found out later that the idea had actually come from Will's younger brother Ian, who, figuring rightly that a successful contestant would have to have an edge, created a persona for Will as a "puppetmaster" controlling the other houseguests, who would be his marionettes.

The strategy worked: thousands of applicants sent in videos, a number were interviewed in their home towns, a smaller number were flown to Los Angeles for further interviews, and at the beginning of July, a dozen finalists moved into the Big Brother house, where their every word and movement was captured twenty-four hours a day by CBS cameras and microphones. Houseguests were forbidden all contact with the outside world. Every Saturday, the houseguests selected a "head of household" from among their number; every Tuesday, the head of household nominated two of the others for eviction; every Thursday, one houseguest was shown the door. The last one left would walk away with half a million dollars.

From the very beginning, it looked as though Will's days were numbered. Ian's strategy for his brother was contrarian: whereas most of the houseguests sought favor with the others by presenting themselves as friendly and likeable, Ian suggested that Will create a turbulent atmosphere by being obnoxious and untruthful. As a result, Ian guessed, the other houseguests would begin to form alliances to bring order out of chaos. Don't join the main alliance, said Ian, but one of the smaller ones. And even there, make yourself the weakest member, the one with the least power. The big alliance will turn on the small one and pick it to pieces, one person at a time. But by the time they get to you, Ian told Will, they'll start to smell the money and they'll turn on each other. Which is exactly what happened. Which is why, counter to everyone's expectations, including mine, Will Kirby walked out of the Big Brother house on September 20 with a check for $500,000.

Between the rise and fall of the curtains on this particular drama, there was plenty of action. I learned quickly that when you're the father of a celebrity, you're a celebrity yourself. My students loved the show, especially the young women. One said, "Saw Will getting out of the shower the other day, Doctor Dave, and—two thumbs up!"

As it did with other members of the houseguests' families, CBS asked me to sign a release consenting to the "use and re-use . . . in perpetuity, of my voice, actions, likeness (actual or simulated), name, sobriquet, appearance and biographical information." The quaint "sobriquet" appealed to the word-lover in me. Why CBS didn't simply use the more common "nickname" was a momentary puzzle, though later its use of the more legalistic term would take on a special significance for me.

As I faxed the signed release to CBS, I became excited about the prospect of my simulated likeness being marketed. It would be a sort of immortality to be an action figure, complete with professor's tweed jacket and pipe, sold in drugstores and supermarkets everywhere—used and reused in perpetuity, as it were.

Then came the request for a network interview (I said yes). And one for a web site interview (I said no).

And then the real fun began.

The July 10 show was devoted almost entirely to Will; the update on CBS's web site the next day was titled "Will Powers His Way into Spotlight." Within a few hours, the hate messages began to show up on my e-mail.

Here are some excerpts:

"Your son is the most hated man in America, next to Gary Condit." (Condit was the U.S. Congressman from California who had had an affair with an intern who had recently disappeared.)

"Your demented son . . . is mentally deranged and should probably seek psychological help."

"You should be ashamed of your son and yourself for raising such a vain . . . psychotic and dangerous son."

Though they varied in length and viciousness, most of the e-mails were anonymous, as was the call from the flat-voiced man who simply said "Your son is a loser" into my answering machine and hung up.

From the wording of the messages, I guessed that most of my correspondents were not only males but also loners; one of the good things about a wife or girlfriend is that when you say "I think I'll harass a total stranger on the internet," she's likely to ask if you wouldn't rather go out for tacos. Surprisingly, my correspondents seemed pretty well-educated; at least they could throw words like "narcissism" and "sociopath" around facilely if not accurately. They couldn't spell all that well, but that doesn't mean anything anymore, since most people can't spell these days.

What surprised me about these people was their naïveté. One of my correspondents reported that Will had said on the show that he'd stolen carloads of Butterfingers "and stored them in YOUR refridgerator [sic] and sold them door to door, claiming he represented the Make a Wish foundation." After I read this, I asked my wife if she ever remembered having carloads of candy bars in our freezer. Like me, she drew a blank: pork chops, yeah, but no Butterfingers.

Of course, I said to myself, Will would have to elicit this kind of reaction if his strategy were to be successful. After all, we're talking art here: pop art or mass art, but art nonetheless. I remembered what a colleague said about Salman Rushdie when the ayatollah condemned him to death for writing *The Satanic Verses,* which is that the ayatollah's fatwa was a sign that the novel was taken seriously. You can't say "Lighten up, it's just a novel," because that means novels aren't important. Similarly, people would have to believe Will was a villain for the show to be entertaining; they couldn't simply say, "What a good actor he is."

At the time, of course, this consolation meant nothing to me. The best I can say about the flood of insults is that it was so awful it was almost wonderful. As a friend said, it was like being in *Rosemary's Baby:* you go to bed feeling safe and warm and you wake up surrounded by hooded strangers muttering in a cryptic tongue.

Ian kept me sane, of course. One of his e-mails during this period read, "Is America more upset with the portrayed Will, or are they going to be more upset when and if they learn that he is actually a very nice, pleasant fellow?"

And then there were messages such as this from Nova Scotia Mom, who wrote: "I just thought it would be nice for you to receive a note from someone that likes Will and want you to know that there are many of us out there. We are just not as vocal as the bashers."

But of all the messages I received, the strangest were the ones from someone I'll call Sally. Sally introduced herself as a fan of my poetry, especially my latest book, *The House of Blue Light,* which she had evidently read closely. How, she wanted to know, would I explain the connection between the benign David in the book and the evil Will on television?

I had just replied that both characters were fictions, that both a poet and a reality-show houseguest have to come across a certain way to succeed, when I learned of a chat room in which someone named Sally asked "So who's going to be the first to e-mail David and ask what he thinks of his son's behavior?" Despite the demurrals of others in the room who said family members shouldn't be harassed, Sally said she was going ahead and would "even be civil and polite and non-offensive—anything to see if I can get a reaction" and that "if I get a response, I will post my e-mail and the response here."

When I confronted Sally with her attempt to deceive me, she denied it. I found this interesting: someone able to create her own deception yet unable to imagine that Will was playacting as well.

Then, suddenly, none of this had any significance at all. On the morning of September 11, the terrorists hijacked the airplanes and crashed them into the World Trade Center towers and the Pentagon and a field in western Pennsylvania. For a few hours, nothing seemed to matter any more. By that afternoon, a lot of people were thinking about revenge. I had to take a package to the post office, where a guy in line told me "we need to turn those countries to toast." What countries? I asked. He didn't know, but I could tell he was mad at me for asking. So I quit asking. But everywhere I went for the next few days, I ran into somebody with a we've-got-to-do-something attitude, the idea being that it was better to do something wrong than do nothing at all.

CBS debated whether or not to cancel *Big Brother 2*. I know this because I and the other families of houseguests were privy to that debate, just as we were always informed about every aspect of life in the house. By noon on the day of the attack, my CBS liaison, a wonderful woman named Kerry Hardy, called simply to ask where I and the other members of Will's family were, i.e., to make sure we weren't in New York or Washington.

Sadly, the catastrophe did touch the houseguests directly. By this time there were three left of the original cast, Will and two women, Nicole and Monica. Monica had a cousin who worked in one of the Trade Center towers and who was declared missing.

In an understandable departure from the rule about isolating houseguests from the outside world, Monica was told what had happened to her cousin, and she elected to continue with the program anyway.

And so did CBS, in a decision that was denounced as callous by some observers at the time but that now appears as the correct choice. After all, barber shops, strip joints, tattoo parlors, bookstores, art galleries, and coffee houses all stayed open, and people continued to visit them. Sports teams didn't cancel games; they delayed and rescheduled them, just as CBS delayed the final few episodes of *Big Brother 2* and then began to run them as people recovered from their initial shock and resumed the activities that give our lives color and flavor.

Those include daily work, caregiving to loved ones and oneself, attendance at church and synagogue and mosque, charity to the newly bereaved, and such artistic and cultural pursuits as reading, writing, and watching television and movies. More than usual, people found themselves involved in serious political discussions. There will always be a place in such discussions for the Manichaean viewpoint that sees the world as divided into black and white, the bad guys over there versus the good ones in our corner. But that outlook grew less clamorous as government officials, educators, media figures, and the average Jane and Joe began to see the breadth of the problem and to reflect that there was more to this new world than a simple us-against-them conflict. Even those who argued at first that the attack was just a broadening of the Israeli-Palestinian dispute began to acknowledge that the terrorist network responsible for the carnage in the United States had arisen in large part in reaction to brutal, corrupt, undemocratic regimes in the terrorists' home countries.

Meanwhile, back in Hollywood, the three houseguests continued doing what they usually did, which wasn't much: working out, shooting baskets, swimming, playing backgammon, and, mainly, talking. As far as I could tell, there was not a single book in the Big Brother house; after all, the houseguests were supposed to interact. Like yours and mine, their conversation in those days of mid-September was somber, often horror-filled, and, more often than not, blessedly trivial in nature.

By that time I was watching the action on the live internet feeds, which is a very pleasant activity for a parent: I could watch my child sleep, get up, and cook an omelet without nagging him to make his bed or wash the skillet. After a while, I began to notice discrepancies between what happened on the daily live feeds and what made it onto the edited thrice-weekly TV broadcasts at night. For example, one of the other houseguests would ask Will what he'd like to do, and he'd say, "I want to see my dad. And I'd like to hang out with my brother." But only one of these statements would make it onto the TV show. Or I'd hear the houseguests discuss an eviction that had already taken place and later see an ad urging viewers to watch the show in a few days to learn who would be evicted "live" that evening.

Still, as many as twelve million viewers tuned in to some episodes. Why? I wouldn't have watched the show at all had Will not been on it. But as the guy who trims my trees said the other day, I don't eat chocolate ice cream, either, and they sell a lot of it. Intellectuals have said little about reality TV in this country, but in France, Julia Kristeva, commenting on France's *Loft Story,* its first reality show and one based on the original *Big Brother,* says: "It offered a solution. It was a televised and manipulated representation of what people cannot express, but it responded to people's needs. Parents wondered, 'Why do my kids need this?' It's because at home they cannot express what they feel about life, about sex, about their friends. [At home] there is no conversation to absorb the psychic malaise."

I even got to manipulate the representation myself once. One day I noticed that I could hear Nicole clearly (Nicole had evicted Monica by this time) but Will not at all. From what I could see on my computer screen, it looked as though he wasn't wearing his microphone, as the houseguests were supposed to do at all times. So I called Kerry Hardy in California.

"Oh, my God, you're right!" she said. A few minutes later, a disembodied voice came over my computer speakers, saying, "Will, will you please put your microphone on?" Will looked up startled, then found his mike and put it in place. "Sorry!" he said. "How's this?" Thousands of miles away, I, who had typed my first graduate school term papers on a Royal manual typewriter, felt like a master of the high-tech universe.

And there was more going on in that universe than even I knew at the time. A half dozen web sites had sprung up devoted entirely to Will, both pro and con, and twice as many made reference to him. One site proposed a "Willennium Institute" and quoted Will's every observation as though it were gospel; at the other end of the spectrum was www.killwill.com, the name of which says everything. There was also www.WillsShorts.com, which devoted itself to speculation on which pair of shorts Will would wear on a given day.

I mention these web sites in hopes of lowering the bar of the reader's credulity to the point where he or she can imagine the one I am going to describe now, the site whose webmaster had taken from the live feeds an image of Will grimacing as he lifted weights and used it to depict my beloved son having consensual sex with, among others, Thomas Jefferson, Mr. T., Yosemite Sam, Bill Clinton, George W. Bush (being observed by *his* father), Rodney Dangerfield, the duck from the AFLAC commercial, Ben Affleck, Ellen De Generes, Godzilla, Bela Lugosi, The Mummy, Arnold Schwarzenegger, Dennis Rodman, and, in the webmaster's ultimate test of his artistic license, Will himself. Suddenly the days of the Royal manual typewriter didn't seem so bad. I've never seen anything as revolting as this web site in my life, I thought. That was just before I forwarded it to all my friends.

Because ultimately this web site didn't bother me; it was too over the top for that. (I mean, come on—Yosemite Sam?) Far more irritating to me personally was a site on which the webmaster had reproduced a poem I had written about Will's birth. Actually, the poem is about the nuns who delivered him; I'd written it mainly to honor them and to keep in memory their glowing faces as they handed me my newborn son. Here it is:

The Little Sisters of the Sacred Heart

I'm bouncing across the Scottish heath in a rented Morris Minor
    and listening to an interview with Rat Scabies, drummer
of the first punk band, The Damned, and Mr. Scabies,
    who's probably 50 or so and living comfortably on royalties,
is as recalcitrant as ever, as full of despair and self-loathing,

but the interviewer won't have it, and he keeps calling him "Rattie,"
    saying, "Ah, Rattie, it's all a bit of a put-on, isn't it?"
and "Ah, you're just pulling the old leg now, aren't you, Rattie?"
    to which Mr. Scabies keeps saying things like
"We're fooked, ya daft prat. Oh, yeah, absolutely—fooked!"

Funny old Rattie—he believed in nothing, which is something.
    If it weren't for summat, there'd be naught, as they say
in that part of the world. I wonder if his dad wasn't a bit of a bastard,
    didn't drink himself to death, say, as opposed to a dad like mine,
who, though also dead now, was as nice as he could be when he was alive.

A month before, I'd been in Florence and walked by the *casa di cura* where
    my son Will was born 27 years ago, though it's not a hospital
now but a home for the old nuns of Le Suore Minime del Sacra Cuore
    who helped to deliver and bathe and care for him when he was just
a few minutes old, and when I look over the gate, I see three

of these holy sisters sitting in the garden there, and I wave at them,
    and they wave back, and I wonder if they were on duty
when Will was born, these women who have had no sex at all,
    probably not even very much candy, yet who believe in something
that may be nothing, after all, though I love them for giving me my boy.

They're dozing and talking, these mystical brides of Christ,
     and thinking about their Husband, and it looks to me
as though they're having their version of the *sacra conversazione,*
     a favorite subject of Renaissance artists in which people who care
for one another are painted chatting together about noble things,

and I'm wondering if, as I walk by later when the shadows are long,
     will their white faces be like stars against their black habits,
the three of them a constellation about to rise into the vault
     that arches over Tuscany, the fires there now twinkling,
now steadfast in the chambered heart of the sky.

Now it wouldn't be appropriate here for me to argue the merits of my own poem. I'll simply say it appeared in *Agni,* a journal which, according to the most recent volume of *The Directory of Poetry Publishers,* publishes only one-half of one percent of the poems submitted to it each year. But this is what the webmaster who posted the poem on his site said about it: "Here's a poem [Will's] father wrote for him. I think it's good, but I'm just not sure. I just don't get that poetry stuff, because this is essentially a story, no rhymes, just broken up to LOOK like a poem. I'm sure all those hip poets out there are already snapping their fingers." In other words, someone who admits he knows nothing about poetry wants my poem to be what he thinks poetry should be, though he can't say what that is. At the same time, he confesses he "thinks it's good." Why doesn't he simply trust his own instincts? Here's a guy smart enough to create web sites, which I can't do, yet poetic language throws him—to him, the poet is a hooded stranger, muttering in a cryptic tongue.

    I've found that, when I'm thinking about something, usually I can clarify my thoughts by thinking about what that thing is not. As I thought about poetry and why it stymies so many otherwise intelligent people, CBS's use of the word "sobriquet" in the release I'd signed kept coming back to me. And it occurred to me that maybe the opposite of poetic language is legal language.

Art and the law are opposed fundamentally, of course. The law is bold, profoundly so; in the second sentence of chapter 1 of *The Scarlet Letter*, Hawthorne writes: "The founders of a new colony, whatever Utopia of human virtue and happiness they might originally project, have invariably recognized it among their earliest practical necessities to allot a portion of the virgin soil as a cemetery, and another portion as the site of a prison." Art, on the other hand, bides its time; later in the same novel, the reader is told that ornaments are a luxury in a world that can barely provide the basic necessities.

What the law and art have in common is that, in order to live, both must be interpreted, which means that both will always subject to misinterpretation. Thus those who know nothing about poetry are nonetheless quick to hamper it, just as those who know nothing about the law are quick to begin bombing without even knowing where the targets are.

Philosophically, art maintains its utility by staying some distance from society so it can comment and critique. Because art situates itself on the margins, it can afford to be provocative; indeed, it has to be provocative if it is to be noticed. But because the law is at the center of our social order—because it *is* the center of our social order—it must move slowly, cautiously. The law says, "Take your time." Art says, "Take a chance!"

That latter-day Puritan men's club the Taliban was notoriously anti-art; it forbade the playing of music and dynamited centuries-old statues. And as far as the law goes, what the Taliban offers was more like a parody than the real thing. I needn't go into detail but will simply say that among the piteous photos appearing in the media during the war in Afghanistan, some of the saddest (and most hopeful) were of twelve-year-old refugee girls standing a head taller than their classmates in a first-grade classroom in Pakistan, girls who weren't allowed to go to school in their own country. Amidst the destruction of real targets the terrorists hated, it's worth pointing out that they directed the hijacked planes toward symbolic targets as well: toward Washington, the center of law in this nation, and New York, its artistic capital.

In a recent article in the *New Yorker,* a middle-class Afghan was asked what he wanted for himself and his family, and the first thing he said was "to have electricity." He also said "there is no time for entertainment, or sports, or travel." And then he said it again: "What I dream about for the future of Afghanistan, is . . . to have electricity." No electricity means no television, no computers, no press—no freedom of ideas and, just as important, no freedom from ideas. That's the best thing about any cultural artifact, be it a novel or a poem or even (maybe especially) a TV program picked in *USA Today*'s end-of-the-year roundup as the worst show of 2001: it reminds us just how civilized we are.

In America, we've come a long way from seventeenth-century Boston. In Afghanistan, the Taliban brought back the pre-Enlightenment and then some. Under the Taliban, stupidity was institutionalized; in this country, it's a constitutional privilege. If you flew a kite, applied eyeliner, or played the radio too loud in Kabul, you'd be flogged in the streets; over here, if you watch junk television, misread a poem, or post an obscene web site, you're simply exercising your democratic rights. Ours is a country of many freedoms. The greatest of these is the freedom to be dumb.

I Never Said What They Say I Said,

OR EVERYTHING YOU ALWAYS WANTED TO KNOW
ABOUT PULL QUOTES BUT WERE AFRAID TO ASK

For years I was the only David K. Kirby I knew. But then I began to think the middle initial seemed pretentious, so I became just David Kirby, of which, as it turns out, there are many. Ever since, my life—our lives—haven't been the same. Not only are there lots of David Kirbys, but an uncomfortable number of them seem to be writers, and I've received calls, letters, and e-mails for all of them. There's the David Kirby who edited a book about the Hewlett-Packard corporation, for example, or the one (a Dave, actually) who writes music criticism for a Boulder newspaper. When I reviewed regularly for the *Times Literary Supplement* of London, I was mistaken occasionally for another David Kirby who did the same. Once he got me a bigger paycheck when he was sent a check that should have come to my house; when he returned it and said there'd been an error, the editors assumed his note was a frosty comment on the insufficiency of the fee and sent him a larger check, which he passed on to me. My least favorite Other Dave is an on-line poet whom my students sometimes praise, confusing his greeting-card verse with mine. And then there's the David Kirby who writes on gay issues for the *New York Times;* from time to time I'll get a note from someone saying, "Nice piece on the club scene in Atlanta—and how *is* Barbara these days?"

And then there's this: on page 15 of the July 25, 2004, *New York Times Book Review,* there was a Little, Brown ad for David Foster Wallace's story collection *Oblivion.* Beneath a photo of the book appear these words: "'Superb.' David Kirby, *Chicago Tribune.*" Yes, I did review the book for the *Tribune.* But I didn't say it was "superb."

It was the middle of the summer blockbuster season, a time of full-page ads for popcorn movies and beach novels that feature eye-catching graphics, the names of celebrity actors and authors printed in fonts usually reserved for national catastrophes, and a fistful of favorable "pull quotes" or statements lifted from reviews. Like most people, I've never taken pull quotes at face value and regard the practice as a harmless attempt to deceive the gullible.

This was personal, though. This time the word was being put in *my* mouth.

So I e-mailed people in various fields to see what they know about pull-quoting. One correspondent reminded me that *Mad* used to parody pull-quoting by showing how self-serving film producers used ellipses to distort the actual reviews. So when you read ". . . highly . . . entertaining . . . see this one!" you were supposed to know that the original review said, "This dud of a movie is highly overrated. In fact, it's the least entertaining film of the season—so whatever you do, don't see this one!"

Reminding me that life imitates art, someone who once worked in publishing wrote: "I remember when I was at Random House that it was common practice for the publicity department to definitely pull words and phrases out of context for the quotes on the back of the book jacket (from the responses they got back from bound galleys)." Thus a jacket might trumpet "'Amazing . . . constantly surprises . . . great fun for the reader' when the actual quote was something like 'Amazing piece of drivel that constantly surprises with its total and complete inanity, thus providing great fun for the reader who truly knows the difference between competent writing and complete ineptitude.'"

That's not what happened in my case, though, since I hadn't used the word "superb" at all. What I did say was that *Oblivion* is an extremely demanding read, a hyperrealistic type of fiction with sophisticated philosophical underpinnings and a worthy book in many ways, though one intended for readers with very specialized tastes—in other words, not a beach novel. For that reason, maybe Little, Brown felt it needed an extra push: "hyperrealistic" probably wouldn't lead to long lines at Borders, whereas "superb" might make a reader on the fence think twice.

But since I hadn't used the word, where had it come from? The Random House insider suggested, "But since you didn't use the word 'superb' at all, maybe they took an 's' from 'annoying piece of silliness,' a 'u' from 'unbelievably dull,' a 'p' from 'pain in the neck writer,' an 'e' from 'enervating in the extreme,' and so on.'"

Maybe so. But why me? Another correspondent suggested that Little, Brown "might be trying to turn you into a publishing company creation—like the fake reviewer some major film companies were quoting several months ago and got busted for." A web search turned up a March 9, 2004, article by Emanuella Grinberg of Court TV that begins "a group of disgruntled moviegoers will settle their suit out of court against a nonexistent film critic, whose glowing reviews of mediocre films prompted a class-action suit alleging filmgoers had been 'tricked' into theaters." It turns out that Sony Pictures Entertainment, through their subsidiary, Columbia Pictures, distributed the films as well as advertisements featuring quotes from a fictitious critic, "David Manning," who purported to write for a real Connecticut newspaper, the *Ridgefield Press*. "Manning" had proclaimed Heath Ledger "this year's hottest new star" and said that the turkey *Hollow Man* was "one hell of a scary ride." More Googling turned up several tongue-in-cheek web sites by writers claiming to be the real David Manning.

My quest for phony pull quote stories brought dozens of responses; apparently there are few seasoned critics out there whose words haven't been used in this way. One of the funniest was from the *New York Times* music critic Jon Pareles, who said he once reviewed an Elvis impersonator who excerpted the remarks Pareles made about Elvis and used them in his publicity. Pareles also led me to a review of *Riverdance* by Jennifer Dunning that had been misquoted by advertisers. Overlooking such phrases as "dreadful stuff" and "soupy clichés," not to mention the sentence "the show looks as if it is unfolding in an olde-Irish parking garage," the ad people changed Dunning's weary "But there will always be, it seems, a 'Riverdance'" into the exuberant "THERE WILL ALWAYS BE A RIVERDANCE!"

One might expect this sort of thing on Broadway, but it seems there is no depth to which even a respected academic press will not descend in promoting its works, as Eric McHenry points out in the September 13, 2004, issue of *Slate,* where he notes that, after he wrote in a review of a book by poet George Starbuck that "it's impossible to resist the language of masonry and carpentry when describing Starbuck's work," the University of Alabama Press pulled only the words "it's impossible to resist the language" for its ads. As McHenry observes ruefully, "distorting a positive review in order to gin up a positive blurb seems kind of pathetic."

The most sophisticated example of fraudulent pull-quoting came from novelist Katharine Weber, who wrote that, before she ever wrote any novels, she interviewed an established author for *Publishers Weekly* in 1985. Fifteen years later, when Weber herself was established, the author came out with a new book accompanied by a blurb from "Katharine Weber, author of *The Music Lesson.*" True, the language of the blurb was taken from the interview, but it appeared now "as if newly-minted," Weber wrote me, "offered as a blurb for this new book mixed with other blurbs from other people, which is especially deceptive since I was not the author of that novel when I wrote those words as a journalist some fifteen years earlier." So this isn't a case of a mistaken attribution but of the words of one Katharine Weber being mouthed by another Katharine Weber, even though they're both the same person.

When I called Little, Brown to get their side of the story, the publicity person I talked to was so insouciant that I wondered if this sort of thing didn't happen all the time. Eventually I ended up chatting with someone who had assured me that, no, this kind of mix-up had never happened before. She also had an explanation for me, which is that, about a month before my review appeared, the *Chicago Tribune* had run a summer reading special that covered more than thirty books, one of which was *Oblivion,* which the Tribune writer called a "superb collection," and somehow the fateful adjective flew across cyberspace and ended up in my mouth.

I asked my Little, Brown contact if the ad was slated to appear elsewhere (it had already appeared in the *New Yorker* as well), and she said no. I asked if the company would like to run a correction, and she said she didn't see how that was possible. So here's the correction.

In the end, little harm was done. If one or two readers buy *Oblivion* because of the phony quote, they'll still be better off than the moviegoers who bought tickets for *Hollow Man* on the advice of "David Manning" or the music lovers who went to see the Elvis impersonator under the misconception that he had all the feline grace and musical mastery of the King.

Personally, I'm still a little miffed, though probably I would have forgotten about the whole thing had it not been for a final bizarre turn. The day after the mystery was cleared up, I got a Little, Brown catalog in the mail advertising a January 2005 book, *The Ha-Ha*, by first-time novelist Dave King. Since I am the author of a 2003 poetry collection also called *The Ha-Ha*, it appeared that Little, Brown not only put words in my mouth but is also publishing a book containing all of my title and half of my name. When I called my Little, Brown contact and told her this, she gasped, "Are you *that* David Kirby?" And thus I joined the army of multiple David Mannings and Katharine Webers, trudging across the faces of America's newspapers and book covers, flinging real and phony praise as they wonder if they themselves are real or not.

Sounds to me like a subject for that superb Czech writer Franz Kafka.

Mornings With Travis,
Evenings With Dick

OR LUCKY BUCK AT THE QUESTURA

Florence, August 18—I am in line outside the Questura, the main police station, waiting to apply for my *permesso di soggiorno*. Here's what I have with me: my application for the *permesso*, my passport, my work visa that allows me to stay in Italy for five months, my letter from the Ministero di Lavoro giving me permission to work, a tax stamp for 10.33 euros, three photos of myself, a photocopy of a credit card, a photocopy of my Blue Cross card, a photocopy of the *permesso* belonging to Sue Capitani, who directs the Florida State Study Center here, and a photocopy of something that appears to be the study center's business license.

In the dim light (it's 7:00 a.m.), I can make out the faces of the thirty or so people who lined up outside the Questura even earlier than I did. Actually, "lined up" is not the right word: ten or so people have formed a ragged file, while the rest position themselves along the wall or pace nervously. Each has a thick packet under his or her arm, presumably with documents roughly analogous to mine. My guess is that my fellow applicants are Russian, Scandinavian, Albanian, German, African, and Central American, especially the latter: more than during my past stays in Florence, there seem to be lots of short, dark women with high cheekbones, come, no doubt, from Guatemala and Honduras and Ecuador to sweep and clean and take care of the old ladies I see them leading down the street like white-haired, black-sweatered children. Each person has a look on his face of either boredom or terror or, as their moods change, both. Not a soul here looks like me.

By the time the Questura opens at 8:15, the crowd has more than doubled in size. Almost everyone has lined up like obedient schoolchildren, though a couple of nervous latecomers try to barrel in as the others cry, "*La fila! La fila!*" ("The line!") As I pass the policemen at the door, one of them gives me a ticket like the one you get when you're waiting to buy cold cuts at the grocery store. I am carried along by the tide of *permesso* seekers through several more doorways until we arrive at a room with numbered windows. An electronic number board begins to ding loudly as it sends this number to that window and so on; as I have ticket 29, I figure it won't take that long to get to a window.

It takes an hour and fifteen minutes. Okay, the earth is 4.55 billion years old, plus or minus 1 percent, so an hour and a quarter isn't that long. What makes it seem longer is that the room, which is designed to seat fifty comfortably, contains roughly a hundred. No one looks bored now, because all look terrified. Some clearly haven't had a bath in month, and as the temperature in the unventilated room rises, so does the odor level. The times being what they are, half of these people have cell phones, and the fetid air is filled with a hullabaloo like the one that arose from the bricks of Babel as the dust cleared and people wondered what the hell the guy next to them was saying.

From the linguistic standpoint, the most disheartening thing to me is that everyone seems to be speaking fluent Italian once they get to their assigned window and began to present their documents. It goes without saying that the odds against showing up on the right day and the right moment at the right window with all the right documents are daunting, and fully half of the applicants are trying to jawbone their way into Italy by saying "Yes, this is what a what an insurance card looks like in my country" or "Wait a minute, I put my tax stamp in my wallet" or "Even if the photos aren't identical, you can see that they're all of me, can't you?"

Over the past twenty years, I have lived in Italy for perhaps two years total, and while I never took a class, I have managed to pick up enough of the language to ask directions, order in restaurants, and even make simple conversation about the weather and current political leadership, Italian as well as American. And for a year now, I have been listening to my six basic-to-intermediate-level Italian tapes as I drive around Tallahassee and feel pretty darned confident about my ability to sling the two major past tenses as well as much of the conditional and, on a good day, the subjunctive, at least in first and third persons. I figure I'm the best-educated person at the Questura this morning, yet people who are obviously going to be selling cheap art posters on the sidewalk this afternoon are spouting Italian as though they were born here.

The electronic board dings, and my number is up.

◆

If I were in Tallahassee right now, I'd be in the throes of rehearsal for an event called *An Evening With Dick,* a benefit to raise money for prostate cancer research. The idea is to write a revue like *The Vagina Monologues,* have it hosted by Theatre School Dean Emeritus Richard Fallon, and call the show—get it?—*An Evening With Dick.* There would be two chief writers, me and a novelist who sometimes teaches at the university and who, according to virtually everyone who knows him, including his wife, is "not the easiest person in the world to get along with." A writer for the *Tallahassee Democrat* is supposed to chip in. Other writers would contribute sketches and songs, and Theatre School personnel have volunteered to provide set design and props.

Calls were put into Ted Turner and Burt Reynolds, both of whom have ties to FSU. But most of the actors and singers will be lawyers, politicians, professors, and businessmen. The police chief has said he'll take part. Several doctors are involved, including, of course, a urologist. The presiding genius is Chef Eric Favier, who, with his wife Karen Cooley, owns and runs Chez Pierre, Tallahassee's most elegant restaurant.

Eric is everything you hope a Frenchman will be: spirited, good-natured, and always giving you the impression that, no matter how much fun you're having right now, there's more just around the corner. Decades of American life have neither erased his accent nor prevented him from making original contributions to our native grammar; the past participle "putten" comes to mind, as in "I putten zuh new menu in your mailbox, Keerby." Eric is one of those people who cheers up a room just by putten his head in the door.

Even better, he owns a restaurant, which makes meetings a lot more attractive. Well, not to everybody. The first meeting is set for five o'clock, but only three people show up on time: Eric, me, and the manager of the auditorium where *An Evening With Dick* will be staged. Over the next hour and forty-five minutes, other principals drift in: the director (the only woman involved), host Dick Fallon, two set designers, publicists. Neither my coauthor nor any of the other writers are present. By now it is almost seven o'clock; Chef Eric has been pouring the Bordeaux for almost two hours, and most of us are hungry or tipsy or both. So the main outcome of the first meeting is to fix a time for the second.

Since the first meeting obviously started too early for everyone, the second meeting begins at six o'clock. The good news is that five people show up on time; the bad is that none of the other dozen principals come that night, including Chef Eric. In fact, the Chez Pierre staff is baffled and can't quite figure out what to do with us, so the five of us commandeer an empty room, order a bottle of Bordeaux (at our own expense), and set a time for a third meeting. None of the other writers appear.

By now I'm getting panicky, so I figure I'd better contact the other writers to see if anybody's going to be working on this script besides me. I call the novelist with the reputation for testiness, and he tells me he's only going to write one sketch; it'll be about his father's dick. I've heard that years ago, his father had molested children, including family members. Now the father has Alzheimer's but was recently restrained for raping another resident in his nursing home; the ideas I have for the script have been leaned toward the comedic, so I'm wondering how easy it's going to be get integrate the novelist's idea with mine. I leave messages for the writer at the *Democrat*. I run into someone who will be one of the actors; he tells me he plans to contribute a sketch as well, one in which two men are sitting in a car, and the first guy tells the other to suck it, and the other guy says he doesn't want to suck it, and the first guy says the other to just stick it in his mouth and suck it, and the other guy says he can't, it's too big. It turns out they're talking about a cigar. The actor/writer is so proud of himself that I can't tell him how close I am to tears.

The Vagina Monologues actually played in Tallahassee and made a ton of money for the women's shelter; Jane Fonda and Margot Kidder were among the celebrities who took part. I buy a copy of *The Vagina Monologues* and start to read it, but it keeps falling out of my hands. I'm glad it's a money-maker for good causes, but the sketches are either creepy or offensive or have an Angry Doormat quality. Or all three; typical is the one in which the woman complains how her husband forces her to shave her pubic hair so he can pretend he's fucking little girls and ends up leaving her for a younger woman. (Did the phrase "leave the bastard" never occur to her?)

The main problem is that, as I see it, the tone of *An Evening With Dick* is going to be completely different from that of *The Vagina Monologues*. The subtext of *The Vagina Monologues* is, "I have a secret garden, but you and only you may go there if you're very, very sweet to me." Whereas the text (there is no subtext) of *Dick* is "Look out, mama, the big boy's back in town!" The most promising thing so far about *Dick* is that, no matter how horrible it is, Chef Eric has promised to throw a big party at the restaurant after the show. As one of the set designers says, "Either every one of us is going to get laid that night or none of us will ever get laid again." Puns fly at the meetings; since everybody's contributing their services, I've proposed that the show be termed a Pro Bono© Production. If I drop the script somewhere, I'm not sure I want it traced back to me, so I keep it in a folder I got a student paper in last term; the folder says "WHATLEY" on it.

None of the other writers come to the third meeting, either, but by now I'm nervous enough to have written an entire script myself. It consists of seventeen scenes and will run, I figure, to about seventy minutes; if the other writers contribute what they've promised to, we'll have a full-length production. My script includes prose sketches, poems (and not just limericks, though there are several of those), long lists of synonyms for the male sex organ, jokes, stream-of-consciousness riffs, and a song by me titled "It's So Nice To Have A Penis In The House" which is to be not sung so much as growled in a sort of Rex-Harrison-in-*My-Fair-Lady* way.

The way I've planned it, "It's So Nice To Have A Penis In The House" will both open and close *An Evening With Dick.* It'll be sung as a solo at the beginning and, at the end, by the audience, who'll have the lyrics in their programs. In fact, I want them to sing it standing, as though it were the "Hallelujah" chorus in Handel's *Messiah.*

♦

At the same time that I am trying to get a grip on *Dick,* I am also spending one morning a week tutoring a first-grader in reading. I feel a bit unsettled about volunteer work; it seems too much like a way to advertise yourself as a good person.

I do have a noncharitable motive, as it turns out, which is that I'd like to know how people learn to read. Memory is of no use, since I can't ever remember not reading. And since I spend my days in a rarefied atmosphere of reading and writing at the highest levels, I feel as though I should know how I and the professionals around me got started.

Beyond that, I want to do something on the south side of town, where the schools are that have the poorest readers. If I want to be able say what's going on in *the* world instead of just *my* world, I need to shake up my routine. I can easily go for days along an undeviating path of home-work-laundry-groceries-home-restaurant-movie-home without seeing anyone different from myself.

Every child at Bond Elementary School is as different from me as anyone can possibly be. With the exception of a few teachers, there are no white people at Bond, and a disproportionately high number of children are on the free-lunch program. The ones who have been singled out for tutoring have names like those of Shakespeare's minor noblemen: Dayzannier, Rantarius, Jaquez. I am assigned to a first-grader named Travis, who has beautiful brown eyes and a shock of hair that sticks up like the crown of a royal palm.

Travis can't read worth a lick. Actually, that's not fair: our first day, it's clear that he can read simple words like "I," "he," and "was." The problem is that he doesn't always get them right the first time: he'll read "I" as "he," and it might take a try or two for him to come up with the right monosyllable. While Travis isn't overactive and is content to sit and work patiently with me, I sense his problem is a deficit in concentration rather than intelligence. I get the sense that he is somehow above all this, that he is a little bored with the whole process and will get down to reading once he has taken care of more important matters.

These mainly involve future issues, such as work and travel. When I ask him what he wants to do when he grows up, Travis says he wants to work with "bugses": not, as I'm thinking might be appropriate, as an exterminator but as a scientist with a magnifying glass and a collection jar and other bug-related stuff, one who spends his days not in the library trying to learn to read but out in the real world, crawling through the grass and turning over rocks in search of interesting new specimens.

Travis also likes to look at the atlas with me, because I'm planning the trip later this year to Italy, where I'll be stuck in the Questura for what seems like days (and will actually turn out to be). So when the lessons get too hard or we just get fed up with each other, often we'll look at maps of the world and plan how I'll get to my destinations and back again. If anyone ever wants to know about the overland route from Tallahassee to Florence, I've got it for them; from village to village, over river and mountain, Travis and I worked it out in detail.

I've never been to a school like Bond Elementary; I certainly didn't attend a school like it as a child, and while I'm often asked to visit classrooms to talk to children because I coauthored a couple of books for young readers a while back, the schools I visit tend to be pretty middle-class. The thing I like most about Bond is that the halls and sidewalks all have names, like "Attitude Avenue" and "Success Road." My favorite is called "Perseverance Street," a name that conjures a work ethic yet has a good-timey New Orleans sound to it. Like most writers, I'm always in the market for a head shot, so I resolve to come back with Barbara on a day when I'm not tutoring so she can take a picture of me standing under the Perseverance Street sign. But something I find unsettling is the fact that the walkways are marked like pedestrian highways, with borders on each side and a center stripe so that, say, eastbound traffic doesn't veer over the line and mingle with the westward flow. Every day I am at Bond, I see entire classrooms lined up in order, ready to march to the gym or the music room. My first day there, a teacher says to her charges, "Now can you children all behave yourselves today?" and twenty voices cry in unison, "YES, MISS JOHNSON, WE CAN!"

When I go to Travis's classroom to pick him up for our tutoring sessions in the library, I wonder if he might be embarrassed to be singled out for extra help; since they have so little status in the first place, schoolkids can be notoriously vicious to the "dummies" in their midst. But the first graders at Bond Elementary are too young for this kind of cruelty. To the contrary, Travis is regarded as something of a celebrity, and when he and I set off together, often I have to gently disentangle myself from two or three children who cling to my leg like kids trying to keep their parents from going off for a night on the town and sticking them with the babysitter. "Naw, naw!" says Travis as he pries somebody's hand off my ankle. "I'm going with David!"

◆

Things start to come together at the fourth *Evening With Dick* meeting. Other than me, we still don't have any writers, but just about everybody who has been asked to participate agrees; now that they have a good cause as their excuse, there are lots of guys who want to get up on stage and act stupid. The publicity people have been working overtime and have set up a shoot for a promotional video to run on local television; I get to write the script for the video.

Earlier there had been talk that the Florida State public relations office might want to film *Dick* for its archives, a decision that wouldn't affect the show's success or failure but would be welcome insofar as it would lend institutional approval to an undertaking certain to be risqué. Now we learn that FSU is dragging their feet. "They've seen the script," says Peggy, the director, and I think, Uh-oh.

But it turns out that what the FSU people are balking at is the use of the word "cock" in a fourteenth-century poem authored by the world's most prolific author, Anonymous, and titled "I Have a Gentle Cock." Clearly the poem is about a rooster—well, and a cock, too, but mainly a rooster. "I have a gentle cock, / croweth me day," it begins, and then there's lots of rooster description ("His comb is of red coral, / His tail is of jet"), even if the last lines hint that we're talking about more than a bird here ("And every night he percheth him / In mine ladye's chaumber"). Still, the poem's about a cock! Not a "dong," "dork," "German helmet," "beef bayonet," "heat-seeking moisture missile," or any of the other synonyms for the male member that I got off the Web and have worked into a sketch that comes later in the show, but a cock. Why this squeamishness, I wonder, then slide into a low-grade depression when I remember that "I Have a Gentle Cock" is the first number; obviously the FSU people never got beyond the first page.

Now whereas *An Evening With Dick* is a proudly amateurish production, Florida State does have an ambitious and widely respected School of Theatre. During the period I'm writing about, the Theatre School is staging *Prymate* by Mark Medoff, author of *Children of a Lesser God.* In *Prymate,* the African American actor André De Shields plays a gorilla who, among other developments, engages in "a shockingly blunt sex act" with a female sign-language interpreter. That quote is from a condescending article by *New York Times* drama critic Bruce Weber, who is clearly disappointed that a controversial play didn't create more scandal in what he terms "a conservative Southern capital." Okay, nobody ever confused Tallahassee with midtown Manhattan, but it's a white-collar town with two universities, and theatre-goers here aren't going to pass out if things get a little steamy onstage.

Weber's dismay that "the opening passed without a murmur of controversy" doesn't surprise me, since most New Yorkers seem convinced that Southerners eat dirt and sleep with their kinfolk; what does startle me is that the play's director and the theatre dean seem to agree with him. The dean jokes about losing his job in the article, and director Edwin Sherin wonders, "Who knows how the religious right will respond? . . . I've got my bag packed and a ticket purchased. When they go out and lynch somebody, they can look for me, but I'm on a plane out of here." Hey, Tallahassee survived *The Vagina Monologues,* didn't it?

Language: can't live with it, can't live without it. About this time there's an article on me in *Research in Review,* FSU's magazine on faculty achievements, entitled "Sho' Like to Ball: David Kirby Hits 'Em High and Low in a Galloping Career through the Quirky World of Free Verse." The magazine's editor tells me that more than one person has called his office to ask him if he knows what "ball" means and how he has to profess shock when they tell him. In the article, a poem of mine is quoted in which I use the word "fuck," though it appears as "f__k" in the pages of *Research in Review.* The poem originally appeared in an issue of *Southern Review,* but when I pull up the on-line version to see how the offending word is treated there, I find that the entire poem has been deleted.

As I will be teaching in Italy in the fall, I listen to language tapes in the car wherever I go, trying to master the present conditional of *potere* and *dovere* at the same time I am attempting to teach Travis the difference between "tree" and "three" and also get the right words into the *Dick* script. Foreign language study, tutoring, script writing: so far I'm not having that much success in any area, yet in all three, the only solution I can come up with is to keep plugging away.

This term I'm also teaching Poetic Technique, the most difficult course in the English Department. Poetic Technique is open to anyone who wants to take it, and since, as far as I can tell, every human being ever born either thinks they are a poet already or can write a poem without much effort, the class can be a nightmare. This term, half of my white students and all of the African Americans want to be rappers. Fine, I say, but here we write poems, not rap lyrics. Fine, they say, then give me a sheet of unpunctuated fragments better suited for club shout-outs than the poetry classroom. The only solution? Keep plugging away.

An editor at the *Tallahassee Democrat* asks me to talk to the writers about style, how to make it lively and fresh. I tell them that the great writers like Shakespeare and Dickens and Whitman all use a range of rhetoric, from the loftiest Latinate polysyllables to the lowest Anglo-Saxon barnyard grunts. You can get away with whatever you want, I tell the journalists, by creating a context in which any sort of language works. We try, they say, but the editors don't want to alienate the readership, so most of the language we use ends up being pretty middle of the road. Well, keep plugging away, I tell the journalists.

After its premier in Tallahassee, *Prymate* goes on to New York, where it folds after five performances.

◆

A breakthrough: I tell Travis to write a sentence, any sentence, and he writes "The fat rat scats" on a 5″ × 8″ card and takes it around the library, proudly showing it to everyone.

Travis tells me he will be going to the circus later this week because he has been "good," though not his brother Renardo. In fact, Renardo has been so bad lately his mother came to his fourth-grade classroom to whip him; he tried to run, Travis reports gleefully, but his mother caught him and "whipped him good!" "What did the teacher do?" I ask. "She laugh!" says Travis. On an earlier occasion, he tells me, Renardo hid in the car before his mother drove to work, so she "beat him down!" Another time, Renardo tried to *drive* the car but was caught, with the usual outcome.

I'm not as horrified as some would be at the beatings. Our mother regularly used a switch or a slipper on my brother and me, and he became a medical school dean and I a professor; neither of us ever used corporal punishment on our own children. What bothers me more is Travis's joy at Renaldo's anguish, which recalls the Medieval church doctrine called the "abominable fancy," whereby the pleasure of the saints in heaven is increased by their ability to witness the sufferings of the damned in hell. When I tell him maybe he should try a little tenderness, Travis puts his chin in his hand and his elbow on the table and looks at me as if to say, Man, you just don't get it.

Just as Travis's ideas on morality are a lot more cut and dried than mine, so are his opinions on the relations between the sexes. One thing I've learned is that I can discipline him by using words that are hateful, such as "girlfriend" and "kiss." The first time I used the former, he closed his eyes and held up his hand, like a Victorian dandy who'd just been invited to a tractor pull. "Don't . . . don't," he said. So now when his attention wanders, I bring him back to the task at hand by saying, for example, "Hmm, I wonder who Sammy is cooking the six sizzling sausages for, Travis. Do you think it could be his . . . GIRLFRIEND?!?"

Once he and I are walking from his classroom to the library, and he looks behind us and notices that we are being followed by the other tutors, all of whom are young women. Travis tugs on my sleeve: "They got a buncha girls back there." "Hmm?" He jerks his thumb over his shoulder: "A buncha girls." "Whoa," I say, taking a look. "I sure hope they're not planning to catch us and . . . KISS us!" Travis shoots me a brief look of terror and then breaks into a toothy grin. We look at each for a moment and then, as though an invisible official has fired an inaudible starter's pistol, we start to hightail it, a fifty-nine-year-old white man and his little charge lighting out for the territory like Huck and Jim with the ages and races reversed, away from women and everything they stand for.

Yet I notice that Travis looks up every time Rori passes through the library to see how we are doing. Rori supervises the tutors; she's short and shapely, and when she smiles, her green cat's-eyes flash like cut glass. One day, Travis grabs Rori around the waist in a bear hug, wiggling his shoulders back and forth with joy as he burrows into her sweater. Rori gives Travis a quick kiss on the top of his head and then sinks her fingers into his bony body, which she kneads as though it were bread dough.

Later, I tell him he did the right thing, that not only is it nice to hug the ladies but they like it, too. Travis says, "Why you don't hug her?" I say I have a wife, and I hug only her. "Aaaah!" he screams; "that's nasty!" Why is it okay to hug Rori, I ask with my wise-guy logic, but not Barbara? Just is, obviously. On some level, Travis may know that hugging just one woman, especially when there's no one else in the room, can lead to the unthinkable—certainly the unutterable.

The course of Travis's relations with women does not run smooth, however. One day I enter the classroom, and from his seat, Travis looks up at me, folds his arms across his chest, sticks his shoulders in his ears, and says, "Unn-UHH!" "What's wrong?" I ask. His little friends rush up and, with all the glee Travis used in describing Renardo's various beatings, shout, "He don't want to go witchoo today!" When I ask why, he just sulks. So I tell him to come along, that we'll just do a little work, not too much.

On the way to the library, Travis begins to cry; ashamed of his tears, he pulls his jacket over his head. When we get there, I ask if he feels bad. Head-shake. If someone's been mean to him: nod. His mother? Shake. Renardo? Shake. Another child? Shake. His teacher? Nod. I ask if he has been bad: vigorous shakes. Did she fuss at you? Nod. Did she hit you in the head with a stick and knock your brains out? He laughs and then remembers that he's sad and pouts again and says, "Noooo!" Well, did she pull your pants down, dip your heinie in chocolate, let it dry, and then stick you in an ant bed so the ants could bite you? This just about kills Travis, who grabs his ribs and falls over, yelling with joy. At least it distracts him enough that we can read about Gary Gopher, who gobbles gobs and gobs of grass and grapes and green beans.

We end up doing about as much work as we always do. On the way back, we see Ms. Hansen, walking fast, hunched over, arms crossed in front. "There my teacher!" shouts Travis with glee, and waves vigorously. Ms. Hansen gives us a sour look and as weak a wave as possible; following their run-in, nobody had cheered *her* up. Travis is feeling great now, though I'm not sure he has learned anything about right and wrong.

In late March, I go to Travis's classroom one day to find a celebration in full swing. It's a birthday party for Travis, who tells me he is nine today. "*Nine?*" I say before I can catch myself, and he grins up at me as he nods with obvious pride at his achievement. After the tutoring session, I ask Ms. Hansen what the deal is, and she tells me that Travis has been through kindergarten twice and this is his second time in first grade; moreover, except for a single year, she's been his teacher all that time. She waves her hand to take in the chalkboard, the coatrack, the bookshelves, the gaudy drawings that are hung everywhere, the little desks where the students eat their hideous-looking lunches. "And he's been in this same classroom for three years—I don't know what he's going to do when he has to leave!"

The week before, I'm asked to visit a classroom at Holy Comforter, a private school on the north side of town. From the parking lot, Holy Comforter looks more like the campus of Amherst or Williams than an elementary school. Its gabled brick buildings are set in verdant fields, and until one sees the children and teachers, it's easy to imagine scholars finishing up some task in Latin or Greek and then rolling up their sleeves for an afternoon of gentlemanly games in the meadow. There are no paths marked out on the sidewalks and no teachers giving drill-sergeant instructions to children lined up in military formation. The sidewalks do not have allegorical names; here, it's assumed that one will have a positive attitude and persevere and succeed and needn't be reminded to do so. The classrooms are high-ceilinged and well-appointed, and the children work in them happily. Money talks: compared to the classrooms at Holy Comforter, Travis's room at Bond Elementary is a cell in a third-world prison.

After nearly four months with Travis, I ask Rori how he's doing, and she asks me what manual he's on. When I say manual #2, Rori's eyes widen; by now he should be on manual #6, she says. I'm not going to let a deficit of four manuals get me down, though. We've made it through two of the sons of bitches, and there are days when I actually *do* feel that Travis has made progress. During one of our last sessions together, I tell him to write "I read books very well" on a 5″ × 8″ card and then stubbornly insist he put an exclamation mark at the end of the sentence. Without looking at it, I slip the card in my folder, give Travis a good-bye hug, jump in the car, pop in an Italian tape, and head home. Later that day I'm looking over our work and find the card, on which Travis has written "I read books very well?"

♦

At the next *Evening With Dick* meeting, eight people show up—on time! None of them are the other writers, though; for better or worse, it looks as though this is going to be my baby. I wonder aloud if the script is gay enough. No, somebody says, probably not, so I say I'll make it gayer. Then somebody else says they have a great idea. How about something on alien dicks? Yeah, I say, I can probably write something in that line. And then someone says, ohh, ohh, I know! How about the difference between Republican dicks and Democratic dicks? This one I turn down; I'll do alien dicks, but I don't want to make any Republicans mad since they tend to have more money than Democrats and are likely to be our biggest contributors.

How are ticket sales going? says someone. Glances are exchanged, shoulders shrugged. The publicity guy tumbles in, apologizes, and then announces he's lined up a TV spot for us, so all we need now is a script. Everybody looks at me. The spot's only twenty seconds, so I decide to call the script for it "20 Seconds Of Dick." I'm told to write lines for five people: me, restaurateur Eric Favier, Dean Emeritus Dick Fallon, and two others.

If you've ever written a twenty-second script for a TV spot, you understand what I went through. The first draft only fills one page, but it takes ninety seconds to read aloud. Reading a second time as fast as I can, I get it down to eighty seconds, but I still have three times as much script as I need. By printing draft after draft and reading and slicing and slicing again, I finally get the script down to just under twenty-five seconds and figure, Good enough. I base the script on Abbott and Costello's "Who's on First?" routine, and as these things go, I tell myself, it's not bad, even though it's the only one I've ever written.

On the day the TV spot is to be shot, Eric and I show up at the studio on time. Dick is fifteen minutes late, but given our record, that's not bad for an *Evening With Dick* meeting. The problem is that the other two guys don't show. So I rewrite the script for three, and we start shooting.

Even though I am the author, to my shame, I am the one who consistently flubs his lines. Perhaps I should say "blows" his lines—the puns that cropped up in the meetings have made their way not only into the main script but also the one for the TV spot as well, and the video team eggs us on. Soon we are talking about what an "upstanding" cast we have and how the whole show just "bulges" with talent. After an hour and at least thirty takes, the chief videographer says, well, we've got enough to work with here, though there's something in his tone that suggests less a desire to spend a week splicing bits of tape together in hopes of coming up with a halfway decent clip and more the fervent wish that Eric, Dick, and I will get lost and let them turn their talents to more profitable use.

A night or two later, I have an anxiety dream in which I'm

with Barbara and my parents in a group of two hundred people or so and I make the mistake of telling a Junior League type that I have a fantasy of planting a dozen friends in a crowd like this one, pretending to start a brawl, and then announcing that it's all just a big joke. As time goes by, I notice that people are shunning me; obviously the Junior Leaguer has told everyone that I'm intent on causing trouble. In the end, only a few people turn out to be stupid enough to believe her (even though she's right). The rest lock arms and begin to sway from side to side and sing, "Bad old, bad old, bad old, bad old, good old Lucky Buck!" That's me, I hope: shooting off his mouth, trying to make people laugh and failing, yet somehow managing to escape with his hide intact.

◆

After tutoring has officially ended but before school lets out for the summer, I e-mail Ms. Hansen and ask her what's likely to happen with Travis. She replies that he didn't do well on one reading and math test that he took; the test took place in a room he'd never been in before rather than in the classroom where he'd spent a third of his life, and he usually does better in familiar settings. He did better on a second test, though, and Ms. Hansen put him in for "placement for cause," which means that a group of experts would look at his scores and decide his fate. The likely outcome is that Travis will go on to second grade but continue to receive intensive tutoring.

Throughout her e-mail, Ms. Hansen refers to Travis as an "ESE student." That afternoon, I'm meeting with Laura, a student of mine who has done a lot of substitute work in the public schools, so I ask her what ESE means. Exceptional Student Education, as it turns out. Laura tells me she subbed once in a class that had an ESE kid in it, and the principal said sweetly, "If Darren gets a glazed, manic look on his face, just get all the other kids over to one side and call me; I'll deal with him." Right on schedule, Darren's face turns into an expressionless mask, and he jumps up on a table and begins kicking things off. Laura finds out later that he is one of nine children, that his mother and her boyfriend are always in and out of jail, and that more than once the boyfriend has put Darren in a Hefty trash bag and beat it with a baseball bat.

In April, there is a banquet for everybody who tutored this term. Two of the children who made a lot of progress attend with their parents and give touching demonstrations of their new skills; Travis is not one of them. At my table, I sit next to a specialist from Leon County Schools and tell her about my difficulties with Travis. "Oh, you're not from the Supreme Court, are you?" she asks. Not . . . exactly, I say; why? She tells me that was surprised I stuck with him because she thought I was with the Supreme Court, which sponsors Bond Elementary, and she said she always told the coordinators not to give difficult students to the judges and lawyers because they (the judges and lawyers) always called up and complained and insisted on being assigned to easier students—they wanted to "win."

One day in early spring, I had taken a camera to school and photographed Travis. After the tutoring had ended, I blew up one of the shots into an 8″ × 10″ and framed it and drove over to Bond to give Travis a copy. I thought he might like to have a memento of our time together, which mainly involved a lot of eat-your-spinach schoolwork but also a fair number of belly laughs.

As I walked into his classroom to give Travis the photo, I imagined him saying, "Hey, here's my old buddy again!" Instead, he does a horrified double take and holds his hands out like one of Dracula's house guests as the count bears down on him. "I thought it was over!" he cries.

◆

Florence, September 29—On my first visit to the Questura, when my number came up, I approached the window I'd been called to in mounting terror. I'd been over my documents a hundred times. I had everything. Everything was in exactly the right order. Yet I'd seen one after another of my fellow applicants sent away in tears that morning, and surely they'd come prepared, too. Now they were looking beyond the ceiling at an empty sky, like broken souls making their way through the stones of a fallen world, crying, "Why, God?" in a dozen tongues.

At the window, an unsmiling officer goes through my application and its twenty pages of supporting documents with agonizing slowness, then, taking up an official seal of some kind, begins to ink-and-stamp with impressive zeal: fwomp-WHACK-fwomp-WHACK-fwomp-WHACK! She tears off a strip of paper with a serial number on it, hands it to me, and tells me to come back in forty days, a number that sounds curiously Biblical. "*Quaranta giorni?*" I ask, wanting to add, "You mean like the time Noah had to wait for the waters to recede?" Surely my home-brewed Italian has let me down again; surely she means four days. "*Quaranta giorni!*" she barks but then throws a little yeah-I-don't-get-it-either grin to the nice American man. And then the electronic board dings, and another tortured sinner steps forward.

If everything had gone ahead the way it was supposed to, this would have been the day before the production of *An Evening With Dick.* When I left Tallahassee, the planning was in its habitual state of enthusiastic disarray, but there were six weeks to go, and the show didn't have to be all that great as long as people bought tickets and nobody got arrested or divorced; being slapped hard on both cheeks was a possibility but one that fell within the range of acceptable fallout.

Yet I'd heard nothing about the upcoming show. There was an e-mail list for *Dick* contributors, but e-mails had been sporadic in August and then stopped altogether. When I go to the web site that had been set up to publicize *Dick,* I see "THIS EVENT HAS BEEN CANCELED." It had been postponed before; originally scheduled for February, the show had been moved to June. Now it was called off for good. Even when I return to Tallahassee in January and ask around, no one seems quite sure why. *Dick* has dropped from the collective memory; the cancellation of a production of *Oedipus Rex* probably would have generated some comment, but no one seemed to want to remember a failed evening of wanger jokes.

From Florence I e-mail Ms. Hansen to see whether Travis made it to the second grade or not, but she doesn't reply. I wonder if I have her e-mail address wrong, so I write not only to hansenbeth29@hotmail.com again but also to the same prefix at Yahoo and AOL. Again there is no response, not even an automatic "Message Undeliverable" reply from the three servers. The other two Beth Hansens must have wondered what the hell I was talking about, but they didn't answer, either.

Once I'd found out about Travis's placement, I wanted to go on from there and ask Ms. Hansen a lot of other questions. Like How do you learn to read? and What if you're not smart enough? and What is intelligence, anyway? During some of my mornings with Travis, I felt like Lavoisier or Buffon or some other eighteenth-century savant studying a wild boy who had been found by peasants; I knew that I knew a lot, but I also knew that I didn't know a thing about the mind of the child I spent all those days with. Like most university professors, I'd only taken classes in my specialty. Yet schoolteachers have to pass courses in reading and language acquisition and IQs and learning disabilities in order to be certified. With that background plus her own years in the classroom as well as our shared experience with Travis, I figured Ms. Hansen would have been able to tell me what I wanted to know. But she'd have to answer my e-mail first, and she didn't.

Forty-three days after my first visit to the Questura (the fortieth day is a Sunday), I return to pick up my *permesso di soggiorno*. Since it's simply a matter of collecting a piece of cardboard with my photo on it, I arrive at 9:00 a.m. instead of 7:00, figuring the process will go a lot faster this time. At the door, the policeman gives me ticket number 607. Inside, the light on the electronic board indicates that customer 547 is being served. Okay, there are only sixty people ahead of me, but I don't have to be in the office until 11:00, so I find a place against the wall and then, when a young man with Slavic features gets up to look for a toilet, dash for his seat, barely beating out a woman in head-to-toe Arab dress; because she has to peer through a slit, I have a slight advantage and see the seat first.

Even though the outside air has a touch of fall in it, the atmosphere inside the Questura is stifling, thick with heat and fear. Again, I am made aware that not everybody bathes on the same schedule; again, cell phone chatter, never welcome anywhere, adds to the feeling that one is getting a foretaste of hell. A pregnant woman gets up and puts both hands on her belly and begins to breathe noisily through her mouth; one or two people eye her seat, but unmannerly behavior has some limits.

A half hour has lapsed, and the number on the board is now 550. At this rate, I reckon it will be 7:00 p.m. by the time my number is called. But I have a class to teach in an hour and a half. Do I really need this damned permit? My time in Florence is nearly half up, and I haven't been arrested yet; for better or worse, guys who look like me don't get stopped in the street here. And then my inner jackass kicks in. I might not be able to teach Travis to read or to get *An Evening With Dick* on stage, but I'll be goddamned if I'm going to let the goddamned Italian immigration police beat me down, goddamn it. I close my book and put it in my shoulder bag; since the Questura closes at 5:00 anyway, I figure I'll come back another day.

◆

Tallahassee, February 10—When I went back to the Questura at 7:00 a.m. one October morning, I was the second person inside and got my *permesso di soggiorno* within a matter of minutes. After I return to the states, I sign up to tutor again, and now every Wednesday I go over manuals and flash cards with a first grader named Mario, who can read much better than Travis but is so hyperactive that nobody else will work with him.

An Evening With Dick has been revived and is scheduled for production in May.

Notes

Never one to search for an endnote when the text itself gives me all the information I need, I have tried to work as much bibliographical data into my essays as I could without turning them into something that looks like those Ezra Pound cantos with the Chinese ideograms. What follows is the material that couldn't be gracefully worked in earlier: additional source books, other essays, web sites, and the occasional editorial aside.

First Words

The interview with Primo Levi is from *The Voice of Memory: Primo Levi, Interviews, 1961–1987.* "Gabfest," where the term "ultra-talk" originates, appears in volume 26 (2002) of *Parnassus.* The Michael Frayn profile is "A Dry Soul Is Best: Friendship, Espionage, and the Plays of Michael Frayn," Larissa MacFarquhar, *New Yorker,* October 25, 2004, 64–73.

On the subject of American intellectuals valuing Europe over their own country, an excerpt from an interview with the writer Michael Martone is pertinent. As an apprentice, Martone entered a rarefied graduate writing program at an Eastern university and began to write imitations of academic fiction but soon found out that what the other students really loved were his stories of life in his home town: "The first time I ever left Indiana was to go to graduate school. And, you know, I was writing my polite imitation stories. And then we'd go to a place like . . . someone's basement or a coffee shop or to the grad lounge. And most of the people in my class were from the East and they knew Europe better than they knew most of America. And I would just tell them, you know, well in Fort Wayne, this happened. And they were fascinated. Riveted. Much more taken. And in class, they'd been politely encouraging about my stories. So I just stopped, and said, I'm going to write about Indiana, because an audience is interested in this." The interview was conducted by Sara Jane Stoner and appears in volume 26 (2004) of *Indiana Review* as "A Prose Aesthetic of Progress: An Interview with Michael Martone."

Viktor Shklovsky's war memoirs are entitled *A Sentimental Journey: Memoirs, 1917–1922.*

Jon Schneider is the student who wrote about the beautiful woman sipping a glass of wine.

I Shot A Man In Corleone: How Sicily Explained Johnny Cash To Me

The two books I relied on most in writing this essay were Peter Robb's *Midnight in Sicily* and Michael Streissguth's *Johnny Cash at Folsom Prison: The Making of a Masterpiece.* Other valuable background information on Sicily comes from Danilo Dolci's *Poverty in Sicily,* Alexander Stille's *Excellent Cadavers: The Mafia and the Death of the First Italian Republic,* and the *Sicily* volume in the Lonely Planet travel guide series; I also gleaned much from the various issues of the *International Herald Tribune* and *La Repubblica* that I picked up whenever I came to a town big enough to have a newsstand. I kept three works of fiction with me during the trip: Giuseppe di Lampedusa's *The Leopard,* Elio Vittorini's *Conversations in Sicily,* and Giovanni Verga's *Little Novels of Sicily;* life sprung from harsh soil and made art, these three books were my Sicilian equivalent of the Johnny Cash lyrics. No, I didn't listen to my CD of *Johnny Cash at Folsom Prison* as I made my way through Sicily because I didn't have to; those songs have been playing in my head for years.

"Why Does It Always Have To Be A Boy Baby?"

Throughout this essay, I have given the titles of my principle book and article sources. Taken together, they would make an exemplary reading list for a course in thinking about religion, though their authors' findings should be updated by regular recourse to the media, especially the *New York Times*. The advice Arthur Schlesinger Jr. once gave to would-be Rhodes Scholars applies to the rest of us: read the *New York Times* every day. That includes the *New York Times Book Review* and its valuable Washington counterpart, the *Washington Post Book World,* from which I learned of most of the titles I cite in this essay. Predictably, the Washington paper reflects the political realities of the city in which it is based by reviewing many more books on religion than does the newspaper published in godless New York. Much of my thinking about religion has also been shaped by a weekly column written by now–Professor Emeritus Leo Sandon of the Florida State University Department of Religion that appears in *The Tallahassee Democrat*. As final proof of the ubiquity of religion, I should point out that my hometown bears the only place name in the English-speaking world that, to my knowledge, contains the name of the God of Islam.

The Goat Paths Of Italy: Dante's Search For Beatrice

Some sentences in this essay appear in a short review of Harriet Rubin's *Dante in Love: The World's Greatest Poem and How It Changed History* (New York: Simon & Schuster, 2004) that appeared in the *Atlanta Journal-Constitution*. Other facts of Dante's life were taken from Thomas Caldecott Chubb's *Dante and His World* (Boston: Little, Brown, 1966). The edition of *La Vita Nuova* from which the excerpts are drawn is *The New Life,* translated and introduced by Dante Gabriel Rossetti with a preface by Michael Palmer (New York: New York Review Books, 2002).

Looking For Leonardo

The book that I took with me everywhere was *Leonardo* by Martin Kemp, although Charles Nicholl's *Leonardo da Vinci: Flights of the Mind* provided much helpful information as well, as did articles on Leonardo by Holland Cotter and Carol Vogel in the January 24 and 25, 2003, issues of the *New York Times* respectively. Of course, nothing prepares the reader for the pages in Frank Zöllner's *Leonardo da Vinci: The Complete Paintings and Drawings*. And the value to such enterprises as mine of that Leonardesque machine the World Wide Web is incalculable; when we speak of the greats, it astounds me that few people know the name of its inventor, the recently knighted Sir Tim Berners-Lee (though I didn't, either, until I looked him up on the Web).

I Brake For Richard Petty: Black Water And Boredom In The Talladega Infield

This essay contains paragraphs from two newspaper articles about Talladega that I wrote for the *Christian Science Monitor* and the *Fort Lauderdale Sun-Sentinel*. The most up-to-date source of information on NASCAR racing is www.thatsracin.com. And even if you decide not to buy that motorized bar stool, at least you owe it to yourself to look at the pictures on www.rocketstool.com.

Bang The Drum All Day

The relatively few books and articles I used are cited in the text; my main print resources are the anonymously authored concert program whose notes I cribbed shamelessly. Obviously, my favorite taiko CD is *Tsunami* by Seiichi Tanaka and The San Franciscon Taiko Dojo; an informative taiko Web site is http://www.taiko .com/rollingthunder.htm. An excellent gamelan CD is *Music of the Gamelan Gong Kebyar, Vol. 1,* recorded by the musicians of STSI Denpasar, Bali's National Institute of the Arts, under the direction of I Wayan Beratha ("the Beethoven of Bali"). Michael B. Bakan's book *Music of Death and New Creation: Experiences in the World of Balinese Gamelan Beleganjur* is not only an authoritative guide but also contains a first-person account of Bakan's studies with the master musicians of Bali. The web site http://www.lifeinkorea .com/culture/samul/samul.cfm tells more about SamulNori; sadly, SamulNori's two CDs are listed as out of stock on Amazon.com.

Anyone who has ever written nonfiction knows how hard it is to change a name; if "Harry Morris" holds up a liquor store, it's just not the same if you say the perpetrator is "Henry Moffett." So here I've changed the names only of the guilty; if someone comes off well, they're sporting their own moniker, whereas anyone involved in a disreputable act is pseudonymous.

Shrouded In A Fiery Mist

To hear my poem about Bernini's *Ecstasy of St. Teresa*, click the audio link on www.davidkirby.com. For an image of the statue, go to www.wga.hu/index.html.

Like A Twin Engine Bomber

The authoritative book on striptease is Rachel Shteir's *Striptease: The Untold History of the Girlie Show* (New York: Oxford University Press, 2004). Some sentences in this essay appear in a brief review of that book I wrote for the *Ft. Lauderdale (FL) Sun-Sentinel*. The newspaper article referred to is "Many Who Voted for 'Values' Still Like Their Television Sin," Bill Carter, *New York Times*, November 22, 2004. Early and late, the Uffizi Gallery in Florence as well as the Musée d'Orsay and the Louvre in Paris shaped my idea of what desirable women look like. I have forgotten the names of the New Orleans strip bars I visited as a teenager, which is of no importance: even if they still exist, they aren't what they were when I frequented them. And while I had to look at half a dozen porn Web sites to make sure that sex was depicted there as the humorless, overly compartmentalized affair I imagined it to be, these shall go unnamed.

Index

Acuff, Roy, 6
Adaptations of Shakespeare (ed. Fischlin and Fortier), 54
Adoration of the Magi, The (da Vinci), 127, 128
Adventures of Huckleberry Finn, The (Twain), 53, 71
Adventures of Tom Sawyer, The (Twain), 53
Affleck, Ben, 206
"Alas, Poor Shakespeare!" (Kamps), 47
Alfreds, Mike, 41
"All's Well" (Berryman), 42–43
American Beauty, 31
American Moderns (Stansell), 63
"American Scholar, The" (Emerson), 55
American Scream (Raskin), 63–64
Amis, Kingsley, 48
Andreotti, Giulio, 8
Angels and Demons (Brown), 186
Antony and Cleopatra (Shakespeare), 40
Aquinas, Saint Thomas, 104, 122
"Are You the New Person Drawn Toward Me?" (Whitman), 67
Aristotle, 79, 143
Armstrong, Karen, 109
Ashcroft, John, 97
Asia's Orthographic Dilemma (Hanna), 28
As You Like It (Shakespeare), 34
Auden, W. H., 192

Bacchae, The (Euripides), 56–57
Bacon, Delia, 44

Bacon, Faith, 196
Bakan, Michael, 166–68; *Music of Death and New Creation,* 240
Bakhtin, Mikhail, xv, xvi, 76, 171, 172; *Rabelais and His World,* 76
"Bang the Drum All Day" (Rundgren), 159–73
Baptist church, 106
Bardi, Simone de', 114, 119
Barr, Candy, 192, 197
Barro, Robert J., 103–4
Barthes, Roland, xvi, 194
Baudelaire, Charles, 160
Beale, Simon Russell, 38
Beatles, 163
Beatrice Portinari, 111–12, 114, 115, 116–20, 124
Beatty, Paul, 58
Beaumont, Francis, 35
Beethoven, Ludwig van, 168; *Ninth Symphony,* xi
Bell, Virginia, "Ding Dong," 189
Bellamy, Edward: *Looking Backward,* 62
Bell Curve, The (Murray and Herrnstein), 103
Bellini, Vincenzo, xiii
Bellochio, Marco, 87
Beratha, I Wayan, 168
Bernard, Saint, 124
Berners-Lee, Sir Tim, 240
Bernini, Gianlorenzo, xiii, 174–75, 176, 178, 179, 190
Berryman, John, 42–43
Berryman's Shakespeare (Berryman), 42
Bertrand, Bill, viii, 164

Better Angel, The (Morris), 72

Bible, 53, 71; Exodus, 97; Job, 57, 60; John, 122; Poetical Books, 57; Psalms, 45, 57, 59

"The Bible is an antique Volume" (Dickinson), 184

Bicci, Neri di, 112

Biden, Senator Joe, 102

Big Brother 2, 199–210

"Birthplace, The" (James), 35–36

Bittman, Dr. Barry, 170

Blake, William, 57–58

Blithedale Romance, The (Hawthorne), 62

Bloom, Harold, 42, 48

Blue Dahlia, The, 89

Bly, Robert, 170

Boniface VIII, Pope, 111, 119

Borges, Jorge Luis: "Everything and Nothing," 36–37; "Shakespeare's Memory," 37–38, 48–49

Boromini, Francesco, 174

Borsellino, Paolo, 9

Bowles, Jane, 192

Bowles, Paul, 192

Bowles, Samuel, 176

Bradford, William, 100

Bradley, Henry, 29

Brahe, Tycho, 127

Brecht, Bertolt, 47, 54

Bridge, The (Crane), 58

Britten, Benjamin, 192

Brown, Dan, 186

Brunelleschi, Filippo, xi, xviii

Bruner, Jerome, 142–44, 145–46

Brusca, Giovanni, 8–9, 10, 22–23

Buffon, Georges-Louis Leclerc, Comte de, 235

Buñuel, Luis, 89

Buongiorno, Notte (Bellochio), 87

Burke, Edmund, xviii

Burke, Kenneth, 143

Burroughs, William, 58

Bush, Barbara, 101

Bush, George W., 84, 100–102, 206

Cahill, Thomas, 102–3, 104

Campbell, Mrs. Patrick, 127

Canova, Antonio, 189

Cantos (Pound), 58

Caravaggio, 118

Cardano, Girolamo, 132

Cardenio (Shakespeare), 35

Carson, Ciaran, 123

Carter, Bill, 241

Carter, June (Cash), 11, 20–21; "If I Were a Carpenter," 21; *Press On,* 21

Cash, Johnny, xix, 1–26; "Folsom Prison Blues," 2–3, 17, 25; "Give My Love to Rose," 11–12; "I Don't Like It But I Guess Things Happen That Way," 25; "If I Were a Carpenter," 21; "I Walk the Line," 25; "Long Black Veil," 7; "Ring of Fire," 25

Cats, 52

Cavallini, Pietro, 118

Céline, Louis-Ferdinand, 58

Cézanne, Paul, 192

Chapman, Mark David, 145

Charisse, Cyd, 88

"Charlie and the MTA," 165

Chase, Chevy, 169

Chaucer, Geoffrey, 49

Chekhov, Anton, 31–33

Chicago, 52

Chien Andalou, Un (Buñuel), 89

Child That Books Built, The (Spufford), 142, 144–45

Chirac, Jacques, 85

Choice of Emily Dickinson's Verse, A (ed. Hughes), 176

Chopin, Frédéric, 192
Chubb, Thomas Caldecott, 239
Ciardi, John, 123
Cimabue, 93
Clark, Gladys, 192
Clark, Katerina, 76, 171, 172
Clinton, Bill, 206
Closing of the Western Mind, The
(Freeman), 96
"Codex on the Flight of Birds" (da
Vinci), 130
Codex Turin (da Vinci), 130, 131
Coen brothers, 168
Cohen, J. M., 75, 77
Comedy of Errors, The (Shakespeare),
35, 39
Condit, Gary, 201
Confidence-Man, The (Melville),
62–63
Conrad, Angela, 182–83
Conversations in Sicily (Vittorini), 6,
238
Cooley, Karen, 218
Copland, Aaron, 192
Corio, Ann, 193
Coriolanus (Shakespeare), 34
Corro, Maria del, 179, 185
Costello, Elvis, 161
Cotter, Holland, 140, 239
Craig, Pastor Mark, 100–101
Crane, Hart, 58
Cruise, Tom, 98
Cymbeline (Shakespeare), 33

Dali, Salvador, 192
Dangerfield, Rodney, 206
Dante Alighieri, xi, xiii, 49, 71,
110–24, 125, 126; *The Divine
Comedy*, 110, 112, 113, 118–19, 120,
121, 123, 126; *The Inferno*, xix, 119,
123; *La Vita Nuova*, 113, 114–15,

239; *The Paradiso*, 111, 119, 123; *The
Purgatorio*, 111, 119
Dante and His World (Chubb), 239
Dante in Love (Rubin), 110, 118, 121,
122, 239
Danti, Giovan Battista, 131
"David Manning," 213, 215
da Vinci, Leonardo, xi, xiii, 125–41;
The Adoration of the Magi, 127, 128;
"Codex on the Flight of Birds,"
130; Codex Turin, 130, 131;
drawings related to flight, 138;
Mona Lisa, 127
Da Vinci Code, The (Brown), 186
Debussy, Claude, 192
Declaration of Independence, 103
Decline of Hell, The (Walker), 100
Def Poetry Jam, 58
De Generes, Ellen, 206
Delusion and Dream (Freud), 145–46
Derrida, Jacques, xv, 47
Desdemona (Vogel), 54
Desmet, Christy, 46, 54
Devena the Aqua Tease, 193
Dickens, Charles, 45, 110, 226
Dickinson, Austin, 177
Dickinson, Emily, 175–77, 280–85;
"A solemn thing—it was—I said,"
183; "He fumbles at your Soul," 181;
"The Bible is an antique Volume,"
184; "Title-divine—is mine!," 177
*Dionysiac Poetics and Euripides'
Bacchae* (Segal), 57
Divine Comedy, The (Dante), 110, 112,
113, 118–19, 120, 121, 123, 126
Dolci, Danilo, 5, 238
Donatello, xix
Donne, John, 59
Dostoevsky, Feodor, 58
Doubt: A History (Hecht), 96
Dowd, Maureen, 84

Drum music, 159–73
"Dry Soul is Best, A" (MacFarquhar), 237
Duck from AFLAC commercial, 206
Dunning, Jennifer, 213
Duvall, Robert, 20
Dylan, Bob, 16, 62

Eagleton, Terry, 47
Earnhardt, Dale, 153
Ecstasy of St. Teresa, The (Bernini), 174–75, 176, 190
Edwards, Carl, 153
Eliot, George, 121
Eliot, T. S., 58, 121
Emerson, Ralph Waldo, 35, 184; "The American Scholar," 55; "History," xvi; *Representative Men,* 34
Endo, Kenny, 160
English Patient, The (Ondaatje), 1, 134–35
English Traveller, The (Heywood), 48
Essays (Montaigne), 75
Euripides, 56–57
Evangeline, the Beautiful Pearl in the Half Shell, 193
Evans, Dixie, 196
Evening with Dick, An, 218–21, 223–26, 230–32, 234, 236
Excellent Cadavers (Stille), 4, 238

Faith of George W. Bush, The (Mansfield), 100
Falcone, Giovanni, 9
Fallon, Dick, 218, 219, 231
Farr, Judith, 184
Farrar, F. W., 100
Faulkner, William, 53
Favier, Eric, 218–19, 220, 231
Feinstein, Elaine, 54
Finnell, Carrie, 193

Fischlin, Daniel, 54
Flaubert, Gustave, 145
Fletcher, John, 35, 48; *The Woman's Prize,* 53, 54
Flowering of the Soul, The (ed. Vardey), 187
"Folsom Prison Blues" (Cash), 2–3, 17, 25
Fonda, Jane, 220
Fortier, Mark, 54
Foucault, Michel, xv, 46
France, Anatole, 75
Franchetti-Sonino report, 5
Francis of Assisi, Saint, 121
Frayn, Michael, xv
Freeman, Charles, 96
Freud, Sigmund, xviii, 47, 105, 121, 127, 137–38, 140, 194, 197; *Delusion and Dream,* 145–46
Furnivall, Frederick James, 29

Galileo Galilei, 117, 127
Gans, Herbert, 195
Gargantua and Pantagruel (Rabelais), 74
Geography of Thought, The (Nisbett), 28
Gift of the Jews, The (Cahill), 102–3
Ginsberg, Allen: *Howl,* xix, 58, 63–64; "A Supermarket in California," 73
Gioia, Dana, 70–71
Giotto, 93, 121
"Give My Love to Rose" (Cash), 11–12
Glass Key, The, 89
Gleason, Ralph, 16
Glennie, Evelyn, 160
God, 93–94, 105, 108, 139, 143, 180, 187, 188
God: A Biography (Miles), 93–94
God Against the Gods (Kirsch), 101

Godzilla, 206
Goethe, Johann Wolfgang von, vii,
    xii, xiii, 71
Gordon, Jeff, 150, 153–54, 155
Gore, Al, 100
Goya, Francisco de, 149
Granger, Stewart, 88
Greene, Robert, 45
"Greystone Chapel" (Sherley), 24
Grinberg, Emanuella, 213
Guido Bevisangue, 132
Guido Guerra, 132
Guinness, Alec, 43
Gutenberg, Johannes, xiv
Guthrie, Woody, 16

Hajdu, David, 162
Hall, Fitzedward, 30
Halliday, Mark, xv
Hamby, Barbara, ix; in a dream, 232;
    and *The Ecstasy of Saint Teresa,*
    175; in Florence, xi, xviii, 125; and
    music, 159, 160; and the OED, 27,
    30; in Paris, 80, 83, 85, 86; in Sicily,
    9, 15, 17, 18, 20, 22
Hamlet (Shakespeare), 40–41, 44, 46,
    71, 78
Hamlet-Machine (Müller), 54
Handel, George Frideric, 221
Hannas, Wm. C., 28
Hansen, Ms. (teacher), 228–29, 235
Hardy, Kerry, 203, 205–6
Hare Krishnas, 107
Harold II, King, 43
Harrison, George, 97
Harrison, Rex, 221
Hawthorne, Nathaniel, 121, 178, 188;
    The Blithedale Romance, 62; "My
    Kinsman, Major Molineux," xvi;
    Our Old Home, 44; *The Scarlet
    Letter,* 209

Hebbel, Friedrich, xv
Hecht, Jennifer Michael, 96
"He fumbles at your Soul"
    (Dickinson), 181
Hegel, Georg Wilhelm Friedrich, 47
"Helping Shakespeare Make an Easy
    Crossing" (Jefferson), 42
Helping the Dreamer (Waldman), 58
Hemingway, Ernest, 156–57
Henry V (Shakespeare), 41
Henry VIII (Shakespeare), 35
Hentoff, Nat, 16
Herrnstein, Richard J., 103
"Hey, Joe," 7
Heywood, Thomas, 48
Higginson, Thomas Wentworth, 176,
    180–81
Hinckley, John, 145
"History" (Emerson), xvi
History of Hell, The (Turner), 95,
    99–100
History of King Lear, The (Tate), 54
Hollow Man, 213, 215
Holquist, Michael, 76, 171, 172
Hopper, Edward, 68, 70
House of Blue Light, The (Kirby), 202
Hover, Herman, 195
Howard, May, 189
Howl (Ginsberg), xix, 58, 63–64
Hughes, Ted, 176
Human Accomplishment (Murray),
    103
Hummer, T. R., 73
Hutin, Francisque, 191, 196

"I Don't Like It But I Guess Things
    Happen That Way" (Cash), 25
"If I Were a Carpenter" (Cash), 21
"I Have a Gentle Cock," 224
Inferno, The (Dante), xix, 119, 122, 123
Ingres, Jean Auguste, 189

Interior Castle, The (Saint Teresa of Avila), 180, 182
Irenaeus, 97
Iron John (Bly), 170
Isabella of Aragon, 128
Isherwood, Christopher, 192
"I Walk the Line" (Cash), 25

Jackson, Janet, 195
James, Henry, 121; "The Birthplace," 35–36
Jefferson, Margo, 42
Jefferson, Thomas, 206
Jehovah, 98
Jenkins, Gordon, 7
Jenkins, Jerry B., 95
Jerusalem (Blake), 58
Jesus Christ, 105, 106, 117, 118, 119, 180
Johnny Cash at Folsom Prison (Streissguth), 3, 6–7, 11, 21, 238
Johnson, Robert, 7
Johnston, Bob, 11, 21
Johnston, Ian, 56
Jonson, Ben, 35
Joplin, Janis, xix
Julius Caesar (Shakespeare), 50, 53
Jung, Carl, 105, 106–7

Kafka, Franz, 215
Kamps, Ivo, 47
Kaufman, Philip, 161
Keats, John, 41, 54, 59, 110
Kemp, Martin: *Leonardo*, 127, 128–29, 136, 138–39, 140–41, 239
Kennedy, Robert F., 17
Kepler, Johannes, 127
Kerouac, Jack, 58
Kerry, John, 83–84
Kidder, Margot, 220
Kidnapped (Stevenson), 4

Kill Bill movies, 103
King, Dave, 215
King Lear (Shakespeare), 35, 46, 50, 54, 71, 78
King's English, The (Amis), 48
Kingston Trio, 162–65; *Close Up,* 163
Kirby, David, 211–15; *The Ha-Ha,* 215; *The House of Blue Light,* 202; "Little Sisters of the Sacred Heart," 207–8
Kirby, Ian (son), 199–200, 202
Kirby, Will (son), 199–208
Kirkland, Elizabeth, 48
Kirsch, Jonathan, 101
Kiss Me Kate, 53
Kristeva, Julia, 205
Kristof, Nicholas D., 95–96
Küng, Hans, 96

LaHaye, Tim, 95
L'Amour, Louis, 106
Lampedusa, Giuseppe de, 6, 18, 238
Lang, Fritz, 88
Lavoisier, Antoine-Laurent de, 235
Lazarus, 106
Lear's Daughters (Women's Theatre Group and Elaine Feinstein), 54
Leaves of Grass (Whitman), 55, 64, 68, 71
Lee, Gypsy Rose, 192
Left Behind novels (LaHaye and Jenkins), 95
Leo X, Pope, 140
Leonardo (Kemp), 127, 128–29, 136, 138–39, 140–41, 239
Leonardo da Vinci: Flights of the Mind (Nicholl), 131, 239
Leonardo da Vinci: The Complete Paintings and Drawings (Zöllner), 138, 240
Leopard, The (Lampedusa), 6, 18, 238

Leopardi, Count Giacomo, vii, xii, xiii

Les Miserables, 52

Lessons from a Father to His Son (Ashcroft), 97

Levi, Primo, xi–xii, 237

Levis, Larry, 73

Life of Emily Dickinson, The (Sewall), 176

Linden, Eugene, 145

Lindfors, Viveca, 88

Lippi, Filippo, 94

Little Novels of Sicily (Verga), 238

"Little Sisters of the Sacred Heart" (Kirby), 207–8

Lodge, Thomas, 34

"Long Black Veil" (Cash), 165

Longinus, 117

Looking Backward (Bellamy), 62

Lorca, Federico García, xviii, 54

Lord, Judge Otis Phillips, 185

Lucas, Charlie "Tin Man," 68, 69, 70

Luciano, Lucky, 2

Lucretius, 79

Ludwig (Visconti), 89

Lugosi, Bela, 206

Macbeth (Shakespeare), 10, 38, 39, 40, 46, 50, 53, 54, 71, 103, 191

MacFarquhar, Larissa, 237

Machiavelli, Niccolò, xi, 117, 125; *The Prince,* 126

MacNeice, Louis, 192

Making Stories (Bruner), 142–44, 145–46

Mamma Mia, 51–52

Mandela, Nelson, 53

Mandelstam, Osip, 111

Manet, Edouard, 189

Mani, 99

Manichaeism, 99–100, 204

Mansfield, Stephen, 100

"Many Who Voted for 'Values' Still Like Their Television Sin" (Carter), 241

Marcus, Greil, 62

Mark, Saint, 117

Marlowe, Christopher, 35, 36, 127

Márquez, Gabriel García, 43

Marquis de Sade, 122

Marriage of Heaven and Hell, The (Blake), 57

Martin, Mark, 154

Martone, Michael, 237–38

Marx, Karl, 47, 156

Mary (mother of Jesus), 105, 118, 119

Masaccio, 94

Masolino, 94

McCleary, Rachel M., 103–4

McHenry, Eric, 214

McLuhan, Marshall, 194

Mears, Casey, 153

Medici, Lorenzo de, 1

Medoff, Mark, 224–25, 226

Medwick, Cathleen, 178, 179, 186

Meisner, Sandy, 20

Melville, Herman, vii, xv, 58, 71, 171; *The Confidence-Man,* 62–63; *Moby-Dick,* xiv–xv, 6, 53, 62, 71

Memories, Dreams, Reflections (Jung), 105, 106–7

Menand, Louis, 96

Mendes, Sam, 31–32

Mercier, Claude, 75, 82–83, 91

Mercier, Marie, 82, 91

Merry Wives of Windsor, The (Shakespeare), 34, 53

Metaphysical Club, The (Menand), 96

Michelangelo Buonarroti, xi, 1, 117, 125, 127

Midnight in Sicily (Robb), 5, 9–10, 21; 238

Midsummer Night's Dream, A
(Shakespeare), 40–43
Mikhail Bakhtin (Clark and
Holquist), 76, 171, 172
Miles, Jack, 93–94
Miller, Henry, 58
Milton (Blake), 57
Milton, John, 40, 123
Mimesis as Make-Believe (Watson),
33–34
Minor, William Chester, 29–30
Minsky brothers, 194, 195
Mirandola, Pico della, 1
Miserables, Les, 52
Moby-Dick (Melville), xiv–xv, 6, 53,
62, 71
Molière, 49
Mona Lisa (da Vinci), 127
Monroe, Marilyn, 196
Montaigne, Michel de, 78, 85, 86, 90,
91; *Essays,* 75, 78–79; "On Cruelty,"
86; "On Idleness," 79, 91; "On
Solitude," 80; "To Philosophize is
to Learn How to Die," 79
Moonflight (Lang), 88
Moonies, 107
Morley, Sheridan, 33
Moro, Aldo, 87
Morris, Roy, Jr., 72
Morris, Tracie, 58
Mother Elms, 195
Mr. T., 206
Msomi, Welcome, 54
Müller, Heiner, 54
Mummy, The, 206
Murder in the Cathedral (Eliot), 58
Murray, Charles, 103, 104
Murray, James Augustus Henry,
28–30
Music of Death and New Creation
(Bakan), 240

*Music of the Gamelan Gong Kebyar,
Vol. I,* 240

NASCAR, xx, 147–58
"Native Moments" (Whitman), 66,
68
Newfield, Jack, 16
"New Prophets of Revelation, The,"
95
Nicholl, Charles, 131, 239
Nietzsche, Friedrich, 47, 58, 63
Nisbett, Richard E., 28
Nixon, Richard, 98
Nuyorican Café, 58

Oates, Joyce Carol, 127
Oblivion (Wallace), 211, 212, 214–15
Odyssey, The (Homer), 11
O'Keeffe, Georgia, 63
Olivier, Laurence, 43
"On Cruelty" (Montaigne), 86
Ondaatje, Michael, 1, 134–35
O'Neill, Eugene, 57
"On Idleness" (Montaigne), 79, 91
"On Solitude" (Montaigne), 80
Othello (Shakespeare), 46, 50, 53, 70
Our Old Home (Hawthorne), 44
Oxford English Dictionary, 27–30

Palmer, Michael, 239
Pandosto (Greene), 45
Papp, Joseph, 48
Paradiso, The (Dante), 111, 119, 123
Pareles, Jon, 213
Parker, David, 104
Party Girl (Ray), 88
Pasolini, Pier Paolo, 89
Paz, Octavio, xvii
Peck, Gregory, 20
Peckinpah, Sam, 89
Pericles (Shakespeare), 34, 35

Perkins, Carl, 11
Peter, Saint, 117
Petty, Richard, 149, 157–58
Phantom of the Opera, The, 52
Picasso, Pablo, 47
Piranesi, Giovanni Battista, 50
Plato, 1, 35, 143; *Symposium*, 77
Plautus, 46
Polanski, Roman, 89
Politian, 1
Pollock, Jackson, 39
Pompidou, Georges, 85
Pontormo, xviii–xix, 49
Positively Fourth Street (Hajdu), 162
Pound, Ezra, 58
Poverty in Sicily (Dolci), 5, 238
Presley, Elvis, 213, 215
Prince, The (Machiavelli), 126
Professor and the Madman, The
    (Winchester), 29–30
"Prose Aesthetic of Progress, A"
    (Stoner), 237–38
*Protestant Work Ethic and the Spirit of
    Capitalism, The* (Weber), 103
Protocols of the Elders of Zion, The, 144
Proust, Marcel, 145
Purgatorio, The (Dante), 111, 119

Quiney, Richard, 46

Rabelais, François, 75, 76, 86, 90;
    Gargantua and Pantagruel, 74,
    77–78, 80–82
Racine, Jean, 52, 192, 197
Rand, Sally, 192
Raphael, 127
Raskin, Jonah, 63–64
Ray, Nicholas, 88
Reality television, 199–210
Reed, John, 63
Reid, Don, 4

Religion, 92–109
"Religion and Economic Growth
    across Countries" (Barro and
    McCleary), 103–4
Representative Men (Emerson), 34
Reynolds, Burt, 218
Reynolds, David S., 61–62
Rice, W. C., 68–70
Richard III (Shakespeare), 39, 50, 78
Ricotta, La (Pasolini), 89
Rigoletto (Verdi), 10
"Ring of Fire" (Cash), 25
Riina, Totò, 8
Rising Sun (Kaufman), 161
Riverdance, 213
River of Diamonds (Polanski), 89
Road to Perdition, 31
Robb, Peter, 5, 9–10, 21, 238
Rodgers, Jimmy, 7
Rodman, Dennis, 206
Roger II (king of Sicily), 12, 19
Romeo and Juliet (Shakespeare), 40, 70
Rosalynde (Lodge), 34
Rosemary's Baby, 202
Rossetti, Dante Gabriel, 239
Rothko, Mark, 68, 70
Rowland, Rose Zelle, 196
Rowse, A. L., 45
Royce, Rosita, 193
Rubin, Harriet, 110, 118, 121, 122, 239
Rundgren, Todd, 159, 173
Rushdie, Salman, 202

Sade, Marquis de, 122
Sandon, Leo, 239
San Francisco Taiko Dojo:
    Sokobayashi, 171, 240; *Tsunami*
    (with Tanaka), 240
Sanger, Margaret, 63
Sargent, John Singer, 68, 70
Satanic Verses, The (Rushdie), 202

"Satin Doll," 163
Sawyer, Robert, 46, 54
Scarlet Letter, The (Hawthorne), 209
Schlesinger, Arthur, Jr., 239
Schwarzenegger, Arnold, 206
Sciascia, Leonardo, 4–5
Scientology, 98
Segal, Charles, 57
Seneca, 46, 79
Sentimental Journey, Memoirs, 1917–1922, A (Shklovsky), xvi–xvii, 238
Sewall, Richard B., 176
Sex Pistols, 162
Sforza, Gian Galeazzo, 128
Shakespeare, William, xix, 28, 31–54, 68, 70–71, 78, 79, 121, 127, 222, 226; *Antony and Cleopatra,* 40; *As You Like It,* 34, 50; *Cardenio,* 34; *The Comedy of Errors,* 35, 39; *Coriolanus,* 34; *Cymbeline,* 33; *Hamlet,* 40–41, 44, 46, 71, 78; *Henry V,* 41; *Henry VIII,* 35; *Julius Caesar,* 50, 53; *King Lear,* 35, 46, 50, 54, 71, 78; *Macbeth,* 10, 38, 39, 40, 46, 50, 53, 54, 71, 103, 191; *The Merry Wives of Windsor,* 34, 53; *A Midsummer Night's Dream,* 40–41–43; *Othello,* 46, 50, 53, 70; *Pericles,* 34, 35; *Richard III,* 39, 50, 78; *Romeo and Juliet,* 40, 70; *The Taming of the Shrew,* 41, 53; *The Tempest,* 110; *Twelfth Night,* 31–33, 35, 39–40, 41–42, 43, 44, 50; *Two Gentlemen of Verona,* 35; *The Winter's Tale,* 33, 35, 49, 51
Shakespeare Alive! (Papp and Kirkland), 48
Shakespeare and Appropriation (ed. Desmet and Sawyer), 46, 47, 54
"Shakespeare and the Norman Conquest" (Watson), 43–44
Shakespeare for All Time (Wells), 46

Shakespeare in Love, 35
Shakespeare: The Invention of the Human (Bloom), 42–48
Shakespeare the Man (Rowse), 45
"Shakspeare [sic] in America," 70
Shaw, George Bernard, 192
Sherley, Glen, 24–25
Shklovsky, Viktor, xvi–xvii, 238
Shteir, Rachel, 189–96, 241
Sicily (Lonely Planet series), 12, 13, 238
Sidney, Sir Philip, 59
Silent Partners (Linden), 145
"Sleepers, The" (Whitman), 67
Snyder, Gary, 63
Sokobayashi (San Francisco Taiko Dojo), 171
"A solemn thing—it was—I said" (Dickinson), 183
Solotaroff, Ted, xiii–xiv
"Song of Myself" (Whitman), xiv, 59–60, 65, 67, 72–73
"Song of the Rolling Earth, The" (Whitman), 67
Southern Baptist church, 99, 106
Spielberg, Stephen, 167–68
Spiral Staircase, The (Armstrong), 107
Spufford, Francis, 142, 144–45
Stalin, Joseph, 48
Stallone, Sylvester, 157
Stansell, Christine, 63
Starbuck, George, 214
Starr, Blaze, 192
Statler Brothers, 11
St. Cyr, Lili, 192, 193
Stein, Edith, 187
Stevens, Wallace, 110, 153
Stevenson, Robert Louis, 4, 66
Stieglitz, Alfred, 63
Stille, Alexander, 4, 238
"St. James Infirmary," 163
Stone, Robert, xii–xiii, 135

Stoner, Sara Jane, 237–38
Storm, Tempest, 192
Strand, Mark, 123
Stravinski, Igor, 168
Straw Dogs (Peckinpah), 89
Streissguth, Michael, 3, 6–7, 11, 21, 238
Striptease, 189–98
Striptease (Shteir), 189–96, 241
Summa Theologica (Aquinas), 104
"Supermarket in California, A" (Ginsberg), 73

Taming of the Shrew, The (Shakespeare), 41, 53
Tanaka, Seiichi, 160, 240
Tate, Nahum, 54
Taylor, Robert, 88
Tempest, The (Shakespeare), 110
Tennyson, Alfred, Lord, 59
Terence, 46, 91
Teresa of Avila (Medwick), 178, 179, 186
Teresa of Avila, Saint, 174–75, 178–80, 185–88; *The Interior Castle*, 180
"There Was a Child Went Forth" (Whitman), 67
"They Call the Wind Maria," 166
This Gun for Hire, 89
Tirza the Wine Girl, 193
Titian, 189
"Title-divine—is mine!" (Dickinson), 177
Todd, Mabel Loomis, 177
"Tom Dooley," 163, 165–66
"To Philosophize is to Learn How to Die" (Montaigne), 79
Transformation of American Religion, The (Wolfe), 106
Travis (student), 222–23, 226–30, 232–33, 235–36

Travolta, John, 98
Tsunami (Tanaka), 240
Tubb, Ernest, 6
Turner, Alice K., 95, 99–100
Turner, Ted, 218
Turner Diaries, The, 143–44
Twain, Mark, vii, 45, 49; *Huckleberry Finn*, 53, 71, 78; *Tom Sawyer*, 53
Twelfth Night (Shakespeare), 31–33, 35, 39–40, 41–42, 43, 44, 50
Two Gentlemen of Verona (Shakespeare), 35

uMabatha (Msomi), 54
Uncle Tom's Cabin (Stowe), 143, 191
"Unexpress'd, The" (Whitman), 71
Upanishads, The, 95

Vagina Monologues, The (Ensler), 218, 220, 225
Van Gogh, Vincent, 192
Vardey, Lucinda, 187
Venus of Urbino (Titian), 189
Verdi, Giuseppe, xiii, 53
Verga, Giovanni, 238
Verlaine, Paul, 110
Vincent, Gene, 10
Virgil, 49, 111, 122, 123
Visconti, Luchino, 89
Vita Nuova, La (Dante), 113, 114–15, 239
Vittorini, Elio, 6, 238
Vogel, Carol, 239
Vogel, Paula, 54
Voice of Memory, The (Levi), xi–xii, 237

Waiting for Godot (Beckett), 2–3, 20
Wakoski, Diane, 58
Waldman, Anne, 58
Walker, D. P., 100

Wallace, David Foster, 211, 212, 214–15
Wallace, Kenny, 154
Walt Whitman in Hell (Hummer), 73
Walt Whitman's America (Reynolds), 61–62
"Waste Land, The" (Eliot), 58
Watson, Billy, 189, 197
Watson, George, 43–44
Watson, Kendall, 33–34
Wayward Nun of Amherst, The (Conrad), 182–83
Weber, Bruce, 225
Weber, Katherine, 214, 215
Weber, Max, 103
Wells, Stanley, 46
West, Evelyn, 189
West Side Story, 53
"Whitman:" (Levis), 73
Whitman, George, 72
Whitman, Walt, vii, xv, xix, 45, 55–73, 156, 226; "Are You the New Person Drawn Toward Me?" 67; *Leaves of Grass*, 55, 64, 68, 71; "Native Moments," 66, 68; "The Sleepers," 67; "Song of Myself," xiv, 59–60, 65, 67, 72–73; "A Song of the Rolling Earth," 67; "There

Was a Child Went Forth," 67; "The Unexpress'd," 71
Wilber, Rick, 99
Wilbur, Crane, 6–7
Wilde, Oscar, 192
Wilkins, George, 34
Williams, Tennessee, 57
Williams, William Carlos, 61
William Shakespeare (Eagleton), 47
Willis, Bruce, 157
Winchester, Simon: *The Meaning of Everything*, 27–30; *The Professor and the Madman*, 29–30
Winter's Tale, The (Shakespeare), 33, 35, 49, 51
Wittgenstein, Ludwig, 47
Wolfe, Alan, 106
Woman's Prize, or The Tamer Tamed, The (Fletcher), 53, 54
Women's Theatre Group, 54
Wordsworth, William, 183
Wright, Richard, 192

Yevtushenko, Yevgeny, 58
Yosemite Sam, 206

Zöllner, Frank, 138, 240
Zoroastro (Masini di Peretola), 131–32